EMPATHIC VISION

Cultural Memory
in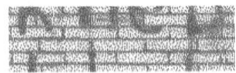
the
Present

Mieke Bal and Hent de Vries, Editors

EMPATHIC VISION

Affect, Trauma, and Contemporary Art

Jill Bennett

STANFORD UNIVERSITY PRESS

STANFORD, CALIFORNIA 2005

Stanford University Press
Stanford, California

Printed in the United States of America
on acid-free, archival-quality paper.

Library of Congress Cataloging-in-Publication Data

Bennett, Jill.
    Empathic vision : affect, trauma, and contemporary art /
Jill Bennett.
        p.   cm.—(Cultural memory in the present)
    Includes bibliographical references and index.
    ISBN 0-8047-5074-2 (cloth : alk. paper)—
ISBN 0-8047-5171-4 (pbk. : alk. paper)
    1. Violence in art.   2. Art, Modern—20th century—
Political aspects.   3. Political violence—Psychological aspects.
I. Title.   II. Series.
N8257.B46   2005
704.9'493036'09045—dc22   2004018550

Original Printing 2005
Last figure below indicates year of this printing:
14   13   12   11   10   09   08   07   06   05

Typeset by James P. Brommer in 11/13.5 Garamond

For my three inspirations:
Luc, Lita, and the memory of my father

Contents

Illustrations

Acknowledgments

Research for this book was undertaken with the support of a Large Grant from the Australian Research Council and was in other ways supported by the College of Fine Arts, University of New South Wales.

A short version of Chapter 2 was published as "The Aesthetics of Sense Memory: Theorising Trauma Through the Visual Arts," in *Trauma und Erinnerung*, ed. Franz Kaltenbeck and Peter Weibel (Vienna: Passagen Verlag, 2000), and in *Regimes of Memory*, ed. Susannah Radstone and Katharine Hodgkin (London: Routledge, 2003). A section of Chapter 3 was published as "Art, Affect and the Bad Death," *Signs* 28, no. 1 (Autumn 2002): © 2002 by the University of Chicago. All rights reserved.

The excerpt from Karen Finley's *Constant State of Desire* is reprinted by permission of City Lights Books © 1990 Karen Finley, and the text of Willie Doherty's *The Only Good One Is a Dead One* courtesy of Alexander and Bonin, New York, and Matt's Gallery, London.

I am grateful to many friends and colleagues for discussions that have contributed to this book. Above all, I thank David McNeill for sharing his best ideas and worst jokes.

I thank many generous hosts in South Africa for their hospitality, guidance and conversation—in particular, Yazir Henri, Heidi Grunebaum, Nkululeku Booysen, and the Direct Action Centre for Peace, Cape Town; William Kentridge, Anne Stanwix, Anne McIlleron, Jane Taylor, Rayda Becker, Fiona Rankin-Smith, Gavin Younge, and Glenda Younge.

I am grateful to Ian McLean, Gordon Bennett and Leanne Bennett who read and offered useful comment on Chapter 6, and to all the other artists who were willing to talk about and provide information on their work.

Many colleagues in Sydney and around the world have advanced theoretical thinking on affect in art and helped my work; in particular, it has been a joy to work with Jennifer Biddle, Anna Munster, and the organizers the 2001 Art Association "Affect and Sensation" conference. I am also indebted to the work of Ernst van Alphen and Marianne Hirsch—both warm, generous colleagues.

I thank Mieke Bal for her enthusiastic support and for the opportunity to publish in this series, Donna Brett for her calm efficiency and help with the manuscript, and Peter Dreyer for his excellent copyediting.

This book is dedicated to the memory of my father, who could only dream of the opportunities I have had, and to my inspiring children—Luc and Lita—in the hope that no obstacle will ever prove too big for you!

EMPATHIC VISION

1

On the Subject of Trauma

Trauma Art

I don't think it's an ontology we need, but a desmology—in Greek
desmos means connection, or link. . . . What interests me is not so much
the state of things but the relations between them. I've concerned myself
with nothing but relations for my whole life.

—Michel Serres

Some years ago, I co-curated an exhibition of art relating to the topic
of trauma and memory.[1] In planning that project, it seemed viable and
productive to identify a thematic category, especially since my co-curator
and I were aware of a number of interesting artworks that emerged from
an engagement with traumatic memory but weren't immediately recognizable as such. These works had eluded classification as trauma works largely
because they in some way evoked the processes of post-traumatic memory
without declaring themselves to be about trauma; and, indeed, in many
cases, they would appear to be about something else. The trauma, it often
seemed, was not evinced in the narrative component or in the ostensible
meaning, but in a certain affective dynamic internal to the work.

The artworks concerned, then, were not usually identified prima facie by their testimonial function; they did not clearly communicate an account of a trauma experienced by a particular individual, as the testimonies
of Holocaust survivors in Claude Lanzmann's nine-and-a-half-hour film
Shoah (1985) do, for example. Nor, in most cases, did they even manifest a

set of symptoms that could be definitively ascribed to the artist as trauma survivor. Many of these trauma-related pieces, in fact, incorporated fictional or fantasy elements, even when the artist might lay claim to expressing an affective truth. Insofar as they could be deemed to promote understanding of trauma, their contribution tended to lie in the endeavor to find a communicable language of sensation and affect with which to register something of the experience of traumatic memory—and, thus, in a manner of formal innovation. This led us finally to frame the exhibition in a way that reflected process—a coming into language—rather than the subject matter of trauma discourse. In doing so, we hoped to move away from evaluating art in terms of its capacity to reflect predefined conditions and symptomologies, and to open up the question of what art itself might tell us about the lived experience and memory of trauma.

This theoretical distinction is, in effect, the rationale for this book, which looks at art as a kind of visual language of trauma and of the experiences of conflict and loss. It is a distinction that throws up a range of methodological problems. How, for example, do we conceptualize trauma and identify its presence in an artwork, if not through the application of existing clinical or theoretical models of trauma? Much recent work on the literary expression of trauma draws on psychoanalytic models to interpret trauma within a text, although this application of psychoanalysis has been rather more limited in the visual arts. But I would like to take up the question "What does art tell us about trauma?" in a somewhat different vein, adopting a theoretical perspective that owes as much to the work of Gilles Deleuze and Michel Foucault as to literary or psychoanalytic trauma studies. I draw on philosophers such as Deleuze, in particular, to focus on the specifics of the visual art medium and to identify what it is that art itself *does* that gives rise to a way of thinking and feeling about this subject.

When I first began work on art and trauma, people would often infer that the kind of art I was researching was that produced by survivors in therapy. The implicit assumption was that professional artists are a breed apart from survivors or those living in war zones—not least, I think, because of a perceived separation between those (artists) who direct their attention toward particular content and those focused on cutting-edge developments within art itself. Correspondingly, a show on trauma might be expected to appeal to special interest groups rather than to those wanting to see new developments in art. In identifying itself by theme, an exhibition on trauma is ipso facto orienting itself to concerns beyond the disciplinary boundaries of fine arts.

Trauma has now had its moment, however. In 2001 a British exhibition of prominent international artists, simply titled "Trauma," was accompanied by a catalogue affirming that "trauma—both individual and collective—has given rise to some of the most compelling art of recent years."[2] Explicitly distancing the show from "art as therapy or exorcism," the curators emphasized that few of the artists involved drew on personal experience. But still there remain a number of theoretical implications to framing such an exhibition—or, indeed, a monograph—in terms of this subject matter, which have led me to focus this inquiry, not on trauma itself, but on the affective operations of art and on the ways in which these situate art in a certain relation to trauma and to the kind of conflict that may engender trauma.

To identify any art as "about" trauma and conflict potentially opens up new readings, but it also reduces work to a singular defining subject matter in a fashion that is often anathema to artists, who construe the operations of their work as exceeding any single signifying function. Although this refusal of meaning embodies a more general challenge to art historical methods that define art principally in terms of its representational or signifying function, it seems to me that there are particularly compelling reasons to question those methods in the case of trauma. This is partly because trauma itself is classically defined as beyond the scope of language and representation; hence, an imagery of trauma might not readily conform to the logic of representation. But it also has to do with the interests of the primary subjects of trauma. If art purports to register the true experience of violence or devastating loss—to be about a particular event—then it lays claim to an experience that is fundamentally owned by someone. Moreover, it invites a wider audience to partake of this experience in some way.

There is a certain hubris in colonizing such experience—and particularly, as Leo Bersani argues in *The Culture of Redemption*, in art's claim to *salvage* damaged experience and thereby redeem life.[3] But what is at issue here—even more than the moral aspirations of a redemptive art—are the *realist* underpinnings of this kind of claim. A form of philosophical realism grounds the notion that art can capture and transmit real experience. This realism sits uneasily with a politics of testimony. I want to propose that such a politics requires of art *not* a faithful translation of testimony; rather, it calls upon art to exploit its own unique capacities to contribute actively to this politics.

In perhaps the most sustained theoretical argument to date for art's contribution to trauma politics, and to Holocaust studies, in particular,

Ernst van Alphen counters that we cannot limit the function of art—be it pleasure-producing or redemptive; what is important is that art itself challenges rather than reinforces the distinction between art (or the realm of imaginative discourse) and the reality of trauma and war.[4] Correspondingly, I intend to focus on work that operates on this boundary. This work does not transparently constitute a genre of trauma art and is not clearly representational. Although it addresses the realm of real experience in some sense, I argue that it is ill served by a theoretical framework that privileges *meaning* (i.e., the object of representation, outside art) over *form* (the inherent qualities or modus operandi of art).

In the 1990s, a number of literary theorists turned their attention to trauma and formed the core of a new interdisciplinary field, identified as trauma studies. Kali Tal's suggestion that the literature of trauma constitutes a distinct "marginal literature," like feminist or African-American literature, implicitly compares the formation of trauma studies to the emergence of areas such as women's studies that subordinate issues of medium to those of a particular object of analysis.[5] This is, of course, a strategy that has a political payoff; women's studies provide a location conducive to the development of feminist projects, just as trauma studies give an impetus and visibility to an important form of testimonial politics. But the danger with such a strategy is that the analysis of the specifics of any given medium is compromised by its subordination to the kind of teleological principles that determine the sociopolitical agenda of the field. Moreover, these principles will inevitably delimit the inclusions of the field.

For me, the question that flows from this is whether thematic or generic classifications—regardless of attempts to interpret the boundaries loosely—are inclined to commit us to a particular set of programmatic understandings about art's relationship to experience and subjectivity. If in fact they do, this may preclude recognition of the possibility that new ways of conceptualizing the politics of experience might actually be derived from the manner in which a visual arts medium can, in distinctive ways, register and embody affect. For this reason, I am mindful of the benefits of retaining some art historical specification—of proceeding from what art itself *does*—an approach that potentially allows into any contingent category of trauma art some unexpected inclusions.

Clearly, however, disciplinary orientation engenders its own problems. Working within an art theoretical framework, we run the risk of succumbing to the pitfalls that Bersani identifies: specifically, the tendency to reduce trauma or painful experience to a mere aesthetic concern. The best-known sustained analysis of the emergence of trauma within the domain of contemporary visual art is Hal Foster's *The Return of the Real*. Foster's conceptualization of the relationship between trauma and art turns on the brilliantly aphoristic notion that trauma discourse continues the poststructuralist critique of the subject by other means. Satisfying two contradictory imperatives—to guarantee identity, on the one hand, and to deconstruct its foundation, on the other—trauma discourse, Foster argues, presents the subject as simultaneously "evacuated and elevated."[6] The experience of trauma paradigmatically encapsulates both direct, unmediated affective experience and an absence of affect, insofar as it is resistant to cognitive processing and induces "psychic numbing." Thus, Foster suggests, it serves as a kind of trope or descriptor for a certain artistic posture: "many artists [today] seem driven to inhabit a place of total affect *and* to be drained of affect altogether. . . . This oscillation suggests the dynamic of psychic shock (of trauma). Pure affect, no affect: *It hurts, I can't feel anything.*"[7]

This focus on the *allure* of trauma discourse is echoed in other branches of cultural studies. Andreas Huyssen argues that the current fascination with trauma is symptomatic of a widespread cultural obsession with memory; Mark Selzer identifies the emergence of a "wound culture," of which the emergency room drama is a symptom; John Mowit, in a twist on Foster's analysis of the seductive appeal of the extreme experience of trauma, talks of the phenomenon of "trauma envy"—and Ghassan Hage provides a motive for this in his account of how postcolonial societies have elevated the figure of the victim to a position of moral superiority.[8]

Foster's analysis thus reflects a more general anxiety engendered by postcoloniality; as he notes, the "abjected" becomes attractive at the moment when the "abjector" is vilified and when it is assumed that "in order not to be counted among sexists and racists one must become the phobic object of such subjects."[9] But his is a diagnostic analysis conducted from within the discipline of art theory, providing an explanation for the way in which the figure of trauma is troped or borrowed to describe a condition that already pertains within the art world.

Unlike the proponents of trauma studies, who manifest an overarching concern with the primary experience of trauma and with the politics of testimony, Foster is not concerned to track the ways in which visual artists have dealt with trauma as a means of expanding an understanding of the nature and experience of traumatic memory. For him there is no imperative to deal with trauma, except insofar as it has become emblematic of a contemporary cultural sensibility. In this dematerialized and radically sublimated conception, trauma is reduced to a set of psychic functions—it becomes a chimera of the real. It is not conceived of as an event that might occur or have an impact within the domain of art; it is not part of the experience of the artist, except in an abstract or figurative sense, but neither is it firmly located elsewhere.

Trauma studies, on the other hand—notwithstanding its roots in poststructuralist literary theory—treats the "real event" as a force that necessarily impacts upon art, literature, and film. The fact that we live in a post-Holocaust world is understood to compel us to deal with Holocaust memory, and to account for the ways in which the Holocaust has touched us either directly or indirectly. Yet if Foster, like others concerned with "trauma culture," describes an aesthetic—rather than political—impulse, and implicitly affirms the separation of art from the traumatic event, trauma studies presumes to place itself at the heart of events that are, in fact, fairly removed from the lived reality of many of its proponents. Writers from Cathy Caruth and Shoshana Felman to Antjie Krog have, in fact, been accused of usurping the position of trauma victim—of appropriating testimony and treating trauma as an available or "unclaimed" experience (to use Caruth's phrase) when, in fact, its ownership is deeply contested.[10] Such writers often make a point of foregrounding self-reflexivity: Krog details the impact on journalists of testimonies delivered to the South African Truth and Reconciliation Commission, and Felman analyses responses to testimonial texts among a class of her own students. But this foregrounding does not always in itself allay the charge of appropriation, insofar as it seems to recast the testimony of another in terms of a drama to which the reader or listener is central.

How, then, might contemporary art engage trauma in a way that respects and contributes to its politics? If trauma enters the representational arena as an expression of personal experience, it is always vulnerable to appropriation, to reduction, and to mimicry. Is it possible, then, to conceive of the art of trauma and conflict as something other than the deposit of primary experience (which remains "owned" and unshareable even once it is communicated)?

What is required here is a framework that challenges the nexus between art and experience and a *realist* aesthetics: a framework that distinguishes the kind of inquiry that art might instantiate from the idea that art is a vehicle for the interpersonal transmission of experience. Narrative film lends itself to a realist interpretation by virtue of characterization—we see a character suffer, and we feel an emotional response—but most contemporary art does not. Even where work proceeds from an endeavor to register lived experience, it rarely configures this experience in terms of characters with whom we can readily identify. Nor does a good deal of contemporary art read easily as the expression of the artist's experience. Thus, the kinds of "transcriptions" of experience one encounters in art do not usually invite us to extrapolate a subject, a persona, from them. Under these conditions, the affective responses engendered by artworks are not born of emotional identification or sympathy; rather, they emerge from a direct engagement with sensation as it is registered in the work.

In this regard, trauma-related art is best understood as *transactive* rather than *communicative*.[11] It often touches us, but it does not necessarily communicate the "secret" of personal experience. To understand its transactive nature, we need to examine how affect is produced within and through a work, and how it might be experienced by an audience coming to the work. But if this affective transaction does not in and of itself convey the "meaning" of trauma, we must also pursue the question of how it might lead us toward a conceptual engagement.

One of the principal theoretical concerns of this book is thus to establish the nexus between art and thought as this is evinced within art practice. In this regard, I take a cue from Deleuze. In his early work *Proust and Signs*, Deleuze coins the term *encountered sign* to describe the sign that is felt, rather than recognized or perceived through cognition.[12] Deleuze's argument is not simply, however, that sensation is an end in itself, but that feeling is a catalyst for critical inquiry or deep thought; we assume, he says, that the best philosophy is motivated by a love of wisdom, but this is not, in fact, the case, since there is nothing that compels rational inquiry. For Deleuze, affect or emotion is a more effective trigger for profound thought because of the way in which it grasps us, forcing us to engage involuntarily: "More important than thought there is 'what leads to thought' . . . impressions which force us to look, encounters which force us to interpret, expressions which force us to think."[13] He quotes Proust directly on this: "The truths which intelligence grasps directly in the open light of day have something less profound, less *necessary* about them than those which life has communicated to us *in spite of ourselves* in an impression, a material impression because it has reached us through our senses."[14]

If art is akin to the sensory impression here, then it might be understood, not merely as illustrating or embodying a proposition, but as engendering a manner of thinking. On this account, art is not conceptual in itself but rather an embodiment of sensation that stimulates thought; the "intelligence," as Deleuze puts it, "comes after," not before.[15] Art is thus not driven by or enslaved by any particular understanding; it is always productive of ideas. But to say that art is not conceptual in this limited sense does not imply that it is only accidentally linked to thought, and I intend to demonstrate that this question of how affect leads us somewhere is carefully addressed within the structure of artworks.

On this crucial point, my theoretical concerns and methods both intersect with and diverge from an important strand of trauma studies that promotes a critical and self-reflexive *empathy* as the most appropriate form of engagement with trauma imagery. Dominick LaCapra, in his various studies of the representation of Holocaust experience, distinguishes empathy in the spectator (the third party, seeing testimony delivered) from the primary experience of trauma.[16] To that end, he proposes the concept of *empathic unsettlement* to describe the aesthetic experience of simultaneously *feeling for* another and becoming aware of a distinction between one's own perceptions and the experience of the other.[17]

LaCapra's arguments concerning historical method clearly invoke particular modes of historiographical practice. On the one hand, he argues against a positivistic tradition that rejects empathy as a mode of writing history; on the other, he resists an opposing tendency, characterized by overidentification with a victim position and the arrogation of survivor testimony.[18] In respect of the latter, LaCapra advances an important critique of an "uncritical, positive transference" that he finds manifested in both Claude Lanzmann's film *Shoah* and Shoshana Felman's response to it.[19] Principally, however, LaCapra's critique is shaped by issues emerging from the mediation (in quasi-documentary form) of actual witness testimony. In contrast, this book is for the most part concerned with work that is nonnarrative and nonrepresentational, although in Chapter 5, I address the question of how testimony might be negotiated within an experimental art practice. Thus, it evaluates contemporary artworks that have found ways of obviating the associated problems of identification, mimesis, and appropriation—problems that remain at issue with regard to the documentary form—and specifically *Shoah*—inasmuch as the presentation of "character" can be said to interpellate witnesses into a particular kind of sympathetic relationship.[20]

The debate around *Shoah* and the representation of Holocaust testimony in general has also given rise to concerns about "secondary traumatization"—or the possibility that trauma imagery may itself be traumatizing. Geoffrey Hartman has proposed that a form of "secondary trauma" is visited upon the viewer of graphic imagery who vicariously experiences a milder version of the shock experienced by the primary witness of the tragedy depicted.[21] LaCapra has similarly suggested that art may enable a secondary witness to experience a "muted" dose of trauma (although he wavers on this point, conceding that it might be preferable to restrict the application of the term "trauma" to "limit cases" that pass a certain threshold).[22]

While there are fundamental problems with the notion that art has the capacity to transmit trauma per se, Hartman invokes the concept of secondary traumatization in a useful discussion of the empathic response, calling for a complex, psychoanalytically informed analysis of this form of trauma, which is, in effect, what Luc Boltanski calls *souffrance à distance.*[23] Precisely because overidentification with a primary victim masks a fundamental *lack* of affinity, we must attend to the affects on which it is grounded, he argues. These may include forms of shame and guilt that may ultimately give rise to negative responses (hate, resentment) if they are not addressed. For Hartman, then, empathy is an indispensable response, but one that must be checked. Art's "truest reason," he argues, is encapsulated in the dictum "Art expands the sympathetic imagination while teaching us about the limits of sympathy."[24]

LaCapra is similarly concerned to rein in empathy, insisting that it be a "virtual, not vicarious, experience . . . in which emotional response comes with respect for the other and the realization that the experience of the other is not one's own."[25] In this regard, he explicitly relates the empathic response to what Kaja Silverman terms (after Max Scheler) "heteropathic identification," a form of encounter predicated on an openness to a mode of existence or experience beyond what is known by the self.[26] My study is premised on similar ethical foundations, inasmuch as it aligns with these critiques of an identification grounded in the effacement of difference but is not concerned with the representation of alterity per se—nor with the relations between given identities (victim, witness, etc.). This is because I do not deal with what LaCapra calls the "aboutness" of art, but with its processes.

The artists I consider may each be understood to produce affective art, although affect in this context does not equate with emotion or sympathy, nor does it necessarily attach to persons or to characters in the first instance. In many of the works discussed, affects arise in places rather than human subjects, in a way that allows us to isolate the function of affect, focusing on its motility rather than its origins within a single subject. This, in turn, facilitates an analysis of the affective transaction in terms other than those of the identificatory relationship.

In effect, then, this study keys into a Brechtian critique of identification (echoed through the work of Hartman and LaCapra), and, specifically, of art that induces what Brecht termed "crude empathy"—a feeling for another based on the assimilation of the other's experience to the self.[27] But rather than concentrating exclusively on the production of a Brechtian alienation effect, on the mechanisms for thwarting any form of identification, the aim of this study is to focus more sharply on affect itself, extracting the affective encounter from generalized accounts of emotional identification.

The book thus moves away from the traps of "crude empathy" to describe art that, by virtue of its specific affective capacities, is able to exploit forms of embodied perception in order to promote forms of critical inquiry. This conjunction of affect and critical awareness may be understood to constitute the basis of an empathy grounded not in affinity (*feeling for* another insofar as we can imagine *being* that other) but on a *feeling for* another that entails an encounter with something irreducible and different, often inaccessible.

Empathy, in this formulation, is characterized by a distinctive combination of affective and intellectual operations, but also by a dynamic oscillation, "a constant tension of going to and fro," as Nikos Papastergiadis has put it, "of going closer to be able to see, but also never forgetting where you are coming from . . . empathy is about that process of surrender . . . but also the *catch* that transforms your perception."[28] It is precisely this conception of empathy as a mode of seeing that underpins this book, which argues for the capacity of art to transform perception. Both Hartman and LaCapra invest art with similar potential, but their studies turn, ultimately, on a concern with the politics of transmission: transmission of meaning and of trauma itself. Here, I focus on art that resists the "danger that the disaster [may] take on meaning rather than body," as Maurice Blanchot puts it.[29]

If we can in philosophical terms refute the argument that art transmits content or meaning intersubjectively, and the associated notion that the substantive condition of trauma might be retransmitted via representation, the prime task for art theory is to determine the specific nature of both the aesthetic experience of affect and the manner in which art is able to open up trauma to an audience. If art cannot communicate the essence of a memory that is "owned" by a subject, it may nevertheless envisage a form of memory for more than one subject, inhabited in different modalities by different people. The instantaneous, affective response, triggered by an image, viewed under controlled conditions, may mimic the sudden impact of trauma, or the quality of a post-traumatic memory, characterized by the involuntary repetition of an experience that the mind fails to process in the normal way. But how does the staging of shock become more than an aesthetic conceit or a kind of metaphoric appropriation of trauma to describe the malaise that Foster describes as permeating the art world? Somehow it must become embedded in a deeper, more extended conception of memory—one that is not confined to a single point in time but that extends temporally and spatially to engage forms of lived experience. Thus, we shall trace the ways in which post-traumatic memory is felt in the here and now, both *internally* and *externally*, as it were. If art registers the shock of trauma (the flashback that one involuntarily revisits), it maintains this in tension with an experience of the present, an encounter with an "outside." I elaborate on this tension in Chapter 2 with reference to Charlotte Delbo's conception of the relationship of traumatic memory to "ordinary" memory.

In highlighting the workings of affect, I shall address responses that subtend those subject to conscious reflection—responses that are, in some sense, autonomic. But this does not entail construing the affective response in narrow cause-and-effect terms, as if the image functioned simply as a mechanistic trigger or stimulus. Certain media forms (e.g., horror films) exploit affective triggers as blunt instruments to engender fear and nothing more, but I steer away here from what has been termed "traumatic realism," tracing instead the conjunction of affect and cognition. Thus, I use specific examples to show that art does not merely assault us, or, conversely, offer a corrective interpretation. When it shocks us, it is the manner of what Brian Massumi has called "a shock to thought": a jolt that does not so much *reveal* truth as thrust us involuntarily into a mode of critical inquiry.[30]

Many of the works I consider—although not all—were produced by artists who are themselves primary witnesses or survivors of trauma. But their work is neither produced nor understood as expressive of a singular subjective account of trauma. In a number of instances, these artists explicitly negotiate relationships with survivors of trauma, loss, and violence, and also with an audience—but even where the subject matter of the work is ostensibly the trauma of a single subject, the artist is concerned less with the integrity of subjective expression than with the complex dynamic of speaking from an "inside" position to an "outside." Trauma, I suggest, is never unproblematically "subjective"; neither "inside" nor "outside," it is always lived and negotiated at an intersection. In this respect, the work I analyze is fundamentally relational rather than expressive in the traditional (communicative) sense of that term.[31]

I present a range of practices that address the fluid boundary between "insides" and "outsides," manifesting trauma not simply as an interior condition but as a transformative process that impacts on the world as much as on bodies. Trauma, in this sense, is conceptualized as having a presence, a *force*. Thus, I argue that visual art presents trauma as a *political* rather than a subjective phenomenon. It does not offer us a privileged view of the inner subject; rather, by giving trauma extension in space or lived *place*, it invites an awareness of different modes of inhabitation.

Embodying this principle, the book's trajectory runs from the local to the global, beginning in Chapter 2 with an examination of artwork addressing intimate or personal experience—experience that nevertheless resists containment within subjective or corporeal boundaries—and culminating in Chapter 6 with an examination of the dynamic by which a personal or local experience can be explored in relation to the global politics of the September 11 attacks.

Chapter 2, then, focuses on the ways in which the boundary between the inner subject and its outside is configured in contemporary artwork, at the same time advancing the central contention that the operative element of the artwork is its affective rather than its signifying capacity. Contemporary work addressing trauma is located within a longer genealogy of affective art, traced through a European and American tradition of performance art, and finding echoes in medieval devotional imagery and practice. Through such precedents, we are able to conceptualize the manner in which sensation might be understood to engender forms of knowing.

Chapter 3 traces the way in which trauma is given extension in the material world in work by artists from Colombia and Northern Ireland, conceived as a response to political violence and murder. Such work is implicitly concerned with audience response—but rather than using the affective trigger to induce a momentary shock, the artists address what might be understood as a mode of "traumatic time." They focus on the duration—rather than the instantaneity—of post-traumatic memory, so as to produce an affective encounter within a temporal framework quite different from that implied by "traumatic realism." Doris Salcedo constructs spaces in which loss is evoked as an embodied experience, yet in contrast to a number of her compatriots, dealing with political violence in Colombia, she avoids showing the faces or bodies of victims or describing the "cause" of trauma and loss. The Belfast artist Sandra Johnston is concerned with the tenuous nature of the relationship between image and affect. Her work points to the failure of graphic imagery or documentary photography to promote enduring empathy, even as it induces an emotive—or visceral —response. But emotions and feelings are not simply manipulated or redirected in the works of these artists; affect is revealed to flow *through* bodies and spaces, rather than residing within a single subject.

Art's capacity to evoke the extrasubjective aspect of trauma is further explored in Chapter 4. Focusing on the lived experience of place in the aftermath of violence and death in both Southern Africa and Northern Ireland, this chapter draws on the work of the philosopher of place Edward Casey. Utilizing Casey's concept of the "chorographic," it describes the practices of artists dealing with an embodied experience of place as it unfolds in time or in memory. A series of "journeys in place" are examined in order to detail the operations of the bodily metaphor in visual imagery, and the ways in which corporeal perception "takes us into" a particular image of place. In this way, the analysis of place extends the broader inquiry into the function of affect, demonstrating how metaphor may promote an examination of conditions of perception, and of the ways in which these are shaped by the social and political forces that structure the body's relationship to place.

Chapter 5 deals with work emerging as a response to the South African Truth and Reconciliation Commission, focusing in particular on the play *Ubu and the Truth Commission*, written by Jane Taylor and directed by the artist William Kentridge, whose animated films are incorporated into the stage production. The play might be seen as a metacritique of the way in which mediation of trauma—in this case in the form of testimony offered in public hearings—induces a form of sentimental identification or "crude empathy." In a Brechtian vein, *Ubu* deploys strategies of estrangement that thwart audience identification, but what is significant about this piece is the way in which these same devices work simultaneously to engender affect. The effect of the spectacle of *Ubu* is thus dependent not on its didactic message but on the creation of an intensity of affect that flows across and between bodies, and that refuses to settle within an ostensive subject. This, in turn, facilitates not identification but an encounter of an expropriative kind in which one *feels into* rather than simply mimics the condition of another.

Chapter 6 draws out the distinction between the *ex-propriative* encounter and the *a-propriative* act, looking at the painting of Gordon Bennett—work that is often characterized in a postmodern context as appropriative in its modus operandi. Bennett exemplifies a new form of political work that operates through empathic—and also expropriative—encounter, addressing his Australian background (which is both indigenous and Euro-Australian) and audience via the work of the late New York City African-American artist Jean-Michel Basquiat. A certain empathic relationship is internal to the work itself, inasmuch as Bennett finds resonances in Basquiat's life—and in Basquiat's experience of the politics of race in the United States—with his own life in Australia. But the works in question also purport to deal with New York City on September 11, 2001. In this regard, they raise interesting questions about ways in which distinct and different traumatic experiences might be linked. Is this work "about" 9/11 or about the politics of race in Australia; if it is "about" trauma, whose trauma—and what is the nature of the metaphorical relationships that link these loci? Again, this discussion moves beyond an analysis of signification to ask how a set of empathic connections that promote a form of transnational politics can be established through the formal language of painting.

Running through these chapters, then, there is a certain notion of the political. And, indeed, many of the artists discussed would describe their work as political even before foregrounding an interest in trauma. Whereas artists are often reluctant to pin down meaning—and hence to concede that a given work is about trauma—to identify the way a work operates within a political field is to make a different kind of interpretative claim. Such a claim emphasizes a dynamic process of intervention: a specific *mode of engagement*, to which the form of the work is integral.

Art, Ethics, Politics

Within trauma studies, the question of trauma's inherent unintelligibility, and consequent "unrepresentability," has itself become something of a trope. Derived from clinical and psychoanalytic accounts of trauma, the

configuration of a realm of traumatic memory outside the normal cognitive process is, as Ruth Leys demonstrates, a discursive organization with
its own genealogy.[32] But it is a modeling that allies trauma with avant-
garde projects in the arts. That which is categorically "beyond representation" may find expression within experimental formal languages. But the
umbrella of the avant-garde potentially provides more than a framework
for the development of a distinct language of trauma. The avant-garde, as
an "outside" with a clearly defined critical relationship to current "'insider"
practices and conventions, offers a rubric for a dialogue with the world of
representation and conventional language and, hence, for the politicization
of "trauma art."

Hal Foster has asked of the abject whether something that is "opposed
to culture" can be "exposed *in* culture"—and whether, in fact, "abject art
[can] ever escape an instrumental, indeed moralistic, use of the abject?"[33]
Yet it is the encounter with the limit case that defines and extends the avant-
garde or politically progressive art practice. Such art seeks out the unrepre-
sentable; thus, in a now famous elaboration of his statement to the effect
that one could not write poetry after Auschwitz, Theodor Adorno was able
to assert that art was compelled to "resist the verdict" that the Holocaust
was inimical to art.[34] Whatever is outside of itself—unrepresented, unthought—is what transforms the language of art. It is, then, the political
imperative—to confront the Holocaust, to confront AIDS, to confront
taboos—that forces art to transform itself and in the process to transform
thought. But does this reduce to an instrumental or moral use of art?

In Deleuze's terms, it is precisely what distinguishes ethical from moral
art. An ethics is enabled and invigorated by the capacity for transformation;
that is, precisely by not assuming that there is a given outside to thinking. A
morality on the other hand, operates within the bounds of a given set of
conventions, within which social and political problems must be resolved.
Thus, as Clare Colebrook argues, politically affirmative Hollywood movies
such as Jonathan Demme's *Philadelphia* (1993), which is critical of anti-gay
prejudice, use standard narrative devices to engender sympathy and manufacture an image of the "moral individual."[35] Homosexuality is thereby effectively recouped by mainstream morality as compassion wins out over fear
and homophobic attitudes are overcome by sympathetic interpersonal relationships. This, of course, leaves intact the larger political formations that
engender fear and prejudice. (A similar critique may be leveled against two
of the films I discuss in distinction to more radical art practice: Aline Isser-

mann's *Shadow of Doubt*—a film about child sexual abuse, and the documentary of the South African Truth and Reconciliation hearings, *Long Night's Journey into Day*, both of which turn on the resolution of conflict through interpersonal relationships.)

Many theorists, from Brecht and Adorno on, have argued for nonaffirmative forms of art to counter this kind of moralism and middlebrow humanism—and the current study is in part located in relation to this tradition. I draw frequently on Deleuze in this and other respects. Yet this is neither ultimately to provide an orthodox Deleuzian reading of trauma in art nor to outline a uniformly Deleuzian art historical methodology. Rather, I use select images and concepts from Deleuze's work—intertwined with references to Delbo, Casey, Brecht, Venna Das, Gayatri Spivak, Arjun Appadurai, Édouard Claperede, José Gil, and others—to suggest a certain set of relationships between art's formal properties and its ethico-political functions. To this end, I look principally to Deleuze's works on aesthetics for a theorization of art and sensation to underpin my analysis of affect in contemporary art. But there is another strand of Deleuze's thought that has some resonance with this study: the theorization of the political, to which the concept of affect is also central.[36]

The effective isolation of affect from character in Deleuze's work finds material extension in the practices of many of the artists I discuss. We see this, in particular, in Chapter 4 in the work of the Belfast artist Willie Doherty, whose video installation *The Only Good One Is a Dead One* evokes a notional "character" who plans an ambush from the security of a surveillance vehicle. Yet this character repeatedly succumbs to fantasies of his own capture and death. Conscience—or empathy—is here revealed as essentially unwilled, arising from a body that is sympathetic in spite of itself. Envisioning the mechanics of death as it will unfold in a particular location has a dramatic effect on the perpetrator's own relationship to space: his surveillance vehicle, the street become threatening to him. But even as it remains clear that he is instigating the single act of violence that induces his fear and discomfort, there is an inevitable, self-perpetuating momentum to this scenario as the video loop repeats. Space itself makes over its inhabitants—and this is the political trope of the work.

Here, characters are not agents precipitating action but are revealed as constituted within affective flows. These flows converge in the present to sustain a kind of web of subjectivities in which the identities of "victims," "perpetrators," and "bystanders" are defined. In this way, the cycle of violence that engenders certain psychological effects is revealed or studied as a political phenomenon. As a means to this end, Doherty locates us within a compressed space of the present. Thus, there is an intensification in his work that is quite at odds with the feel and pace of Doris Salcedo's installations, for example. But at the same time, there are resonances with Salcedo both in terms of this play on the bodily perception of space, and the way that subjectivity is politicized. Although Salcedo's work is produced out of a long-standing engagement with the victims of political violence, it is—as we shall see—less an exploration of the impact of violence on individuals than a more expansive and political description of a world shaped by violence, and of the kind of constraints that operate within such a world.

It is always easy for art and for audiences of art to take the moral line—to feel sympathy and compassion, to use art to confirm us in our humanitarian role. But artists like Salcedo and Doherty are often more concerned to remind us that identifications are not always the result of moral choices. And more than this, that there is an ethical imperative to think beyond the moral role, because as Nietzsche puts it: "[People] confound themselves with their role; they become victims of their own 'good performance'; they themselves have forgotten how much accidents, moods, and caprice disposed of them when the question of their 'vocation' was decided—and how many other roles they might have been able to play; for now it is too late . . . the role has actually become character; and art, nature."[37]

Hence, Doherty presents character poised on a knife-edge. From a single affective base, he effects a pull toward the two apparently opposing poles of killer and victim, so that the polarity collapses. In the process, affect becomes the object of analysis, effectively prized away from character or identity.

Whereas a didactic or moral image might tell us whether a character was bad or good, exploiting character identification to align us with the moral viewpoint, here we are aligned neither with good nor bad. Our propensity for affective investment or bodily identification allows us to oscillate between good and evil, so that we feel different possibilities, we see how a role might *become* character. The register of political analysis is not the act itself but the larger flows within which investments are made, and subjectivities are forged. To put a kind of Deleuzian gloss on this—the politics of such work lies in its understanding of affective investments. We are not looking at already formed subjects and the relations between them —that is, between perpetrators and victims within a given sociopolitical

frame or moral law—but at the way in which politics and morality operate via the coding of affective intensities and the production of identity
grounded in affect.

Salcedo has said of her most recent work—inspired by events in Colombia in the 1980s—that it is an attempt to explore the ways in which
perpetrators, victims, and bystanders are *all* compromised by a cycle of violence.[38] Politics for her cannot be reduced to the intersubjective—to an
analysis of the relationships that pertain between already formed characters. And in this respect, she believes her work to be generalizable; because
it is about the *mechanisms* of constraint, it is as much about the constraints
of the refugee, for example, as of the Colombian victim of terror. In this
sense, we realize that the work does not turn on its capacity to signify or to
represent, or to embody the trace of the individual subject or event. It is
rather the sensation arising in space that is the operative element: its capacity to sustain sensation (to quote Deleuze's definition of art) rather than
to communicate meaning.[39]

By figuring memory in "trauma art" as lived and felt in relation to a
whole series of interconnected events and political forces, rather than as embodied in an atomized subject, we are able to move trauma into a distinctive political framework. Instead of seeing trauma as a condition we might
mimic or appropriate from an aesthetic standpoint, or analyzing the appeal
of traumatic subjectivity (in the manner of Foster and others), we might
now begin to plot this mode of subjectivity on a larger global picture. This
picture needs to be textured with the kind of analysis provided by postcolonial theory—so that any formal analysis proceeds in conjunction with a
reading of global and micropolitics: that is, a sense of our connectedness to
global events and the precise nature of our relationship to others.

. . . since 2001

In the late 1990s, trauma studies was identified by certain commentators as a fin de siècle phenomenon, yet it has flourished rather than
waned in the 2000s.[40] No doubt the attacks of September 11 and the ensu-
ing "War on Terror" have been an important factor in this regard. Writers
like Foster and Hage suggest that identification with the victim of oppression or traumatized subject is a function of a kind of postcolonial anxiety—a social conscience afflicting privileged First World subjects, for whom
trauma is characteristically of the other. But on 9/11 such trauma was de-

finitively visited on the "center," and the West continues to live under the threat of terrorism, reminded through events such as the Bali bombings that no corner of the globe is unreachable. Terrorism now touches us all—to a greater or lesser extent—through what Mike Davis has called the "globalization of fear."[41]

On one level, this suggests that art produced in the context of political violence in, for example, Colombia or Northern Ireland, might be received with a greater sensitivity in the United States in the wake of 9/11; in other words, that global politics have themselves engendered the conditions for greater empathy. But, on the other hand, we might question whether the globalization of trauma does not in itself efface the specificity of experience. New Yorkers or Australians might be more touched by the plight of Colombians these days, but are we any more willing and able to *understand* their situation insofar as this entails an acknowledgment of an alterity, irreducible to our own experience?

Hage's comments on the extension of victimology are all the more pertinent in the post-9/11 context, particularly as they identify a form of cultural investment that works to occlude both difference and political responsibility. Hage argues that the mobilization of binaries that fix the victim in opposition to the oppressor produces an illegitimate extrapolation by which the victim is ipso facto equated with "good." The victim thus acquires a kind of protected status, as if the fact that a victim of oppression or violence was *bad* might mitigate the crimes of the oppressor. This polarization pits passivity against agency; if we are all victims, none of us are any longer implicated in outcomes.

Prior to 9/11, Michel Serres argued that in responding to the problem of evil simply by seeking someone to accuse, we have exhausted the possibilities of accusation, exculpation, and exoneration. Thus the present dispensation may be characterized: "By this global result: evil, hate, or violence has every object but no subject. Rain, hail, and thunder fall on everyone, without there being a hand that dispenses them or controls the electrical current. Active evil is conjugated like an impersonal verb, it is freezing, it is thundering."[42]

The "ultimate" act of terrorism, the one that penetrated the perimeter fence of the home of First World capitalism on September 11, is emblematic in this regard. We are all "victims" of the 9/11 attacks, by some degree of association—or by the laws of globalization that ensure that the economic fallout of an event in New York City affects the lives of those on the other side of the world—but none of us (except Osama bin Laden and a handful of al-Qaeda operatives) are understood to have been in any way implicated prior to this date. In large sectors of the U.S. media, in the aftermath of the attacks, it was heresy to whisper the suggestion that U.S. foreign policy might, in some small way, have contributed to the global scenario that prompted the attacks;[43] that anything other than the abstraction of evil produced "the Evil One" and his affiliates. The laws of global flow seemed to allow that everything was connected to everything else *from* this point, but not before; 9/11 was not the culmination of history but its beginning.

As I try to show through analysis of Gordon Bennett's 911 paintings, it is not that we need to return to an analysis of individual agency in order to understand the interconnectedness of things; global events are all, in some sense, overdetermined (the United States didn't *cause* Osama bin Laden to do what he did, although it may nevertheless have been implicated in his emergence as a terrorist force). The question is rather, in what ways are we (all) invested in, even produced out of, the "flows" or forces (political, cultural, economic, social) in motion across the globe—and how is "active evil" constituted through us? To address such questions, we need to focus not on the interpersonal negotiation but on this bigger picture.

These issues are of concern to many of the artists discussed in this book—particularly those who ask how a cycle of violence is perpetuated in their part of the world, be it in Colombia or Belfast or Johannesburg. As the South African artist William Kentridge says in a discussion of his work *History of the Main Complaint*, referenced in Chapter 4, "there may not be blame but there is responsibility."[44]

If the concept of trauma long ago entered the popular vernacular through the discourse of self-help manuals and television talk shows, it was generalized to an unprecedented degree after 9/11. The term "trauma" came to encompass a range of responses, including those that might more accurately be described as anxiety, shock, fear, sympathy, compassion, and so on. But at the same time, for many "secondary witnesses"—those affected by the tragedy, but not directly involved—the symptomology of trauma offered a means to articulate an affective response—and also to identify as a victim—even at some remove from the locus of the attacks.[45]

What was generally lacking in the popular mediation of emotional identifications with the victims of the September 11 attacks was a conceptualization of empathy that might enable us not simply to feel for those victims but to articulate and understand our difference from them. This might be understood to echo the failure of the First World to think outside of itself—to understand its differences from other places—and to understand the ways in which post-9/11 life in New York City is still radically different from life in Bogota or Jenin.

As a political as well as an affective mode, much of the art I discuss can be seen in a critical relation to this global tendency. Its contribution to trauma studies does not reduce to a further extension of the already attenuated trauma discourse through aestheticization. It does not simply make available a condition of trauma or suffering to a wider audience. Indeed, after 9/11, it seems all the more urgent to counter the notion that trauma can be transmitted or shared through art, as well as the tendency to overidentify with the victims of trauma.

The artwork analyzed here was largely produced prior to September 2001, but its political significance comes into sharp focus in the global social context shaped by the events of 9/11. Moreover, I propose that it is this context that provides the most compelling basis for uniting a group of works that are linked not strictly by theme but by a mode of political engagement. These works often provide a way of thinking about trauma, but they are not symptomatic of a "trauma culture." For the most part, those discussed in Chapters 3 to 6 are the product of a sustained engagement with the consequences of political violence in diverse parts of the world, although they do not offer a clear political statement in the manner of didactic works. Insofar as they warrant generic treatment, they do so because they point to a new way of doing politics in art: one that is characterized by an aesthetic of relations. This mode of politics addresses the impact of trauma on the world—although it is not precisely about the subjective—and it operates through affective connection—although it is not simply concerned with the interpersonal. Principally, it understands or "enacts" the political as a sphere of interconnection, in which subjectivities are forged and sustained, but within which new links might be traced between subjects and places with only limited experience in common.

What I seek to show, then, is how, by realizing a way of seeing and feeling, this art makes a particular kind of contribution to thought, and to politics specifically: how certain conjunctions of affective and critical operations might constitute the basis for something we can call *empathic vision.*

Insides, Outsides: Trauma, Affect, and Art

Seeing Feeling

> It is impossible to feel emotion as past. . . . One cannot be a spectator
> of one's own feelings; one feels them, or one does not feel them; one
> cannot imagine them without stripping them of their affective essence.
> —Édouard Claparède, "La Question de la 'mémoire' affective"

There is a compelling logic to these words, written in 1911 by the
Swiss psychologist Édouard Claparède. Emotions are felt only as they are
experienced in the present; as remembered events, they become representations. The conceptual work implied in the act of remembering—of representing to oneself—entails a kind of distanced perception: one thinks
rather than simply *feels* the emotion. For Claparède, to represent oneself in
memory was to see oneself "from the outside," as one might see another.
"My past self," he wrote, "is thus psychologically distinct from my present
self, but it is . . . an emptied and objectivized self, which I continue to feel
at a distance from my true self which lives in the present."[1]

Claparède's refutation of the possibility of emotional memory is partly
influenced by the work of William James, who argued that although we can
remember undergoing specific emotions, we cannot remember just how
those emotions felt.[2] However, wrote James, if emotions are not retrievable
from memory, they are *revivable*; hence, we don't remember grief or ecstasy,
but by recalling a situation that produces those sensations, we can produce

a new bout of emotion.[3] In other words, affect, properly conjured up, produces a real-time somatic experience, no longer framed as representation.

This opposition between affect and representation also subtends early work on trauma and memory. Pierre Janet argued that in the normal course of events, experiences are processed through cognitive schemes that enable familiar experiences to be identified, interpreted, and assimilated to narrative. Memory is thus constituted as experience transforms itself into representation. Traumatic or extreme affective experience, however, resists such processing. Its unfamiliar or extraordinary nature renders it unintelligible, causing cognitive systems to balk; its sensory or affective character renders it inimical to thought—and ultimately to memory itself. Moreover, trauma is not so much remembered as subject to unconscious and uncontrolled repetition: "It is only for convenience that we speak of it as a 'traumatic memory,'" Janet writes. "The subject is often incapable of making the necessary narrative which we call memory regarding the event."[4]

The argument that trauma resists representation has continued to be made at different times in relation both to psychological process and to aesthetics. Bessel van der Kolk, for example, has been particularly influential in reviving the work of Janet in order to argue that traumatic memory is of a "non-declarative" type, involving bodily responses that lie outside verbal-semantic-linguistic representation.[5] In the humanities, the development of trauma studies in the United States in the 1990s has prompted a revaluation of modernist literary texts, and of poetry, in particular, as forms of Holocaust or war testimony.[6] Such texts, rather than narrativizing traumatic experience, are seen as bearing the imprint of trauma.

Up until now, theorists of trauma and memory have paid relatively little attention to visual and performance art. Yet in those fields, we find a long tradition of engagement with affect and immediate experience, not just as sources of inspiration or objects of representation, but as fundamental components of a dynamic between the artwork and the spectator. In an almost concrete sense, much visual and performance art evokes the possibility—for both artist and viewer—of "being a spectator of one's own feelings." The kind of imagery that operates in this vein—mediating affects, sensations, and traumatic memory—cannot be reduced to a form of representation. And insofar as such imagery serves to register subjective processes that exceed our capacity to represent them, certain of its features might be understood as reflecting those of traumatic memory.

The distinction between narrative memory and traumatic memory thus seems to offer a useful schema for distinguishing a realm of secondary imagery in which affective experience is not simply referenced but activated or staged in some way. By specifying the characteristics of the imagery, we may be able to understand it as contributing to an inquiry into subjective process. But I want to resist reading such imagery purely in terms of a symptomology of trauma—that is, as embodying a pathology or set of symptoms defined exclusively in clinical terms. Such a reading would simply treat artwork as illustrative of memory process. Rather than taking as axiomatic a radical and incommensurable split between traumatic and normal memory, I shall treat these provisional categories as fluid and expansive, considering both their mutually constitutive nature and the ways in which they are extended through art production.

In this chapter, then, I focus on three things. The first is how a practice of art making—which has certain formal resonances with a substantive category of memory—calls for a rethinking of the concepts of affect and expression conventionally used within art theoretical discourse. The second is how new ways of reading this imagery can enhance our understanding of experiences associated with trauma. By demonstrating this, I shall show that artworks can be regarded, not simply as illustrating certain clinical, psychological, or psychoanalytic propositions, but as engendering new languages of trauma that proceed from its lived experience. Third, I want to suggest the ways in which visual and performative languages of trauma and affect operate in dialogue with other discourses of memory. By exploring the relationship between the registration of the subjective experience or trauma and the realm of normative memory or representation, I shall address the relationship between *affective* and *critical* function. Thus, I shall move toward a consideration of the ways in which affective responses to artworks can be thought provoking as well as emotive—and, specifically, how they can produce a form of empathy that is more complex and considered than a purely emotional or sentimental reaction. In this chapter I focus primarily on works concerned with child sexual abuse in order to exemplify the politics and the stakes involved in an analysis of emergent languages of trauma.

Conventional theories of expression are inadequate to the task of describing the mode of image production I have outlined, insofar as they regard the artwork as the transcription or deposit of a prior mental state.[7] The imagery of traumatic memory deals not simply with a past event or with the objects of memory but with the present experience of memory. It therefore calls for a theorization of the dynamic in which the work is both produced and received—a theory, in other words, of affect.

A useful reference point for conceptualizing such a project is provided, in a literary context, by the French poet and Holocaust survivor Charlotte Delbo, whose work following her experience in Auschwitz is interesting not simply for its form and content as survivor testimony but also for the fact that it institutes a category of memory that becomes at the same time an aesthetic category. This category, identified with the terms "deep memory" and also "sense memory," designates precisely the realm of affective memory that Janet regards as nameless—as outside memory proper.[8]

Like Janet, Delbo posits ordinary memory as properly representational; it is the memory connected with the thinking process and with words —the realm in which events are rendered intelligible, pegged to a common or established frame of reference, so that they can be communicated to, and readily understood by, a general audience. But whereas Janet is concerned primarily with identifying cognitive process, Delbo invokes the notion of ordinary or "common" memory to describe a social or popularly understood discursive framework, designated as the site where history is written. Common memory is thus not simply a form of narrative memory inherent in the individual subject but the language that enables such memory to be transmitted and easily understood. For Delbo, the writing of history in the language of common memory, its processing and presentation within an intelligible narrative framework, was of vital social importance. But at the same time, she realized that something integral to the experience of the Holocaust is lost when an essentially traumatic experience is consigned to history, when the imposition of a temporal frame establishes a distance from the present and effects a stripping of affect in Claparède's sense.

For Delbo, sense memory registers the physical imprint of the event. As such, it is always in the present, although not continuously felt: "Auschwitz is there, fixed and unchangeable, but wrapped in the impervious skin of memory that segregates itself from the present 'me' . . . everything that happened to this other 'self', the one from Auschwitz, doesn't touch me now . . . so distinct are deep memory [*mémoire profonde*] and common memory [*mémoire ordinaire*]."[9]

Seen from the outside, Delbo's Auschwitz experience is the property of another self, much like Claparède's "past self." Delbo experiences these two selves as segregated, yet she also speaks of being in the grip of sense memory for periods of several days, during which time the physical pain of her trauma returns. Thus, the Auschwitz self, for all that it is discrete, retains a capacity to touch and affect, to trigger emotion in the present.

As the source of a poetics or an art, then, sense memory operates through the body to produce a kind of "seeing truth,"[10] rather than "thinking truth," registering the pain of memory as it is directly experienced, and communicating a level of bodily affect. The art of sense memory might further be distinguished as a motivated practice. Radically different from timeless or transhistorical expressionism, it aims to constitute a language of subjective process (specifically, of affective and emotional process) to complement history and to work in a dialectical relationship with common memory. Its production thus becomes a contingent and culturally situated practice—linked to social histories—that requires framing against a backdrop of cultural knowledge.[11]

Ethical Investigations and the Issue of Child Sexual Abuse

Michel Foucault reminds us, that *ars*, unlike *scientia*, promotes open-ended inquiry; it can embrace the unknown, the abject, the amoral, the aberrant, the pornographic, not as pathology but as experience.[12] Foucault's notion of an open-ended artistic exploration is, however, at odds with a method of textual or image analysis that would read the artwork through a clinical or psychoanalytic text, simply as a symptomology of trauma. In this respect, Ruth Leys has criticized the application of models of traumatic memory derived from van der Kolk and Janet to the analysis of literary testimony. Leys points out that the concept of traumatic memory embraced in this work— in particular, the idea that victims are revisited by traumatic memories and unable to process them—should not be treated as axiomatic but as part of a larger discursive formation.[13] My interest here lies not specifically in a critique of van der Kolk's model but in arguing for a more expansive reading of the imagery of trauma, unconstrained by singular or pathological models; a reading, modeled, in this regard, according to a Foucaultian ethics.

In the era of postcolonialism, trauma has acquired a certain cachet, and, with it, a moral authority. Increasingly, it is discomforting to find oneself aligned with cultural oppressors; hence, it has become politically desirable to identify with victims of oppression. But as Ghassan Hage has argued, this has produced a tendency to exalt the condition of innocence pertaining to the specific event and to transform it into a moral attribute.[14]

The victims of oppression or terror thus become ciphers of good, simply by virtue of having been subjected to evil.

By co-opting the designation "victim" into a narrative of good and evil, we foreclose on the possibility of elaborating a description of traumatic experience that addresses either the moral ambiguities of lived experience or the inherent tension between the experience of sense memory and that of common memory. It is this tension that fundamentally characterizes the struggle to represent or register traumatic experience. Thus, the art of sense memory is less an art of pure personal or subjective expression than an enactment of the uneasy relationship between common memory and that which threatens its coherence: a manifestation of the lived experience of an inside and an outside. In recent times, we have seen this most clearly demonstrated in work documenting the experience of living with AIDS—work that is concerned with a form of traumatic experience that is beyond the scope of established forms of representation, but that is simultaneously bound up with a continual negotiation of the interface with social and cultural institutions.[15] The language developed to express the particular nature of this experience manifests not only a form of sense memory but a sense of how such memory might cut across common memory, revealing a kind of truth that eludes the moral organization of common memory.

The advantages of an art practice that suspends moral judgment are similarly apparent in relation to the highly charged issue of child sexual abuse. Once unspoken and effectively denied, child abuse is now the subject of a certain amount of moral panic. It tends to be figured in rather stark moral terms in common language, the demonized figure of the pedophile representing the antithesis of the child victim, who becomes, in turn, the cipher of innocence. This framework leaves little space for exploring the subjective experience of either perpetrator or survivor, both of whom frequently confound moral categorization. How can a survivor describe the experience of rape perpetrated by a loved one—or that of "becoming sexualized" at an early age—from the perspective of an innocent? And what of the abuser who is him- or herself the survivor of abuse, a victim of the act s/he now perpetrates? For all that we might concur that child abuse is, categorically, an immoral act, the experience of being abused cannot be contained in the figure of the victim; survivors are necessarily *more* than passive victims of the acts of another in the sense that survivors live and continually negotiate the effects of abuse.

To register and understand the nature of those effects, we need a form

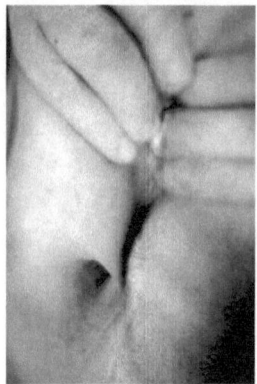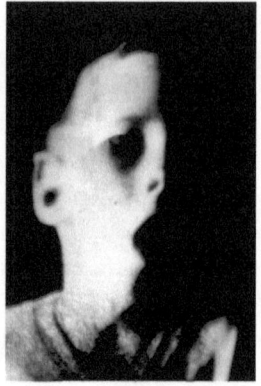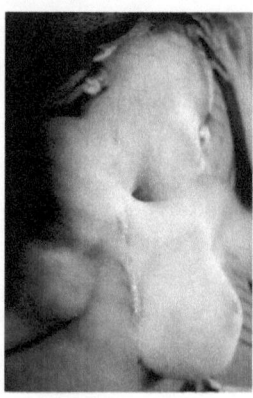

FIGURE 1. Dennis Del Favero, *Parting Embrace* (1997). Detail: *Parting 1, Parting 2, Parting 3.* Type C photographs. Used with permission.

of imagery that proceeds from or, at least, privileges the vicissitudes of lived experience. In other words, we require an approach that pursues the exploration of traumatic memory not as *scientia sexualis* in which moral or medical classification precedes representation, but as open artistic inquiry. This means not only circumventing classification, however, but moving outside a representational practice that aims to comment on its subject matter, treating the event of abuse as a completed past action, toward a practice that sees the artwork as generating sensation so as to produce an encounter in the present. Yet at the same time, such work does require a discursive framework; it operates, in other words, in concert with developing cultural awareness of the issue of sexual abuse.

Dennis Del Favero's *Parting Embrace*, a series of ten large photographs, does not approach the experience of abuse from within a narrative or moral framework (fig. 1). Instead, it seeks to register the pain of abuse as physical imprint. Constructed as an unfolding of memory, the imagery offers a vision from the body, embracing in the process a certain moral ambiguity. The artist says of this work that it incorporates not just the pornography and the violence of memories of abuse, but also an element of love or fantasy, and that these things are not always distinct; the affects of fear, humiliation, shock, and so on, may be tied to the same objects as those of joy and excitement. In other words, "love" may characterize an aspect of the relationship one has with an abuser—particularly in an incestuous relationship where the victim has an emotional attachment to the abuser, notwithstanding the pain or trauma that may accompany abuse. Hence

Parting Embrace actually divides through the center: the first five images in the series constituting *Parting*, the last five *Embrace*. As the titles suggest, the second set of images, which are softer, and more diffused, cast memories in more positive, romantic hues than the more overtly disturbing and hard-core *Parting*.[16] Here, then, the mix of feelings, sensations, and emotions that characterize the experience of abuse for certain survivors is privileged, at the cost of moral clarity.

Part of what the imagery conveys is precisely a condition of confusion. In this respect, the work does not aim to transcribe sense memory into common memory; it offers only fragments of memories, written onto the body. These can be read only in reference to the viewer's bodily sensation. To see these images is to be moved by them—not in the sense that one is touched by the plight of a character in a fictional narrative, but in the more literal sense being *affect*ed, stricken with affect.

The expansive nature of Del Favero's inquiry can be appreciated through a contrast with a more overtly moral—but nevertheless illuminating—representation of the subject of child abuse in which more conventional narrative forms provide a vehicle both for the transformation of the survivor and for effecting a (moral) resolution.

Aline Issermann's 1992 film *L'Ombre du doute* (Shadow of Doubt) is the story of a twelve-year-old girl—Alexandrine—who is sexually abused in her home by her father. Through an exploration of Alexandrine's interactions with various social institutions (the nuclear family, school, social welfare organizations, the judiciary), the film examines the speaking position of the abused child, highlighting the limitations and expectations attached to it. Alexandrine's mother, too frightened to see the truth, is compelled to doubt her daughter's words, punishing her for telling tales when she speaks of the abuse. Similarly, Alexandrine's father fails to acknowledge the reality of the situation, implying that his daughter's feelings are misguided, confused, unfair. Far from validating their daughter's self-awareness, the two parents deny the truth of her statements and thereby the nature of her experience. The reality for Alexandrine at this point is that words fail her. Her spoken accounts fall short of conveying the truth of her experience. Coached by a persistent social worker, Alexandrine is finally able to speak of her ordeal, at first within a private context and subsequently to the courts. To make this last step, however, Alexandrine has to adopt the language of external or common memory—a language designed to translate for others, to render experience a matter of public record.

Once Alexandrine's testimony receives institutional support, it acquires a certain truth status, allowing Alexandrine to move out of what Delbo calls the "world beyond knowledge." Through the act of testifying (albeit under inauspicious conditions), Alexandrine establishes her own presence at a scene to which others now bear witness. But if the film's narrative resolves rather too easily through this reconciliation, it is haunted by the specter of failure embodied in the character of Jean, Alexandrine's father. At the end of the film, we learn that Jean was himself abused by his father as a small boy. This experience leaves him with a facility of denial that enables him thereafter to misrecognize his own activities and to identify himself as a victim rather than a perpetrator. The tragedy of Jean's story lies not simply in his abuse but in the fact that no one bore witness to his experience. He is the Alexandrine that might have been—the child who never got to tell his story and who, as a result, lost any capacity for self-recognition. In adulthood, Jean recreates the scene of his own abuse, continually leaving open the possibility of discovery by his wife. He wants to be discovered. To be seen in the act of abusing his own daughter would at least release him momentarily from the unspeakable, unintelligible realm of his own trauma.

The suppressed core of *L'Ombre du doute* is the issue of unspeakability—or the realm of sense memory. As Alexandrine is reclaimed by the discourse of common memory and thereby rehabilitated into everyday life, the unspoken is contained within the demonized figure of the father whose cause is lost. Whereas in Del Favero's work, affect flows across multiple bodies and body parts, suggesting the failure of this kind of (moral) containment, here narrative order prevails, while good and bad cohere within the fixed boundaries of character. What the film does not tackle is the fragmentation of memory within the subject, the sense in which one must always live with memory and come to terms with it. If post-traumatic memory requires the double articulation implied in Delbo's distinction between sense and common memory, then Alexandrine's story is not simply told in the narrative account she produces as testimony but remains at least, in part, embedded in a sense memory, forged from an initial condition of unspeakability.

The bleak image of Jean, the abusive father, who tells his story at the end of the film, goes some way to dispelling the illusion that languages of common memory are readily available to the survivors of abuse, thus to some extent tempering the harmonizing trajectory of the film. It alerts us to the importance of the reception of speech—or to what the psychoana-

lyst and child survivor of the Holocaust Dori Laub identifies as the necessity of witnessing.[17] In one of the founding texts of contemporary trauma
studies, Laub argues that those who experienced the trauma of life in the
Nazi camps were not at the time, or subsequently, in a position to bear witness to the event of the Holocaust. In spite of—and because of—the fact
that survivors were at the very center of the Holocaust, they are unable to
extricate themselves from the event in order to describe it from the perspective of an external observer—that is, in ordinary or common language.
In Laub's view, this produces a need to tell one's story, not simply so that
others may know the truth of the camps (as is commonly assumed), but so
that the witnesses themselves can come to know and process the experience. The therapist, as listener, or the filmmaker videotaping testimony thus
becomes a key facilitator: the witness who enables the subject to articulate
his or her own experience.

What precisely, then, is documented in the videotaping of testimony
or in the dramatization of the discovery of sexual abuse—that is, when a
witness testifies to camera (as in Claude Lanzmann's film *Shoah*, for example), or when the fictional Alexandrine talks to the social worker who has be-
friended her? Rather than the objects of memory, a process is registered: an
attempt to find a language. These representational forms do not simply
frame the suffering of the individual, an expression in the form of a private
language; they evince a process of coming into view—of moving out of the
realm of traumatic memory through a set of social interactions. As sense
memory is spoken in any given space, it is bound up in a dynamic encounter
with a structure of representation, so that it becomes, in Gilles Deleuze's
phrase, a question of putting "an outside and an inside into contact."[18] And
it is this notion of the interface—of a point of contact to be negotiated—
that is central to understanding the experience of sense memory. What flows
from this is that we cannot automatically presuppose that imagery associated
with traumatic memory will take a particular form—or a pure form in the
sense associated with various kinds of expressionistic art practices.

The value of Deleuze's notion that affect is produced as intensity, by
formal means rather than by narrative, is that it allows us to understand affect as something other than an emotional response to character, and thus
to address the limitations of a narrative organization that contains affect
within certain corporeal and moral boundaries. Rather than prescribing or
implying the necessity of a particular avant-garde form, however, this insight provides us with a means of reading encounters between "insides"

and "outsides"—as between sense memory and common memory—within any given pictorial or performative field.

A painting in a relatively conventional narrative form by the South African artist Motseokae Klas Thibeletsa seems to me to exemplify the attempt to depict the experience of memories of abuse as poised at a point of entry into common language. Into a vivid scene of domestic abuse, Thibeletsa inserts an incongruous witness, Alexandrine's mother, a prim woman in a hat—parodying the image of the churchgoing moralist—who does not want to see the scene she confronts. There is an element of wish-fulfillment about this scene; this is the painting Alexandrine or her father might have produced. Its emotive power lies in the clash that occurs in the imagined moment of discovery: the moment in which sense memory breaks through into a representational economy that cannot entirely subsume it. The authorial subject of such work might be construed, not as *lying behind* an expression or representation, but rather as a nodal point in a dialogue within —but also between—various languages. If the negotiation of sense memory entails an emergence into a designated social space, then it occurs not in a discrete region but as a rupture within the field of representation or common memory.

If Thibeletsa's painting operates in the gap between ordinary language—or common memory—and subjective experience, the work of New York performance artist Karen Finley might be seen as directly testing the capacity of cultural memory to admit a form of testimony grounded in a language of sense memory. Finley has provoked riots, been closed down, and had funding cut for her performance monologues, which have been described by Elinor Fuchs as "a theater of disgust filled with obscene fantasies."[19] Her performances of discontinuous first-person narratives, in which she appears to take on different personae in a trancelike state, are to some degree suggestive of traumatic memory. Paradigmatic of a resistance to moral categorization, they present experience that is inherently amoral and that exceeds the bounds of ordinary language. In *The Constant State of Desire*, for example, Finley takes on the voice of a man fantasizing about the rape of a mother:

I just take that mama and push her against that washer. Then I take her baby, a bald-headed baby, put Downy Fabric Softener on baby's head, strap that baby around my waist till it's a baby dildo. Then I take that baby—that baby dildo —and fuck its own mama . . . 'CAUSE I'M NOTHING BUT A MOTHER-FUCKER![20]

The fantasy progresses to incest—"Then I mount my own mama in the ass"—in the process, mocking the possibility of moral judgment in this context: "That's right, I fuck my own mama in the ass 'cause I'd never fuck my mama in her snatch! She's my mama." The bitter irony lacing such black humor is the only device that enables us to establish any moral distance from the figure of the perpetrator. Unconstrained within the vestigial narrative, this figure is brought to life and allowed to regale us with his disturbing fantasies. If the indulgence of the fantasy of the perpetrator, conveyed through a language of sexual violence, grounded inexorably in a male body, is somewhat mitigated by Finley's own gender, the audience is all the more disturbed by the ease with which Finley allows herself to be inhabited by the figure of the perpetrator. In the next phase, the monologue poignantly evokes the lonely figure of a young girl abused by her father:

And the first, and the first, and the first memory I have, I have of my father is of him putting me into the refrigerator. He'd take off all my clothes on my five year-old body. . . . My feet and fingers would get into the piccalilli, they'd get into the mustard, the mayo. You wonder why I puke whenever I see condiments. . . . My daddy stands behind the icebox door. He smiles wide saying we're goin' to play a secret game, for just me and daddy. Then he says don't tell anyone. It's just our game. . . . He slap slap. He slap slap. I don't know this game. I don't want to play this game. Then he smiles wide. I hold onto my dollies more. Then he leans down to the vegetable bin, opens it and takes out the carrots, the celery, the zucchini, the cucumbers. Then he starts working on my little hole, my little little, hole. My little girl hole. Showing me "what it's like to be a mama," he says. Showing me "what it's like to be a woman, to be loved. That's a daddy's job," he tells me. Working my little hole. Hee. HEE. HEHHEEE. HEE HUHUHU HUH. Working my little hole hee hee heee.

Finley's evocation of the child's eidetic memory, linked to objects and sensations appears at first to effect an acting out of a traumatic memory; but if we are invited to witness this trauma, if the performance is intended to engender what D. W. Winnicott calls a "potential space" in which the trauma of abuse might be discovered, then our position as witness is made all the more uncomfortable by the infusion of self-conscious humor—and by what is usually taken to be the calculated provocation of the performance.[21]

Finley's work seems, in fact, to fit squarely within a tradition of performance art, given to testing the limits of an audience by promoting discomfort. Yet it is not possible to understand the affective impact of art in such instrumental terms—that is, in terms of a simple communicative act, designed to elicit a set response.[22]

Although the trancelike monologue of *The Constant State of Desire* may be understood to touch or affect the spectator, neither Finley nor her "characters" effect an emotional pull on the audience. We are not offered an encounter with a subject for whom we might feel sympathy—because, as in Del Favero's work, affect is not organized in terms of emotion or the expressions of individual characters. Finley's vestigial characters are, indeed, caught in the flows of affect. They are manifestly not the generators of emotion and feeling, but simply subject to sensation. Finley acts out a form of sense memory insofar as she shows how one might undergo sensation—or conversely, a kind of post-traumatic numbing. She speaks from a body sustaining sensation, a body inhabited by different aspects of a self, different facets of memory. In this respect, a certain "corporeal promiscuity" is the structuring principle of the piece.[23] This presents a specific challenge to the viewer. To make an empathic connection with a work that refuses to yield to sympathetic identification, one must adapt to this corporeal promiscuity and *feel into* another.[24] Rather than inhabiting a character, however, one inhabits—or is inhabited by—an embodied sensation: a sensation that is challenging precisely because it is not anchored by character or narrative.

Finley's enactment of a sense memory of trauma does not directly address conventional morality; it simply is outside of any moral bounds. She shows us, in effect, how to crack a joke about abuse. But the affective dynamic of the work does not lie in the joke's capacity to shock us. Finley's work is not concerned purely with testing the limits of bourgeois sensibility; rather, it stages a perceptual experience that threatens to take us outside ourselves.

To understand this function in terms of an art of sense memory, however, we need to explore further the relationship of art itself to memory and affect. Finley registers the imprint of trauma but, at the same time, the operations of art render this more than a transparent acting out. At a conceptual level, and through the medium itself, the work addresses the impossibility of stabilizing affect—not simply within a subject but within a pictorial, performative or representational space. Affect, it demonstrates, is inherently unregulated: "Pure affect, no affect: *It hurts, I can't feel anything . . .* "

The Operations of Affect in the Field of Visual Art

The idea that artwork dealing with trauma can act upon a spectator so that one feels or experiences the work before one reads or recognizes its content has led theorists to equate the structure of such imagery with the operations of traumatic memory itself. While I want to suggest that certain work on trauma operates according to an economy of affect, I do, however, want to distinguish this idea from the notion that such work can engender in the viewer what Geoffrey Hartman has called a secondary trauma.[25] Although it is certainly possible that a viewer might be disturbed by the work, the range of affects that it produces do not simply combine to approximate an experience identifiable as trauma or a specific emotional condition. As Ernst van Alphen has emphasized, the spectator is quite clearly not placed within the traumatic encounter—so that even when one views a disturbing image of the Holocaust, one is under no illusion that one is present at the site of that trauma.[26] Similarly, my argument—following a logic of affective imagery that I outline below—is that affect is not precoded by a representational system that enables us to read an image as "about trauma," then to experience it as secondary trauma. Whereas the autonomic responses induced by affective imagery are, in their instantaneity, outside representation, by the same token, they are not inside trauma. If certain kinds of narrative representation manufacture an illusion of inclusivity, inviting us to mimic or identify with the traumatized subject, the affective works in which I am predominantly interested self-consciously exploit this distinction. Unfettered by narrative framing, the affective devices they deploy are not subordinated to prescribed or didactic ends, but work to stimulate thinking in a different way. A particular conception of the relationship of visual signs to the body and to thought is implied here.

Words, Delbo tells us, are on the side of thought: common memory, narrative memory. Although words can clearly serve sense memory, vision has a very different relationship to affective experience—especially to experience that cannot be spoken as it is felt. The eye can often function as a mute witness by means of which events register as eidetic memory images imprinted with sensation. We see this particularly in relation to childhood trauma, where access to speech is limited, and there is something of the mute witness in Del Favero's portrayal of a boy who appears to cry in anguish (fig. 1).

Visual artists and those who theorize about art and its function have long exploited this allegiance of sight to affective memory. The notion that visual icons were the most effective means of storing and retrieving memories, including those consisting of perceptions mediated through other senses, underpinned medieval understandings of the mnemonic function of art. Devotional imagery was thought by medieval theologians to be effective in acting upon memory, insofar as it could—like the *phantasm*, or memory icon—act as a trigger, inciting an affective response.[27] The images developed from the late medieval period with the express function of inspiring devotion were not simply the "Bible of the unlettered" in the sense of translating words into images. Rather, they conveyed the essence of Christ's sacrifice, the meaning of suffering, by promoting and facilitating an empathetic imitation of Christ. Those who engaged in self-mortificatory devotional practices such as flagellation hoped to come to know Christ through bodily *imitatio*. The conveyance of suffering through imagery in this context is possible only insofar as images have the capacity to address the spectator's own bodily memory; to *touch* the viewer who *feels* rather than simply sees the event, drawn into the image through a process of affect contagion.[28] As I have previously argued, however, the operative element in the medieval devotional image is not the narrative framework but the affective detail (the wound).[29] Bodily response thus precedes the inscription of narrative, of moral emotion or empathy.

At work here is a conception of art, not as aiming to reproduce the world (the Renaissance conception of art as representation), but as registering and producing affect; affect, not as opposed to or distinct from thought, but as the means by which a kind of understanding is produced. This is a formulation that has some resonance with the aesthetics of Gilles Deleuze, which might be brought to bear on a theorization of sense memory and its representation.

In his early work *Proust and Signs*, Deleuze develops the concept of the *encountered sign*, which he distinguishes from a recognized object, insofar as it can only be felt or sensed.[30] The kind of affect the sign incites, however, is not opposed to the thinking process in the sense of supplanting critical inquiry with a kind of passive bodily experience; far from foreclosing on thought, it agitates, compelling and fuelling inquiry rather than simply placating the subject. In its capacity to stimulate thought, the *encountered sign* is—according to Deleuze—superior to the explicit statement, for it is engaging at every level: emotionally, psychologically, sensorially. The importance of this conception of the sign lies in the way it links the affective actions of the image with a thinking process without asserting the primacy of either the affective experience (sense memory) or representation (common memory).

Deleuze's focus, it should be noted, is always on creative production rather than reception, and in this regard, what he says of the philosopher's compulsion is instructive. Attacking the notion of the philosopher as lover of wisdom, Deleuze reasons, with Proust, that critical inquiry is not, in fact, motivated by love so much as by jealousy; the philosopher or truth seeker, he claims, is not a lover but a "jealous man who catches a lying sign" on his lover's face and in doing so "encounters the violence of an impression."[31] An inquiry is set in train when the jealous man is forced by the violence of his own emotions to scrutinize the impression or sign, which itself produces a set of affects—so that philosophy is far from being a dispassionate or neutral activity. Nor is it necessarily willed at the outset, for one may well be thrust into an encounter. "Neither perception nor voluntary memory, nor voluntary thought gives us profound truth," Deleuze says. "Here nothing forces us to interpret something, to decipher the nature of a sign, or to dive deep like 'the diver who explores the depths.'"[32] For Deleuze, as for Delbo, deep thought entails circumventing conventional thought and moving into darker regions; it is also motivated by an affective connection. But, most important, the affective encounter becomes the means by which thought proceeds and ultimately moves toward deeper truth. It is thus also integral to the composition of an artwork, as Deleuze outlines in particular in his work on the painter Francis Bacon.[33]

Deleuze effectively (perhaps even rather willfully) subverts the opposition between thought and sensation, arguing that whereas philosophers think in concepts, artists think in terms of sensations. Sensation is generated through the artist's engagement with the medium, through color and line in the case of the painter, so that it is not the residue of self-expression, or a property of some prior self, but emerges in the present, as it attaches to figures in the image. "Sensation is what is being painted," Deleuze asserts, "what is being painted on the canvas is the body, not insofar as it is represented as an object, but insofar as it is experienced as sustaining *this* sensation."[34]

Painting is thus essentially nonreferential; as the emphasis shifts from expression to production, from object to process, sensation is less subject matter than modus operandi. A Deleuzian framework does not, therefore, allow us to theorize art as a transcription of a psychological state. But this may be of the essence insofar as sense memory is about tapping a certain kind of process; a process experienced not as a remembering of the past but as a continuous negotiation of a present with indeterminable links to the past. The poetics of sense memory involve not so much *speaking of* but *speaking out of* a particular memory or experience—in other words, speaking from the body *sustaining sensation.*

While Deleuze's argument turns on a reading of one figurative painter —Francis Bacon—contemporary art has its own history of the senses, or tradition of engagement with process and affect, in which various means of presenting the body in extremis have been explored. Such work might be understood as staging the body undergoing sensation, but also as inciting an affective response in the viewer; to engage with it is always in some sense to feel it viscerally.

An example is provided by Marina Abramovic's 1975 performance *The Lips of St Thomas*, in which Abramovic sits at a table, eats a kilo of honey, drinks a liter of wine, cuts a five-point star into her stomach with a razor blade, whips herself until she can no longer feel pain, and finally lies on ice blocks for thirty minutes. The most enduring image from this performance is that of the incised star—of the body as a ground of inscription, experienced as sustaining sensation.[35]

But if Abramovic, the artist experiences the body—or the artwork— in this manner, what of her audience? Seeing sensation for an audience surely entails feeling or, at the very least, experiencing a tension between an affective encounter with a real body in pain and an encounter with the body as image or ground of representation. As Abramovic focuses on sustaining the act of incision until the nominal star form is completed, the star promises to emerge as an object, with some meaning or purpose other than as site of pain, even though as it appears the flow of blood spoils the clean lines and obscures its shape. But ultimately one cannot perceive the star except as wounding process. Even as one reads the figure, one winces or squirms, forced into an affective encounter with the image.

The refusal of other meaning here conjures up Kafka's image of a torture machine from *In the Penal Colony*, in which a harrow writes for twelve hours on the body of a condemned man, incising a script into his flesh. In excruciating pain, the man finally comes to determine the text's significance, just before he is impaled completely. The machine operator says:

Enlightenment dawns on the dullest. It begins around the eyes. From there it spreads out. A spectacle that might tempt one to lay oneself under the harrow beside him. Nothing further happens, the man simply begins to decipher the script, he purses his lips as if he were listening. You've seen that it isn't easy to decipher the script with one's eyes; but our man deciphers it with his wounds.[36]

To be a spectator in this instance does not yield true understanding, but the rather Catholic image of revelation is (supposedly) so enticing that it tempts one to lay oneself under the harrow. This is exactly how Christian imagery traditionally operates, the spectacle of crucifixion promoting an *imitatio Christi* or practice of bodily mortification that in turn will yield its own enlightenment. Revelation proceeds from bodily affect; the stigmatic does not read his or her wounds but *feels* their true meaning. Truth is revealed to the body, never to the onlooker, except as the spectator is 'touched' by the image and, through a process of contagion, induced to become the image. The becoming implied in this premodern concept of imitation (as in *imitatio Christi*) entails precisely taking on the pain of the other; seeing from the body so that one *sees truth* in a more profound way. And this is what the art of sense memory may achieve by touching the viewer, bringing him/her into contact with the image. Sense memory doesn't just present the horrific scene, the graphic spectacle of violence, but the physical imprint of the ordeal of violence: a (compromised and compromising) position to see *from*.

Hence the image of pure affect in Kafka: the Darwinian-sounding description of the external features of the body undergoing revelation ("it begins around the eyes" and proceeds with a pursing of the lips).[37] We see enlightenment, but we don't see the cause; we see fear in the figure of the boy with the open mouth in *Parting Embrace* (fig. 1), and we see the scream with Bacon (Francis Bacon paints the scream, not what causes the scream, it has been said).[38] In a similar way, the Australian artist Gordon Bennett, whose work is discussed in Chapter 6, paints the affective experience of colonial regulation in his series *Welts* in which words are rendered in the facture of paint as welts in skin. Words are, for Bennett, not only expressive of pain, but injunctions. In phrases like "Enter at your own risk," "Trespassers Shot," "Private," the law is inscribed directly into the skin— so that the word of law is registered as it is felt by the subjects it constrains.

If thinking in sense memory is a mode of thought like the artist's (the painter's, the performance artist's), the idiom of which is sensation, it does not reflect on past experience—although it is undoubtedly motivated by such experience—but rather registers the lived process of memory. The art of sense memory, then, does not make a claim to represent originary trauma—the cause of the feeling—but to enact the state or experience of post-traumatic memory. In her reading of Freud's *Beyond the Pleasure Principle*, Cathy Caruth emphasizes that "trauma is not locatable in the simple violent or original event in an individual's past, but rather in the way that its very unassimilated nature—the way it was precisely *not known* in the first instance—returns to haunt the survivor later on."[39] Traumatic memory is, in this regard, resolutely an issue of the present.

The photomedia artist Justin Kramer worked for a long time on the experience of child sexual abuse.[40] His memory images relating to this experience were always vivid, but with no pain associated with them, so that one might argue they were ultimately "stripped of affect," easily rendered within common or representational language. For Kramer, his sense memory comprised, not these accessible screen images of scenes from his childhood, but a lived bodily response to trauma. In 1995, he began to experience a new set of physiological symptoms: blackouts, disorientation, vertigo, and a fear of falling, to which his response was always to seek out a chair. Although unconnected in his conscious mind with the photographic memories of abuse, these symptoms were in some sense experienced by Kramer as his memory of abuse, as his body's response to prior events. He began to make photographic images documenting physiological symptoms, visualizing sensations. Acting out slapstick performances in which he balances precariously on a chair (echoing the features of some of Bacon's paintings), the artist produces the source material for a set of images of a body in tumult.

In 1996, Kramer was diagnosed with a tumor in the right temporal lobe of his brain. Although it was successfully removed, Kramer continues to experience the sensation or aura that it produced. He continues to live its symptoms in what he describes as "the manner of a phantom limb," his memory haunted by the former presence of the tumor as it is haunted by the memory of abuse. Was the tumor somehow connected to his abuse? Is it a symptom? he asks. But these are not questions his work can answer. The work is itself about the failure of thought to connect. It is, indeed, an *enactment* of this failure. It is not about the past so much as a haunting of the body; haunting in Blanchot's sense when he says: "What haunts is the inaccessible which one cannot rid oneself of, what one does not find and what, because of that, does not allow it to avoid it. The ungraspable is what one does not escape."[41]

One can argue with Deleuze's disciplinary distinctions when he talks about the differences between philosophy and art, but the advantage of disciplinary specification is that it enables us to ask what art can do that philosophy can't, what art can do that psychology or psychoanalysis can't, what sense memory can see that common memory or conventional language can't. Work like Kramer's that might be identified under the rubric of an art of sense memory does not simply analyze a symptom; it cannot explicitly theorize the links between traumatic memory and originary trauma. But in presenting the process of memory as "sign," it registers the affective experience of memory, enacting a process of "seeing feeling" where feeling is both imagined and regenerated through an encounter with the artwork.

One should ask of a work of art, Deleuze says, not "What does it mean?" but "How does it work?" So the question becomes: How is "seeing feeling" achieved, and how does this process yield information to the body? Crucially, however, there remains the question Deleuze is less concerned with—but which is always a factor in performance work, in particular—of how precisely sensation is encountered by the viewer.

Skin and the Membrane of Memory

Delbo said that her Auschwitz self was encased in the skin of memory so that it could not touch her now. But the skin of memory is notoriously permeable—particularly the skin of traumatic memory, which is at once "tough" and "impervious" (Delbo's words), but also broken, ruptured, and scarred. In dreams, she wrote: "Sometimes . . . it bursts and gives back its contents . . . I see myself again . . . just as I know I was . . . and the pain is so unbearable, so exactly the pain I suffered there, that I feel it again physically, I feel it again through my whole body, which becomes a block of pain. . . . It takes days for everything to return to normal, for memory to be "refilled" and for the skin of memory to mend itself."[42]

It is no coincidence that the image of ruptured skin recurs throughout the work of artists dealing with sense memory—in the details from Del Favero's *Parting Embrace*, for example.[43] And this is particularly the case where artists are dealing with violations of the body such as sexual abuse. The new media artist Linda Dement is another case in point; her CD-ROM *In My Gash* evokes the sensation of abused body as, literally, under the skin, in the inner recesses of the body, by imagining subdermal processes.

If the skin of memory is permeable, then it cannot serve to encase the past self as other. It is precisely through the breached boundaries of skin in such imagery that memory continues to be felt as a wound rather than seen as contained other. One might say also, that it is through the breached boundaries of *memory* that *skin* continues to be felt as a wound rather than seen as contained other, or as "past other" in Claparède's sense; it is here in sense memory that the past seeps back into the present, as sensation rather than representation.

How do we know, then, that what is happening in sense memory (which is after all in the present) is not really happening to us now—if, indeed, there is such a bleed, and if affect cannot be contained within representation?

Sara Chesterman, a student of mine with no surface skin sensation on 90 percent of her body, once told me that now that she couldn't feel her body and had only her brain interpreting what she saw, she found this entirely inadequate for viewing.[44] You need to feel to see images, she said, and in particular you need to feel to know that what is visibly occurring before you is not actually happening to your own body.

Chesterman now relies on her brain to tell her what is happening to her body, so that if she burns her leg, her brain knows this only by seeing the skin damage. Conversely, however—and this was the surprising thing to me—when she sees other bodies in pain, she finds herself *more* rather than less connected to these other bodies, because she cannot readily dissociate herself from the site of pain. "[M]y experience of thrillers and horror films becomes so intense that it becomes almost unbearable," she observes. In other words, sensory images designed to hit the nervous system are experienced, not as "stripped of affect," but with an added intensity of affect felt not on the skin but internally, as a deeper, more invasive process. Bypassing the surface response (galvanic skin response), this viewer has a depth reaction, which may also involve autonomic functions such as fluctuations in heart rate and breathing, visceral sensation, and so on. Such responses, although autonomic, are, as Brian Massumi notes, usually associated with expectation and entail some kind of narrative identification: a level of personal identification that renders the image all the more compromising.[45] Lacking skin sensation as the first line of defense, this viewer finds that the image goes straight to the core—or heart—of her in a quite literal sense.

But what was missing? How do other people—people who take for granted surface skin sensation—watch movies that depict people undergoing extreme bodily sensations, or watch Abramovic? And how does the skin protect us from the intensity of this experience? The answer for Chesterman lies in the squirm: "When people watch films they squirm. I think that the physical act of squirming is one of feeling one's own body, it is an act of distancing the sensual experience being depicted—a way of feeling your own body and sending messages to the brain."

Although the squirm is a recoil, a moment of regrouping the self, it is also the condition of continued participation, the sensation that works with and against the deeper-level response, which on its own is unbearable. The squirm lets us feel the image, but also maintain a tension between self and image. It is part of a loop in which the image incites mimetic contagion acted out in the body of the spectator, which must continue to separate itself from the body of the other. And it is this function that enables one to see feeling as the property of another, and simultaneously to feel it—or at least to know it as felt. The squirm is in essence then, a moment of seeing feeling—the point at which one both feels and knows feeling to be the property of another. It is a trivial, unwilled response that in terms of spectatorship can constitute an experiential link between affect (sensation in the present) and representation.

The recoil, as described above, is not a retreat but a way of negotiating the felt impact of the image—a crucial part of how the affective sign unfolds to the viewer. Such micro-bodily responses enable us to locate ourselves in relation to the image—to "think through the body," in the phrase of the painter Francesco Clemente.[46] By sustaining sensation, we confirm our sense of the ontological status of the image and inure ourselves to its effects—effects that are, nevertheless, felt.

There are, self-evidently, major differences between the genre of the horror film and experimental art dealing with trauma. The former deliberately engages triggers of fear and other sensations; but I have suggested that many artists dealing with trauma and affect conform to the Deleuzian assessment of Bacon who "paints the scream, not what causes the scream." In this sense, the registration of sensation or an embodied affectivity cannot be reduced to the dynamic of a mechanistic stimulus-response trigger. But if the effects of the image may be shaped by narrative and mitigated by a range of bodily responses (I have noted one, in particular), the concentration on feeling sensation—particularly feeling, unconstrained by narrative—ultimately renders perception itself the object of inquiry. The affective image neither draws us into a narrative that simply purports to deliver us into the place of the traumatized subject nor achieves its best effects by inciting a particular kind of "moral" response. Indeed, as examples in the following chapters will demonstrate, by extracting affect from narrative, or by isolating the embodied sensation from character, affective imagery promotes a form of thought that arises from the body, that explores the nature of our affective investment, and that ultimately has the potential to take us outside the confines of our character and habitual modes of perception.

To reflect on sense memory is not to move into the domain of representation (analogous to "ordinary memory") but to move into contact with it. To create a work that activates sensation is a matter of envisaging sensation both from the inside and the outside in the way that Delbo describes— of *calculating the effect* of putting two sides into contact. Thus it can be argued that art registers not the symptom but an interaction within memory. Indeed, it is telling that Deleuze defines memory, or the "world-brain," as "a membrane which puts an outside and an inside into contact, makes them present to each other, confronts them or makes them clash. The inside is psychology, the past, involution, a whole psychology of depths. . . . The outside is . . . the future, evolution."[47]

Memory in this account is neither that possessed by the individual, or that which resides inside (as conventional expressionism holds), nor that which is representational or representable (the outside); it is rather the dynamic of contact: "[M]emory is clearly no longer the faculty of having recollections: it is the membrane which, in the most varied ways (continuity but also discontinuity, envelopment, etc.) makes sheets of past and layers of reality correspond, the first emanating from an inside which is always already there, the second arriving from an outside always to come, the two gnawing at the present which is now only their encounter."[48]

The two parts of memory that Delbo inhabits come together in similar fashion, "gnawing at the present," which is felt like a skin. The rupturing of this skin—the lived experience of it—is not simply an acting out of a memory of past trauma, but the experience of being in the world—of living memory at a point of contact.

As spectators of the imagery of traumatic memory, we might, at certain points, regard our affective encounter from an "outside" in terms of a contact with a concealed "inside." But the model of viewing implied here is not one that maintains a radical separation between an interior subject and its exterior; it evokes instead a form of memory image, echoing Deleuze's conception of a memory for more than one subject, constituted through an engagement with differential positions, colliding in the present. The memory image in this scheme does not express inner trauma in such as way as to make it available to another to take on; rather, it finds a way to activate and realize connections. The question to ask of the artwork is thus, not "What does it mean?" or "What trauma is depicted?" but "How does it work?"—how does it put insides and outsides into contact in order to establish a basis for empathy?

The Force of Trauma

In the opening sequence of M. Night Shyamalan's 1999 film *The Sixth Sense*, unbeknownst to the audience, the central character, played by Bruce Willis, is fatally wounded in a shooting. Thereafter, he lives on in the filmic narrative for a period in which he fails to recognize his own death, until one day he comes upon his wife crying alone in their home. Catching sight of his wedding band in her hands, he understands for the first time that she is mourning his death. It is the recognition of her act of mourning that produces the latent recognition of death, both in Willis's character who touches his own dead body with horror, and in the audience, the majority of whom seemed to experience this moment as a revelation.

In a discussion of violent death, the anthropologist Veena Das refers to Intizar Hussain's story "The City of Sorrow," which has features in common with Shyamalan's screenplay.[1] The story concerns a conversation between three men, one of whom has died in violent circumstances. His companions are trying to uncover the manner of his dying. He is asked if he died when he forced a man at the point of his sword to strip his sister naked; he says, "No." Then the companions ask if he died when he saw the same man forcing another man to strip his wife naked; again, he responds with a "No." So, they ask, was it when he was himself forced to strip his own sister naked? Once again, he says, "No." "It was only when his father gazed at his face and died that he heard in his wife's voice the question 'don't you know it is you who are dead?' and he realized that he had died."[2]

Both of these narratives are, in effect, allegories of the failure to comprehend massive trauma: the traumatized (dead) body leaves its subject radically alienated, so that it is only through the actions of an external witness that it can be perceived in its current state. The subject of the violent death reestablishes an affective connection to his own body when he finds himself interpellated into a scene in which his place is verified by other participants. Death is effectively "lived" by its primary subjects only when they experience their own deaths as lived by others.

Once again, we might say that a kind of bodily knowledge is at stake here; recognition is less a cognitive function than one proceeding from an awareness of embodiment. Truth is revealed to the body, not just by a wounding process in this case, but in the restoration of an affective connection. In addition to exemplifying the modes of bodily understanding discussed previously, this scenario reminds us of Freud's argument that traumatization is not an effect of loss per se but of the absence of appropriate affect; thus, as Eric Santner suggests, the trauma survivor is "locked in a repetition compulsion: an effort to recuperate, in the controlled context of symbolic behavior, the *Angstbereitschaft* or readiness to feel anxiety, absent during the initial shock or loss. . . . This affect can, however, be recuperated only in the presence of an empathetic witness."[3] Here we have two examples of the dynamic by which one gets back in touch with the body via the trigger of the external witness.

But in this imaging of violent death, we are presented, not with the passage of a subject from traumatization into the realm of language or common memory, but with an affectivity that inhabits the body. Indeed, the denouement of *The Sixth Sense* presents a body sustaining sensation (to echo Deleuze's formulation); affect is, in effect, what is depicted as it emerges and attaches itself to the body. In watching this sequence we are moved by the sense of what it is to be reinhabited by affect in this way—*to see oneself feeling.*

This chapter further pursues the question of what it is that art relating to trauma *does*, focusing on the affective dynamic of the artwork. Thus far, I have been suggesting that this entails relinquishing readings of traumatization that foreground the psychic trajectory of an individual or interior subject. Here I shall consider how such a strategy can lead us to a better understanding of imagery that addresses loss and death in the context of political violence, even where there may be an ethical imperative to acknowledge the pain and suffering of specific individuals. Taking this transaction of *The Sixth Sense* as a cue, I want to consider the possibility of thinking of affect—of the pain of loss, in particular—in terms of its own motility and even its own "grammar." What does it mean to understand trauma in terms of affect coming to rest in a body, rather than simply proceeding from a body? We are accustomed by various individualizing discourses to think of pain as something private that emerges from within, and that must be *worked through* if one is to return to a normal life. In her pathbreaking essay on violent death, however, Veena Das turns this proposition around. In a highly evocative formulation, she affirms the agency of pain itself: "In the register of the imaginary the pain of the other not only asks for a home in language but also seeks a home in the body."[4]

For Das, there is a compunction to understand how pain comes into the world, how it inhabits the body but also a culture. To this end, she uses Wittgenstein's analysis of the statement "I am in pain" to elaborate an account of the affective force of its iteration. This phrase, she argues, has the formal appearance of an indicative statement—a referential statement with an inner object—but its function is beseeching. As Stanley Cavell explains, one is not free to believe or disbelieve an expression of pain: "[Y]ou are forced to respond, either to acknowledge it or to avoid it; the future between us is at stake."[5] For Das, then, "this sentence is the beginning of a relationship, not its end."[6]

The important feature of this argument is that it places pain immediately within a nexus of social relationships—so that, like sense memory, pain is seen to be negotiated as a "gnawing encounter." More than this, however, pain conceived of as a "call" is bound up with a response, which, in turn, implies a kind of antiphonic structure. As the examples discussed in the previous chapter have shown, the lived experience of pain is shaped by the language—and also the silences—that surround it. Hence, Das insists, a study of pain must incorporate a study of silence and of the absence of languages of pain—but, most fundamentally, it should constitute a study of the transactions between language and the body.

For me, Das's insistence on the relational—and essentially nonreferential—nature of the iteration "I am in pain" comes close to suggesting that any expression of pain occurs in the mode of Deleuze's encountered sign. Pain conceived of as a call for acknowledgment implies that a response is compelled. And it is compelled at a level that engages affect. That is to say, (the image of) pain touches us viscerally—or, conversely, it reveals a failure of affect in our demonstrated incapacity to acknowledge it. If this is, indeed, the grammar of an expression of pain, then, as with our earlier discussion of the sense memory of trauma, this expression or utterance must be understood to be poised at the intersection of the body and its outside, and in a manner that begins to challenge, in one crucial regard, the notion that trauma exists in the realm of the unspeakable. As Das suggests: "Pain . . . is not that inexpressible something that destroys communication, or marks one's exit from one's existence in language. Instead, it makes a claim . . . which may be given or denied. In either case, it is not a referential statement that is simply pointing to an inner object."[7]

This is, on one level, a statement about the visibility—and audibility—of pain: about the response of a viewer or listener. But it is also an argument that a culture must establish a particular relationship to pain and death. In this regard, Das seeks to counter what she refers to as "simplified images of healing"—particularly those (psychoanalytic) accounts that construe successful mourning in terms of a decathexis from the lost object.[8] For Das, the principal problem with such accounts is that they implicitly treat pain as that which removes one from the social sphere, rather than as a force that fundamentally changes both people and societies. She demonstrates that rather than conceiving of pain as "hidden" (a formulation considered further in Chapter 4) or as confined within the depths of an interior subject, to be revealed to us, fleetingly, through communicative acts and representations, we should focus on the means by which pain itself inhabits a world; that is, on the ways in which pain is precisely *not* contained within subjects. This, then, is the political crux of Das's position: trauma is not something immaterial that happens to the individual, leaving the world unchanged—rather, it has a palpable extension within the world. I take this argument as an exhortation to those of us who study cultural responses to trauma and pain to trace the ways in which pain is constitutive and active, as well as the ways in which it might be made visible.

It seems to me that Das's analysis of the cultural transactions that shape a culture's relationship to death is not inconsistent with the broadly Deleuzian account of the operations of the image outlined in the previous chapter. These two perspectives on essentially different objects may be combined, not simply to provide an account of the social function of images, but to illuminate the way in which an imagery of trauma or loss registers something of the dynamic—or "grammar"—of pain itself. Such imagery might thereby be understood as putting us in touch, neither with the ostensible subjects of trauma nor with a specific inner condition, but with the force of trauma as this inhabits space, both external and internal to the body. This is not to suggest that the trauma of loss can be disembodied and given over to those who are not its primary subjects but rather that its embodiment in art orchestrates a set of transactions between bodies. To this end, I would like to borrow Das's notion of the "antiphony" of mourning as a means of describing both the transactive nature and the politics of images relating to the processes of trauma and loss.

Specifically, I want to consider how art registers pain's call for acknowledgment in the context of a kind of cultural reception—an antiphony of language and silence. The culminating scene from *The Sixth Sense* offers an extraordinarily effective account of pain actively and dramatically finding its home in the body. But the image of an antiphonic structure— a series of calls and responses—also raises the question of art's address to its audience. How can art put us in touch with a certain kind of pain and move us toward a way of thinking about pain and violence? I have been suggesting thus far that it does this, not by interpellating us as a particular kind of subject in relation to what is depicted, but through establishing a manner of affective connection. Affect in art does not operate at the level of arousing sympathy for predefined characters; it has a force of its own. By virtue of its propensity to impact on us *in spite of who we are*, it goes beyond reinforcing the kind of moral emotions that shape responses to a particular narrative scenario. Thus, to understand the call that is made through art, we need to think through the ways in which pain surges beyond the boundaries of any given body.

When Das asks, after Wittgenstein, how we might describe our pain by pointing to the body of another, it is not only the possibility of an embodied pain that is evoked but an imaginary in which pain is palpably conceived of as transferable. There is something innately uncontainable about the phenomenon of pain within representation. If is not transferable as a condition pertaining to a subject, it is apt to "shock" us at the level of inducing an autonomic, prereflective response. But, as I have already indicated, the *shock to thought* requires more than the activation of an affective trigger.

To explore these issues further, I shall focus on work by two artists who deal with the devastating effects of political violence: Sandra Johnston and Doris Salcedo. *To Kill an Impulse* (1993) by the Belfast artist Sandra Johnston consists of two sets of slide footage screened simultaneously from opposing walls onto a single sheet of glass in the center of a room, producing a backwash on the wall behind and on the bodies of spectators wan-

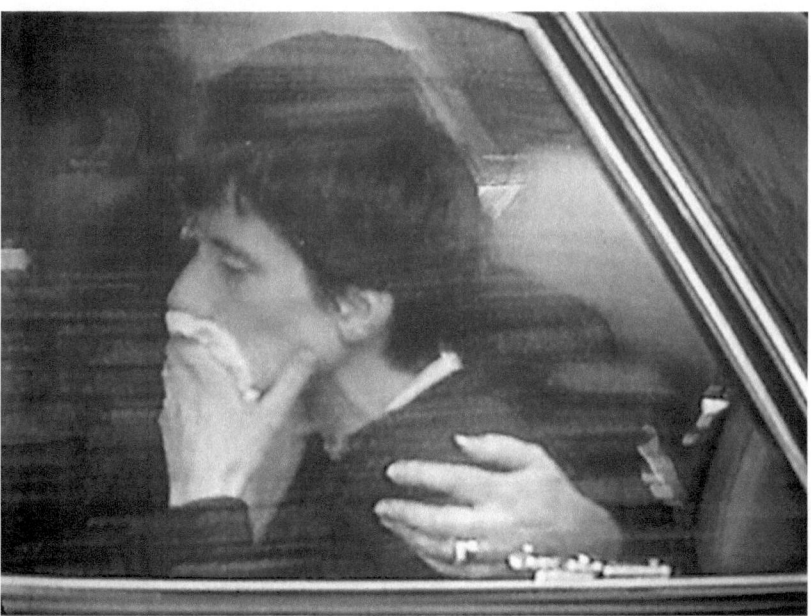

FIGURE 2.   Sandra Johnston, *To Kill an Impulse* (1993). Detail. Used with
permission.

dering through (figs. 2 and 3). This glass sheet manifests traces of absent
bodies in the handprints left in its dust-coating. One set of slides shows
media images of political funerals in Northern Ireland—both Protestant
and Catholic—focusing on women mourners; the other depicts a confrontational performance in a mound of garbage by Johnston herself, intended
in part as a cathartic enactment of grief. As something of a contrast to this
juxtaposition of the public face of mourning and the bodily manifestation
of trauma, the Colombian Doris Salcedo's *Casa Viuda* (1994) and *Untitled*
(1995) evoke the state of loss through inanimate objects (fig. 4). The former
series of installations comprises broken domestic furnishings into which
are embedded fragments of bone, clothing, and so on—traces of individuals who have been driven from their homes and killed; the latter piece is
constructed from a glass-windowed chest, packed with items of clothing
and concreted over.

Although from quite different cultures, Salcedo and Johnston are both
from countries riven by political violence in recent times. Both make work
that addresses the responses of individuals and communities to what Das
has called—after Nadia Seremetakis—the "bad death."[9] The "bad death" is,

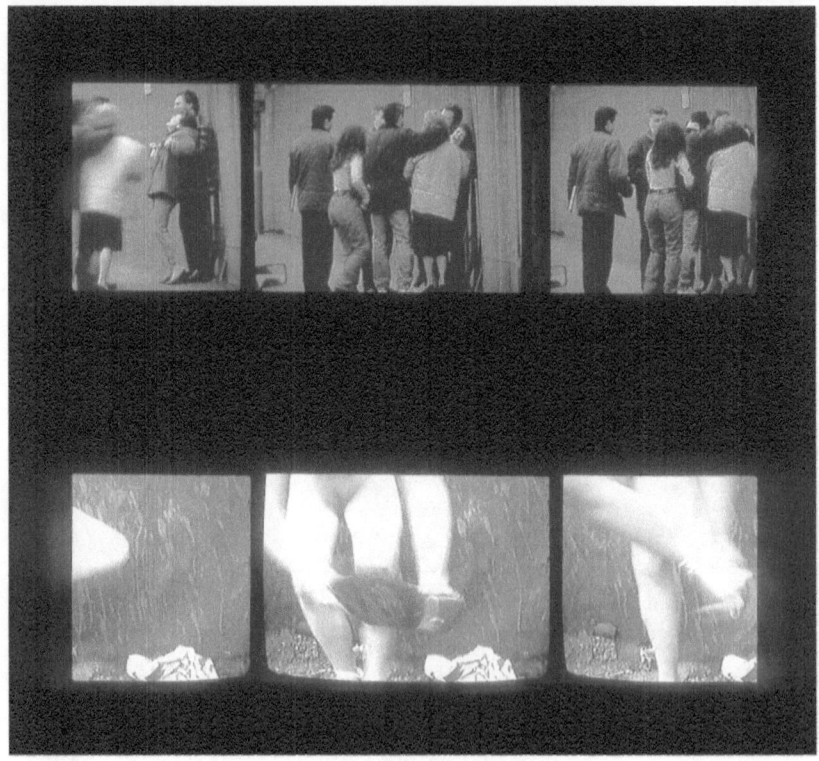

FIGURE 3. Sandra Johnston, *To Kill an Impulse* (1993). Detail. Used with permission.

for Seremetakis, the improperly mourned or "unwitnessed" death ("disappearances" in Colombia would fit this model, since they deprive the bereaved of a body to bury). In a more general sense, as Das has indicated, all untimely and violent deaths are, of course, "bad," and in contexts where such deaths are common, they require a particular kind of marking and a particular kind of study. Salcedo's and Johnston's artwork mourns the bad death, but is, at the same time, more than simply memorial.

The works of these artists move across two domains. Although they are primarily concerned to register the sense memory of grief or trauma, Johnston and Salcedo also address an issue normally outside the purview of artists who are deemed to work in an expressive or subjective vein: that of the interrelationship between the artist and others. That is to say, by exploring ways in which the artist can encounter the trauma of others, they both give consideration to the ways in which a secondary witness—and, by extension, a spectator—is positioned in relation to that trauma, and also to the way in which an affective response might be triggered through visual imagery.

Although both Johnston and Salcedo work on the trauma of others, they approach this task not as outsiders but with a particular cultural affinity. "In a country like Colombia, life is constantly interrupted by acts of violence," Salcedo has said. "There is a reality which is intrusive . . . life im-

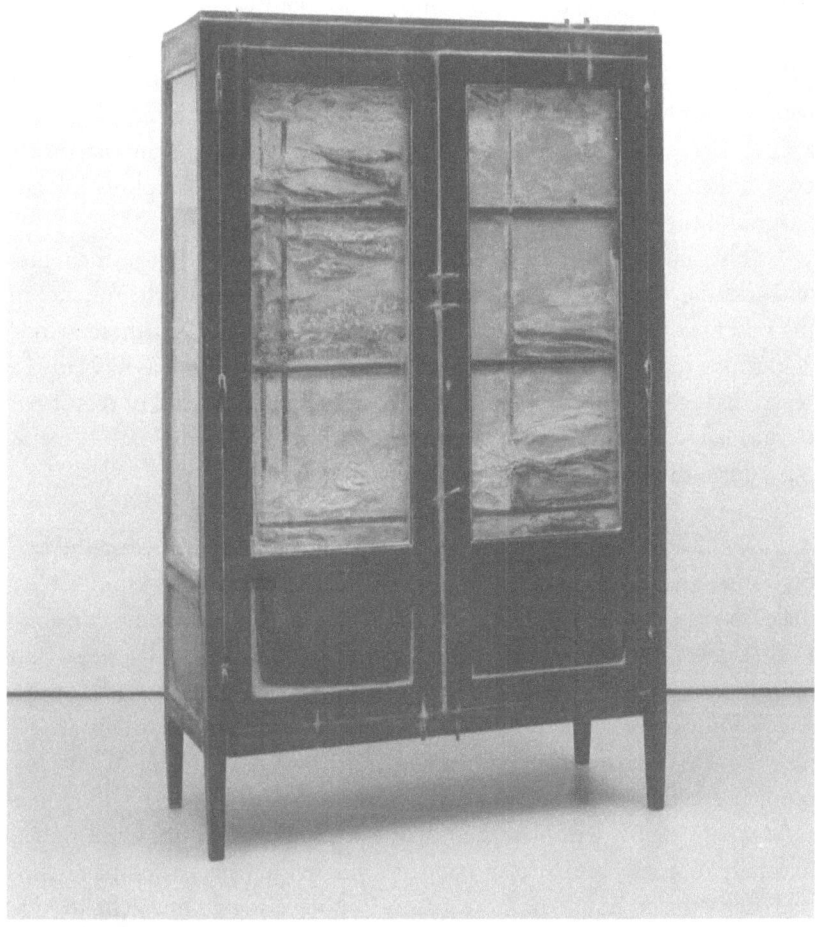

FIGURE 4. Doris Salcedo, *Untitled* (1995). Wood, glass, clothes, cement. Courtesy of Alexander and Bonin, New York.

poses upon you this awareness of the other. Violence, horror, forces you to notice the Other, to see others' suffering."[10] As "insiders" both are concerned with the ways in which memories of the bad death are represented and negotiated within communities. And in each case, their work proceeds from a relationship forged with the primary subjects of violence that enables the artist to enact the state of grief as a form of embodied perception. In response to a grieving process, which Das and Seremetakis understand as engaging the bodies of women in particular, they both strive, in some sense, to "give pain a home." In the case of Johnston, pain is momentarily given body in a performance, which maps the bodily memory of one trauma onto the image of another. In the case of Salcedo, the work proceeds from the artist's sense that she is able to allow the pain of the other to inhabit her—although the body in her work is fugitive rather than figurative, rendered present simply as an elusive trace. In quite distinct ways, then, these two artists reflect Das's proposition that the work of mourning is, in many societies, linked to a gendered division of labor in which an "antiphony of language and silence" is negotiated through "bodily transactions."[11]

This antiphony is explored in different ways in relation to the figure of a grieving woman—in one case in the public domain of the funeral; in the other, in the domestic sphere—so that, in one respect, these artists' works may be understood as actively contributing to what Das has called a "genre of lamentation," in which women are afforded control of their bodies and language.[12] By what means, then, do their works themselves facilitate a form of affective connection between bodies?

Political funerals were a regular occurrence in Belfast before the first cease-fire, and, in a context where most victims of political killings were male, the image of the grieving woman acquired a certain media currency. In the funeral footage that aired for a few brief moments in TV news bulletins, mediating the public face(s) of loss, one of the features that most struck Johnston was the mourners' awareness of the cameras. This awareness is evident in the edited footage included in Johnston's *To Kill an Impulse*. It emerges in what she identifies as the "small but very telling gestures where people withheld their own grief, stalled the impulse to retreat naturally to grief," and also in incidents where mourners attempt to conceal each other.[13] In one frame a man is seen lowering an umbrella to hide a woman in the cortege of a Protestant funeral (Protestant women do not customarily escort the coffin in Northern Irish funerals). For Johnston, this act of concealment is emblematic both of the focus upon women's presence in mourning ritual and of the masking of female grief.

Touched both by pain and the fact of its suppression, Johnston describes wanting to "puncture" the image, to "excavate" the moment of pain, feeling, or stifling.[14] By re-shooting the TV footage with a motor drive and producing a series of stills, she isolated within the footage passages of affective resonance; points of entry that, in light of the artist's invocation of the metaphor of puncturing, might be understood in relation to Barthes's *punctum*, the "sting, speck, cut, little hole . . . that accident which pricks me (but also bruises me, is poignant to me)."[15] When Johnston uses this metaphor she is in part evoking the way an image acts upon her as an affective trigger on a passive viewer—that is, doing a Barthesian reading—but she also points to a more invasive process by which she ruptures the image and renders herself present in the mise-en-scène.

The vehicle for this "excavation" is Johnston's performative response to grief, documented in the second series of slides, juxtaposed with the funeral imagery. This performance was conceived, not as an enactment of—or even response to—the grief of others, but was motivated by the artist's own experience of a violent attack that left her unable to "talk or cry or expel in any way outwardly what had happened." Undertaken in a refuse container, the debasing situation was intended by the artist to recall the abject nature of her attack, but also as a direct reference to the murder of one of the women represented in the footage, whose body was left in such a garbage container. As much as the performance speaks of Johnston's trauma, then, it also reflects upon the cyclical nature of violence in the community, where one person's trauma seems destined to be repeated by another. In this interplay between the public and the personal—the grief of the other and the grief of the self—Johnston finds a connection with the women, both Catholic and Protestant, whom she saw nightly on television. The parallel unfolding of the two distinct sequences does not, however, invite us to decode one trauma through another, or to establish a hierarchy of representation in which one experience could be designated the underlying subject matter of the work and the other a metaphorical account of that subject.

If Johnston is, in some sense, acting out her own trauma in this performance, this is not simply a cathartic act, undertaken for its own sake, but the means by which an empathic experience or understanding is engendered. Empathy in this context is more than the sharing of affective experience, or recognizing another's experience as similar to one's own; it is a mode of thought that might be achieved when one allows the violence of an affective experience to truly inform thinking. In this regard, the artist does not merely *describe* an inner experience but allows such experience to fold back into the world in a manner that can inform understandings both about the nature of relationships to others and about the political nature of violence and pain.

By juxtaposing her body image with the funeral imagery, Johnston does not simply enact her own sense memory of trauma but opens up a critical reading of the media imagery of funerals. She exploits what she perceives as a deficit in public images of funerals—their lack of affect—by reflecting back onto them an image of pain expressed through the body. In documenting her own mode of affective reading, demonstrating the impact of the funeral images upon her, Johnston intends to activate affective triggers within the media images, so that other viewers might perceive these through an embodied imagination. This serves to counteract the processes of familiarization through which "people could too easily watch without being affected or [without] seeing themselves implicated in the mechanisms of violence and its viewings." Johnston is not, however, merely "rectifying" a perceived failing in her audience, directing us to feel in a particular way. In fact, the juxtaposition and intertwining of two accounts of grief serve to fracture and multiply embodied viewpoints. There are visual resonances, a play between what Deleuze would call the "part objects" of feminized bodies: a woman's legs, feet, bits of naked flesh; the shielded face, the concealed body behind the umbrella. All figure as markers of a structure of violence, a political ground in which gender is invested in particular ways, in which we, the audience, are always already invested, and in which violence is destined to be repeated, acted out upon different, new bodies.

The two distinct sequences of slides projected onto the glass "membrane" of memory might, on one level, present an excessively schematic contrast between a form of public and private memory. But this work is not merely a representation of the components of memory. It conveys the operations of memory by virtue of a certain temporal unfolding—a structure that evokes memory as a series of collisions. The progression through the slide sequences itself contributes to the sense of a cyclical violence that co-opts subjects at various points, capturing them within a frame, suggesting certain connections that dissipate with the next change. Each set of contrasts between Johnston's body image and the funeral imagery is designed to push the affective detail to the surface, as it were. The haphazard "part objects" of Johnston's performance throw into sharp relief the motions of hands clutching at faces or resting on shoulders to provide comfort in the funeral images. This dynamic produces a suffusion of affect; the media images that fail to capture the essence of their subjects (who are often literally dashing off, driving away, hiding, or just too distant) are made to bear an affective weight. At the same time, they don't yield their subjects to us; pain is neither expressed in the media images nor even exposed: it simply seems to *alight on* (parts of) human figures.

It is the unerring, mechanical progression of the slides that evokes the surfeit of affect in each frame. Subject to the arbitrary rhythm of the projectors, the affect of these images is unsettled; pain seems to ebb and flow, lurching from image to image.

As we have seen, Delbo, in discussing the aesthetic rendering of traumatic memory, suggested that what made sense memory valuable was the fact that it resisted historicization and preserved within memory the affective experience itself. From her insights we might infer that an art form that seeks to bear the imprint of sense memory must operate in these terms, making the experience of trauma present. In other words, rather than removing the experience to the field of "historical" analysis, it should confront that experience in the realm of the senses. For psychoanalytic theorists, in particular, the notion of transmitting or reliving trauma through art—of making trauma present as opposed to simply representing it—has posed something of a dilemma. To be in the grip of sense memory is, by definition, to remain haunted by memory that resists cognitive processing. Insights are thus yielded not by design or analysis but almost incidentally. As Christopher Bollas argues, repetition in art is not "symbolic elaboration," although it may tell us something about the nature of trauma.[16]

A number of theorists have made use of Freud's distinction between *acting-out* and *working-through* to distinguish the retriggering of trauma from a more self-conscious re-presentation, in which transferential relationships to the past are recognized rather than simply reenacted uncritically.[17] Within such a framework, acting-out is often opposed to any kind of critical strategy. Dominick LaCapra has counseled, however, that it is unwise to see these two stages in diachronic progression, as if acting-out were simply a raw response, giving way to working-through.[18] Rather than proposing a clear-cut opposition between the two modes of remembering, he argues that performativity requires a conjunction of acting-out and attempts to work-through, which should "engage social and political problems and provide a measure of responsible control in action."[19] LaCapra's thinking here seems broadly in line with Delbo's if we understand her commitment to registering a sense of the lived experience of traumatic events as a counterbalance to the necessary production of common memory. LaCapra too, sees narrative history as benefiting from a "muted" dose of trauma, suggesting that artists and historiographers find a way to make history bear its mark, albeit stopping short of abetting a straightforward retransmission of trauma.

Johnston's work would seem to conform to this stipulation, inasmuch as she seeks an antidote for the stripping of affect that she sees occurring through the media. Her aim is precisely to mark the funeral images with the imprint of trauma. She does, however, make an ostensible argument against "muting," in that her project is intended to counteract the forces that promote the suppression of emotion—the processing of grief through "acceptable channels"—and the silencing of women, in particular (the suppression of female grief in funeral imagery is, for her, emblematic of a period in Northern Irish history when many women lived "half lives"). And in her enactment of her own trauma, there is less a muting or toning down than a *reframing* of the process of repetition. Rather than simply injecting a muted dose of trauma into representation, Johnston preserves the ontological distinction between the representational space of the mourning/funeral imagery and the space of her own performance, setting up a dialogic encounter between the two. The languages of sense memory and of common or ordinary memory are thus juxtaposed and brought into touch.

LaCapra's main concern in his discussion of these issues—developed in particular around Claude Lanzmann's film *Shoah*—turns on two points. First, he attacks a certain tendency to uncritical mimicry on the part of the artist, arguing that a "secondary witness" may overidentify with a primary witness. Second, he identifies an associated problem wherein the reactivation of trauma in the primary witness becomes a desirable outcome for a secondary witness in pursuit of what might be termed the art of sense memory.

Johnston neither takes on the grief of another nor indulges solely in an orchestration of other bodies, particularly as she introduces her own body as a surrogate. Thus, she offers an acting-out or repetition of her own trauma as an absorbing, noninteractive performance that because of its lack of self-awareness jars with the ritualistic images of mourning. The body remembering trauma is not, therefore, an unwitting performer but is positioned as an interlocutory figure. Johnston attempts to induce an affective response from her audience, but our awareness of the separation between the mourners and the performer is maintained through a kind of Brechtian "separation of elements." The separateness of each sequence of photographic images might further engender its own pathos by inviting us to regard the actors in each as trapped within the spaces of their respective actions. The mourners are confined by the ritual of the public funeral and subjected to the intrusion of the camera; Johnston herself appears caught in lonely reenactment of a painful and alienating experience. But it is precisely the flow of affect across these two registers that counters any tendency to read these as two distinct portraits of grief; they are not in fact affective images in isolation. They are, in effect, too abstracted to provide narrative foundation for sympathy. It is the encounter with the other that transforms each one; each time we see an image, it is locked in a relationship with its unlike, transformed by an impossible encounter.

The antiphonic structure of this piece might also be understood to play off the simultaneous absence and surfeit of affect, characterizing traumatic experience: the oscillation between feeling and nonfeeling, psychic shock and numbing: "pure affect, no affect: *it hurts, I can't feel anything*" (Foster). But in the generalization of this "condition," in its dispersal across the gap between public and private, sense and common memory, personal and televisual memory, it is located within a political terrain or "placed." Pain reaches across this place, asking for acknowledgment. Johnston's framing of the details of the funeral images functions to create a series of shocks —literally, affective jolts of recognition. But the only violence done to these images occurs through the simultaneous screening of images of the artist. Johnston does not, in the end, co-opt or assimilate imagery; she determines a means of viewing *from* the body.

Johnston's is a kind of orchestrated lament: a series of calls and responses. If the funeral image serves to render death familiar, ordinary—to turn a bad death into a "good" death in Seremetakis's sense—Johnston is here reinventing the process of lamentation, insisting on the strangeness of the traumatic, violent experience and its call for a special kind of cultural mourning—a point to which I shall return in discussion of Salcedo.

Johnston's use of her own body to disrupt the spectator's consumption of familiar media images of funerals serves, on one level, as an analogue for the pain of concealed grief. In this sense, pain might be understood as finding its "home in the body." But the performative body can also be understood to *take us into place*. As Edward Casey argues, the body is "at once agent and vehicle, articulator and witness of being-in-place"[20]—the means by which we understand not simply the pain of the other but the nature of place itself. For Johnston, the body is a means of navigating place—a lived space, marked by events, in which the consequences of violence are felt. It is an "articulator and witness" of being-in-place even more than it is the vehicle for an expression of inner sensation. It is this concern with inhabitation, and with the way in which embodied perception locates us in relation to the world, that also motivates the Colombian artist Doris Salcedo.

Salcedo began to make art after long research trips to the interior of Colombia, during which she spoke to families of victims of violence. She continues to gather testimony, often from very young children who have witnessed the murder of loved ones.[21] Such testimony has inspired a series of works since the early 1990s that engage with the trappings of domestic space, reworking familiar objects in ways that evoke the losses that households have borne and the silences that descend in the spaces inhabited by the bereaved.

Most explicit in this regard are the *Untitled* works of 1995, in which wooden furniture items—such as the chest with glass doors containing folded clothes—are encased and effectively petrified in cement (fig. 4). Salcedo employed similar techniques in the earlier series of sculptural assemblages called *Casa Viuda*, or *Widowed House*, in which partially dismantled furnishings were dispersed around the gallery space. The titling of that series is particularly telling, evoking, as Dan Cameron has put it, "a home grieving for lost occupants."[22] The pathetic fallacy brings to mind Elaine Scarry's description of pain "lifted into the visible world" and "attached to a referent other than the body," so that pain becomes an attribute of something else.[23] Scarry's argument here is based on the premise that the pain of another is scarcely apprehended until it is figured in concrete terms and achieves some kind of analogical verification. Hence, we recognize pain in the visual image of a knife—a fact that Joseph Beuys plays upon in a 1979 piece consisting of a bandaged knife labeled "when you cut your finger bandage the knife."[24]

The furnishings of *Casa Viuda* do not, however, induce the same kind of autonomic response—the skin sensation or shudder—that the body has to a weapon. Like Beuys's knife, Salcedo's objects are subject to a process of anthropomorphization when they are embedded with a sign of personal trauma. *Orphan's Tunic*, a piece from her *Unland* series is the most emphatic in this regard. The work is a response to an encounter with a six-year-old girl who witnessed the killing of her parents. When Salcedo spoke with the girl, she found her unable to recall—or at least express verbally—anything prior to the death of her parents, but on each day that they met, the girl wore a dress made by her mother.[25] By interweaving silk and human hairs and threading strands through holes in a table, Salcedo incorporates the image of the girl's tunic into the body of the work. As a kind of growth upon the form of the table, it constitutes, as Charles Merewether suggests, a "testimonial sign" for the traumatic experience.[26]

But it seems to me that there is a fundamental difference between the knife that induces a bodily memory of physical pain and an object like the table in *Orphan's Tunic* that conveys the psychic trauma of grieving or loss. If one can perceive the essence of a knife wound through the visceral response or skin sensation engendered by its image, the pain of loss is not as easily or instantly apprehended, nor is it necessarily a sensation that can be instantly "remembered" by everyone. (As Johnston shows, we do not automatically read the imagery of mourning through the body—particularly as such images as those of Northern Irish funerals become conventionalized and overfamiliar.)

Unlike the sensation of a cut, grief is not something that can be understood as occurring within the moment; it is a more diffuse and extended process. Correspondingly, in contrast to the concise visual joke of Beuys's piece, Salcedo's work engages a much slower process of perception, in which the transformation of the object is itself gradually apprehended rather than instantly recognized. Hence, what appears at first to be the familiar form of a table is revealed on closer examination to be a conjunction of two tables, one of which is wrapped in silk, tied to the surface with strands of human hair. When we view this work, our affective response to the object plays off a form of recognition: our feeling toward the piece is heightened by the apprehension of human hair. But the *trace* in Salcedo's work always short-circuits the interpretative endeavor, offering too little content to ground a narrative of absent characters, yet too much to obviate an increasing bodily investment in viewing.

When we scrutinize the surfaces of home furnishings in *Casa Viuda*, we discover, merged into them, fragments of plates, clothing, buttons, zippers, and bone. In *Atrabiliarios* (1992), the shoes of women who have "disappeared" are immediately noticeable, encased in niches in a wall, but partially obscured behind semitransparent animal skins sewn across the niches

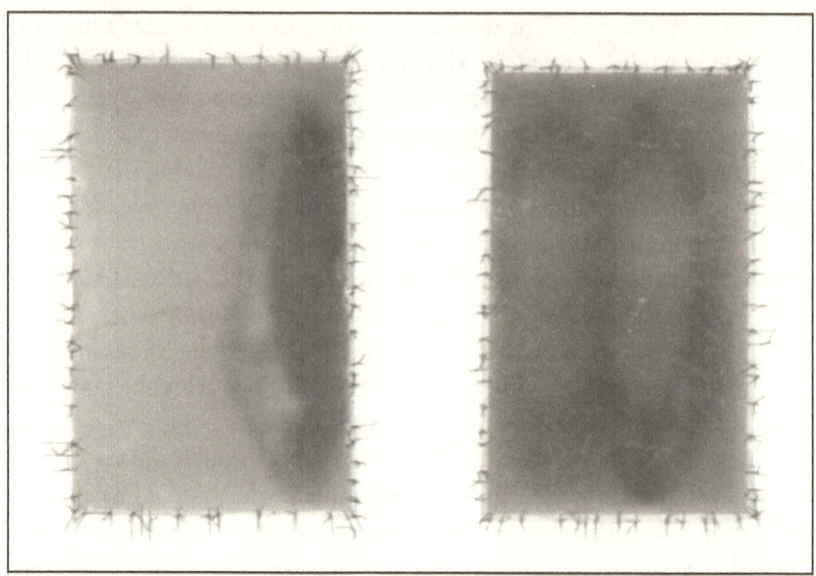

FIGURE 5. Doris Salcedo, *Atrabiliarios* (1992). Detail. Shoes, animal skins. Courtesy of Alexander and Bonin, New York.

(fig. 5). Such personal effects are not incorporated into Salcedo's work as they are into the displays in Holocaust museums, where they serve as shocking reminders of lives taken. Enclosed, occluded, embedded, or encased, they no longer function as mementos of the dead—or as the kind of personal effects that animate family shrines—but are absorbed into a perceptual scene in which they refuse to come to life, fail to signify. The shoes, barely discernible behind the thick hewn skins, are less concrete signifiers of their owners than objects that now cannot be grasped, touched, or brought into focus. The fragments of clothing encased in furnishings (e.g., the lace and embroidered flowers, suggestive of a particular kind of "feminine" taste, in *Untitled*) no longer enliven those objects; instead, they haunt them in a way that does not recall their former use, confirming instead that these items no longer function as they once did.

Salcedo underlines her interest in the changing status of objects when she says that her works are not "monuments" or memorials; in other words, they are not commemorative works that refer directly to something or to someone that existed in the past.[27] Although they are comprised of familiar objects—even to the extent of evoking generalized memories of childhood—they are not fixed signifiers but index a change in the way such common objects are perceived. The visual analogy of *Casa Viuda* registers the way things change when loss is experienced. The work is not simply about evacuated space, but about the continuance of mourning itself. In this respect, Salcedo's methods demonstrate an overriding concern with inhabitation; that is, with the ways in which those left behind learn to inhabit a world made strange and uninhabitable by death. As such, the fabrics in the glass-windowed chest of *Untitled* do not simply read as literal relics; they suggest the way in which a sensation (of pain or loss) attaches itself to objects as to bodies.

It is this emphasis on survivor memory—on "those who have suffered ongoing displacement as individuals, coping with lives that have been disfigured by the tragic encounter with the death of a beloved one"— that distinguishes Salcedo's work from certain other approaches to political violence in Colombia and elsewhere in Central and South America that attempt to image the victims of murders or "disappearances"—or even the survivors themselves.[28] Her compatriot Oscar Muñoz's work *Aliento (Breath)* (1996–97), for example, consists of twelve steel discs imprinted with photoserigraphs. Images of the "disappeared," taken from news photos, are revealed when one breaths on the surface, so that the physical encounter with the image is the means by which one's attention is drawn to the loss or "erasure" of those depicted.

There is, of course, something of a tradition of confrontational work dealing with documentary imagery of violent death, a well-known example being Chilean artist Eugenio Dittborn's *airmail paintings*, which present the faces and bodies of victims in an attempt to force the audience to bear witness to losses and to confront the reality of political murder. Graphic images of the bodies of murder victims operate in a manner more akin to Beuys's bandaged knife inasmuch as they engender an instant affect or shock in the viewer. Hence Geoffrey Hartman has discussed the atrocity photograph as promoting a kind of "secondary trauma" in the process of "educating" an audience.[29] There are, however, several issues at stake here, relating to LaCapra's concern with both art's capacity to reignite the trauma for a primary witness and the role of an artist in triggering this response.

The "truth value" of the atrocity photograph seems to offer some justification for the argument from "education" (to show the photograph is to reveal evidence; to view it is, therefore, to be informed). But artists who make work out of documentary images clearly do more than re-present those images. LaCapra is right to suggest that an artist—or filmmaker, in the case of Lanzmann—must be called to ethical account for the manner in which trauma signifiers function within a work. Yazir Henri has argued that the use of the image of a "victim" as a trigger for an affective response is a violation of the individual depicted.[30] Such a strategy is presumptuous —even if well intentioned—because it fails to respect the dignity and autonomy of the subject, reducing him or her to a cipher of victimhood and thereby enacting a further form of colonization. Henri does not concede that there is any educative benefit in such a strategy; for him, it allows artist and viewer to indulge an unreflective—and ultimately unproductive —sympathy that fails to move toward any understanding of the violence depicted, or of the nature of differential involvement in that violence.

Henri is effectively describing a gap between affect and understanding that the terms "secondary trauma" and "secondary witness" can sometimes mask. Clearly, primary witnesses—in other words, those intimately linked to the victims depicted—are most apt to be traumatized by artworks that use photographs or iconic signifiers of victims (consider, for example, the troubled response of parents of victims of the Moors murderer Myra Hindley to Marcus Harvey's painting *Myra*, constructed from infants' handprints, when this work was shown at the Royal Academy in 1997). It is by no means clear, however, that the affective shock induced by the graphic image in a third party—or "disinterested" viewer—can engender something akin to trauma.

The issue is where an image *takes us* once an initial affective connection is established. And here, I return to Deleuze's notion of the *encountered sign* that propels us into a form of intellectual inquiry through its assault on our senses, emotions, and bodies. The link between sensation and knowledge is, on this account, bridged by a kind of compulsion engendered by the sign. But how "compelling" are violent images? Deleuze's elucidation of an affective compulsion invites us to distinguish between work that functions like the encountered sign and work that is simply "shocking"—and thus to argue that the link between the graphic image and "education" is far from axiomatic.

In a very real sense, conditions of viewing matter. A wealth of evidence indicates that a kind of *failure* to witness can result from viewing disturbing images under conditions that precisely *don't* compel one's continued involvement (hence the phenomenon of "compassion fatigue").[31] The controlled viewing conditions of a gallery offer a defense against the horror evinced by such images; indeed, as the discussion of autonomic reactions such as the "squirm" in Chapter 2 has indicated, our bodies themselves provide defense mechanisms as long as they remain unfettered. Thus, it must be demonstrated that the shock engendered by the image is a hook into a more extended form of engagement. The fundamental error, it seems to me, lies in the aesthetic reduction of trauma to the shock-inducing signifier. While it might be argued that the shock of the (graphic) image mimics, in muted form, the moment of trauma, it does not address the duration of trauma in memory. Salcedo's work does not, of course, enable us to *live out* traumatic experience in an extended sense, but it is concerned to actively engender the possibility of an empathic encounter, where the graphic trauma image might simply leave us high and dry.

In refusing us sight of the atrocity or the murder victim, Salcedo shifts her focus away from the traumatic confrontation and toward a more enduring experience of traumatic memory and grief. In this context, pain is not contained in the single moment but is present in everyday life, in all interactions. Her work is, indeed, a refusal of the temporal collapse implied in the crude use of a "trauma signifier" to trigger a response—and the implication that this moment of shock can stand for trauma itself. Like Das, Salcedo seems to argue for an imagery that evokes a place transformed by pain. Our bodies take us into this place, not as witnesses shadowing the primary subjects of this pain, but in a manner that demonstrates, at the same time, the limited possibilities of either containing or translating pain.

Like Johnston, then, Salcedo is concerned with the ways in which pain imposes itself over time—and with the ebb and flow of affect. This concern with the temporality of affective perception is echoed in other work on political violence in Colombia, such as Silvia Vélez's *Madre Patria/ Motherland* (2000), an installation composed of multicolored miniature viewscopes. These viewscopes are a popular item in Colombia, used as key rings or to contain photos of loved ones, or even sometimes pornography. In either case, they offer an intimate viewing experience, transformed in this work into a public event, because the viewscopes are suspended from the ceiling of the gallery. Vélez fills the viewscopes with photo-journalistic images—of violence and destruction, of street scenes, military parades, and funerals—culled from the press. Some are banal documentary images; others stand out because of the way they capture a moment of grief: a picture of a soldier in tears, his hand raised in a gesture of despair, is captioned: *El soldado Fredy Iturre Klinger llora impotente la muerte de Simón Gómez, su medio hermano. Este fue uno de los 36 militares muertos en los*

combatates con las FARC cerca de la población de Gutiérez, en Cundinamarca
(the soldier Fredy Iturre Klinger cries impotently over the death of Simón
Gómez, his half brother. He was one of the 36 military who died in com-
bat with the FARC near the town of Gutiérez, in Cundinamarca). Like
Johnston, then, Vélez reframes images from popular sources, images saved
for her by family and friends and mailed to her along with family snaps
(the one mentioned above is reproduced in her catalogue with a handwritten message—*"Silvi—este es la foto que mas me ha impresionado!"* ["Silvi—
this is the photo that made most of an impression on me!"]—so that we
get a sense of an ongoing project of reevaluating and collecting). For Vélez,
this is a way of confronting the "extremes" of a culture that one is disin-
clined to see. Indeed, she argues, we can only *see* in a full sense once we intervene in the flow of images, finding a way of "slowing down" and reacti-
vating affective viewing.

Vélez's use of a highly personalized viewing context, like Johnston's
use of the body, is at once a means of evoking both the distance and close-
ness of images of violence in a culture saturated by such images. For her—
as for Salcedo—to make art in a culture riven by violence is to pursue an
understanding of what it is to be caught in a place that can make one over
as victim, bystander, perpetrator. Thus, the manipulation of affective imagery is never simply aimed at revealing or informing; it is always about
"how we are implicated in these horrors."[32] In this sense, it is not concerned with *meaning*, so much as with the processes of immersion and inhabitation. Documentary images alone are insufficient, failing to embody
affect; hence the ongoing need to inscribe them into memory—*this one
made the biggest impression.*

In the past, Salcedo described her "research" process in terms of inter-
nalizing the grief of others—of "allowing their pain to take over me . . .":[33]
"In a way I become that person. Their suffering becomes mine; the centre
of that person becomes my centre and I can no longer determine where my
centre actually is."[34] More recently, however, she has articulated a certain
discomfort with the notion of identification and the implication that one
can move into the place of the primary witness.[35] Although her encounter
with such a witness entails a capacity to *feel into* another, it retains a sense
of the separateness of that person's experience—and of a distance that cannot be entirely bridged. Indeed, the negotiation of duration and physical
distance is a structuring feature of Salcedo's work. A piece, she believes,
"forms itself" out of objects familiar to the person whose experience she

addresses—and, for her, the process of making is a process of encountering these objects.[36] This is in itself a long-drawn-out affair: a single piece can take up to four years to complete. Grief, however, finds symbolic expression in the transformation of objects—so that, for Salcedo, affect is both relational and dynamic *and* inherent in the installation or sculpture.

To some extent, Salcedo treats objects—the components of an installation—as possessing what Christopher Bollas calls a "lexical function"; that is as "mnemic objects" that contain a projectively identified self-experience.[37] Rather than being read in terms of memory narratives, as references to the past, they can be seen as objects enabling the symbolic repetition—or enactment of the sense memory—of trauma. Thus, it is not simply the nature of the object that is important (as is the case with the knife that evokes pain) but the fact of its transformation, its subjection to the process of remaking, its "becoming strange." But, at the same time, these objects do not read in relation to specific characters; they are, in their essence, envisioned from within an embodied imagination, but they are not embodied within a demarcated subject. Their transformation testifies not to a singular experience but (as in Johnston's work) to the cyclical nature of the violence, which is destined to repeat itself.

Unlike the literal signifiers of pain and violence that make an immediate appeal to the bodily memory of the viewer, Salcedo's work unfolds through the gradual negotiation of metamorphosis.[38] The world made strange by death—the alienating and disorienting experience of loss—is thereby slowly revealed to viewers in their own encounters with the objects in transformation, objects that become affective triggers only at particular junctures in a perceptual process. One could argue, then, that like Johnston, Salcedo employs what the Russian formalists called *ostranenie*—a strategy of defamiliarization—drawing attention to the process of transformation that removes the object from the realm of the familiar. But here the shock of recognition has a particularly disturbing effect, activating an affective connection as one senses the trace of human presence in an object. In effect, the viewer is haunted, perturbed by the realization that the space is inhabited, as it would be for those who mourn the dead, for whom every space is suffused with the pain of loss.

Salcedo does not reveal the body of the other. "Memory must work between the figure of the one who has died and the life disfigured by death," she argues, and it is in this gap that the artwork itself functions.[39] This gap may be thought of as a perceptual space in which objects are encountered through the senses and in which—as Salcedo notes—the capacity of vision to make sense of the world breaks down, because one can no longer render present the one who has died. Hence, we see—with a certain lack of clarity—from an embodied perspective, evidence of lives disfigured by death. But as I have previously argued, we are unable to share the perspective of those whose lives are touched by such loss.[40] We occupy their ground, their place—yet the objects that come into view for us as we examine Salcedo's work (the fragments of bodies and identities, the remnants of missing people) are objects already invested with a presence for those who mourn. There is almost a chronotopic reversal in terms of the way that place unfolds over time to different inhabitants: the objects that are gradually revealed to us can be understood to fade from view and rescind from touch for those who mourn, and we remain on radically different sides of a divide. We, as spectators, inhabit this space, not through an identification with primary witnesses (for their identity is never made clear, in any case), but as our bodies enable us to respond to being-in-place, a place where our conditions of perception are themselves challenged.

In transporting us into this world made strange by death, Salcedo addresses the context of a society in which violence is commonplace, although never "understood." Under these conditions, the "strangeness" of death is a shared reality. Consequently, as Das has pointed out in relation to her work in India, the experience of the trauma of loss cannot be conceived of in terms of temporary estrangement from a more stable reality. For those who live in violent communities, there is no stable backdrop. Johnston and Salcedo, it might be argued, focus not only on the alienating nature of violence itself but on the ways in which communities are transformed by the expectation of violence, on the normalization of violence. In this, their work finds echoes in Das's conception of the process of inhabitation in the wake of loss, a process of coming to terms, which does not imply a decathecting of desire from the lost object so much as a reenvisioning of the world. Das, in common with these artists, offers an alternative to individualizing accounts of trauma and loss, insisting upon recognition of the material encounters that occur in the wake of loss, and focusing not simply upon the private aspects of trauma but on the transformation of space itself. Grief is thus thought of in terms of an outfolding into the world that must be remade in the aftermath of tragedy. Languages of sense memory might similarly be understood to transgress intersubjective boundaries and fold back into social memory.

Salcedo and Johnston each actively engender pain's transformation into language; they "lift it into the visible world," as Scarry puts it. And they do this by negotiating the evacuated spaces of the past and the "antiphony of language and silence." If they stop short of giving pain a stable home in the body, they both yield to its call for acknowledgement and play on the capacity of the body to perceive pain. They each attempt, in different ways, to redress a perceived absence of affect by encouraging us to experience their work by relating to our own sense of bodily memory. But this is by no means an easy strategy. If sense memory is particularly difficult to convey, it is because images of trauma and loss do not automatically map onto bodily memories as do images of physical pain (the aforementioned knife, for example). Sense memory calls for active negotiation and, to this end, both artists attend to the ways in which bodily and emotional connections can be established. They do not offer us images that are themselves traumatizing; rather, an image of the force of trauma—of its capacity to infuse and transform bodies, objects and spaces. Both artists present readings of trauma *from the body*; that is, not representations of the body in pain, which serve to induce shock or secondary trauma, but a sense of what it is to see from a series of compromised positions: from the body of a mourner, from the body of one who shares a space with the mourner, from the gap between these two. And it is perhaps, above all, the refusal to reconcile these differential placements that moves us away from a form of sympathetic identification or mimicry toward a critical thinking of loss in this context; toward a way of seeing that changes the terms of our engagement. Through these works, then, we might come to understand how empathic vision is enacted as a modality of seeing.

Journeys into Place

Chapter 3 identifies some of the ways in which artists have engaged modes of embodied perception as a means of understanding mourning as it occurs within a lived space. I now want to investigate further the significance of place in artwork evoking memories of trauma and conflict—and to examine a range of interventions by artists whose concern with inhabitation promotes a form of remembering quite different from that facilitated by the memorial site. To this end, I shall focus on a number of artists who engage in what the philosopher of place Edward Casey calls "chorography": a mapping of the ways in which space is lived and experienced within time.[1] Rather than addressing trauma purely as a psychical or inner phenomenon, these artists treat it as having a physical extension in the world. As well as being a temporal phenomenon, traumatic memory is envisaged as folding into space in a way that leaves manifest traces: not simply marks that tell a story of the past, but indications of a lived present, of a mode of inhabiting both place and memory.

As we began to see in the previous chapter, such a spatial conception of trauma can embody a politics. In constituting places of inhabitation and encounter, visual artworks have the potential to explore the differential terms on which we are "implaced." But, more precisely, by actualizing a set of spatial relationships, art is able to examine the nature of the body's relationship to space—and thus the very conditions of perception that determine various modes of inhabitation. In this chapter I focus on the means by which art addresses a perceiving body in ways that illuminate encoun-

ters within specific postcolonial locations. I explore this question in relation to a range of artworks, through a series of metaphoric journeys across
places where violence and struggle have occurred, and where subjects are
marked—in different ways—by the violence of encounters.

Journeys: 1

*The damaged organ displayed on the scanner metamorphoses into a landscape with a
road running straight into the distance. The scene moves along this road from a fea-
tureless rural landscape into a built-up area. . . . The movement is accompanied by the
regular bleep of the electrocardiograph. This electronic pulse is changed into the sound
of an actual heartbeat . . . as the view is adjusted and shown through the windscreen
of Soho's car. Soho is shown from behind, as if from the back seat of the car, and his eyes
seem to fill the rear-view mirror. In fact, these disembodied eyes look like those of the
artist. . . .*

*The car windscreen is replaced by the medical scanner and the view returns us to a sec-
tion of Soho's body as it is examined by the doctors. The noise of an electrical contact
recurs when their stethoscopes touch the body. Numbers on the screen indicate sites of
bruising and trauma. The sound of the beating heart accelerates as the scanner moves
rapidly through a series of images. . . .*

*. . . Next, Soho is driving down the road—his car windscreen fills the view and the
ambiguous eyes stare back from the mirror. He passes a body lying unnoticed on the
road. Soon the viewer becomes aware of an assault taking place on the road ahead. The
scene briefly cuts back to Soho comatose in the hospital. Returning to the road, the assault comes closer and increasingly violent. The representation of the assault is translated from the view through the windscreen to the medical scanner; and the wounds of
the victim are transposed to Soho's body. The head of the victim fades into an x-ray of
itself, marked by the red crosses that indicate trauma, before rematerializing as Soho's
head, seen for the first time in profile as he continues his drive. Seen from the front, the
windscreen becomes covered with these same red crosses, which Soho attempts to clean
off with his windscreen wipers.*[2]

The above passages are taken from a description by Michael Godby
of the animated film *History of the Main Complaint* by the South African
artist William Kentridge (figs. 6 and 7). The film features a character familiar from earlier Kentridge films, Soho Ekstein, a businessman in a pin-
striped suit, whom Godby describes as standing for "both rapacious business interests and, because of a sense of alienation and displacement, more
generally, for white South Africa as a whole."[3] Soho lies unconscious in a

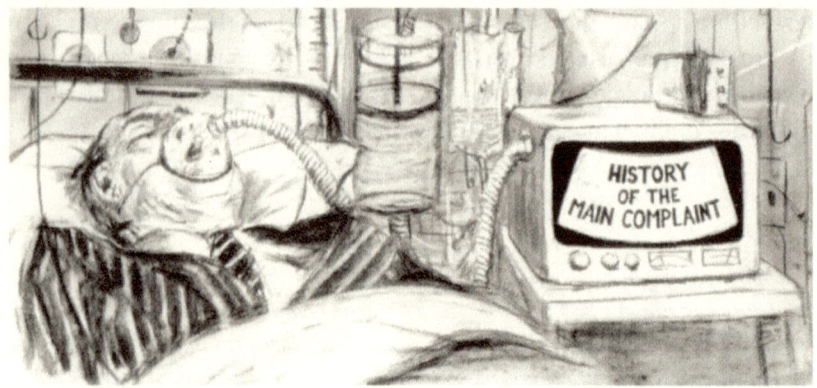

FIGURE 6. William Kentridge, untitled drawing for the film *History of the Main Complaint* (1996). Charcoal on paper, 1,200 x 1,600 mm. Courtesy the artist.

hospital bed, apparently the victim of an accident that has left him with multiple injuries and in need of life-support. In the scene following that described above, he is driving in darkness through a forest. A series of figures emerge from the blackness, darting across the road in front of the car. One of these figures is momentarily caught in the headlights, then smashed by the car, hurled onto the windshield. Suddenly, we are back at the hospital bed, where Soho's eyes flash open. A pair of eyes in the car mirror impassively watch the injured man in the road. Images of this accident victim's body appear on the scanner by Soho's bed. Finally, Soho makes a sudden recovery. As in the opening sequence, the curtains around Soho's bed open, signaling the commencement of an act, a new scene. As his life-support system transforms into office equipment, he is effectively restored to his position at the head of a business empire.

Soho's "recovery"—the reconstitution of Soho the businessman, effected through the literal erasure of the charcoal figure lying wounded on the bed—confounds any straightforward reading of the film as a linear narrative. We cannot be completely sure if Soho was the victim of an accident or its cause. We interpret the scenes of violence on the road as memories, somehow embedded in his unconscious body, undergoing medical procedures; "the tests on Soho's body run parallel to his memories of witnessing the infliction of violence," Kentridge says.[4] But these are not, in any obvious sense, flashbacks. Events are not envisaged from any coherently defined subjective standpoint, much less one that accounts for the current situation of the character of Soho. A pair of eyes in a rear-view mirror appear in the same frame as the road accident, but the watching and the infliction of violence remain unconnected events (fig. 7). The subdermal perspectives, mediated through scanners and stethoscopes, serve to fracture the memory images, rather than ascribe them to a single character, constituting multiple planes, a series of what Deleuze calls "mobile sections" or viewpoints that exceed the subjective or human, so as to expand memory beyond that which might be represented as a linear or temporal flow of events belonging to one person's experience.[5] Kentridge's characters are literally drawn as part of this flow. They emerge as nodal points, which appear to set in train a series of actions, only to disintegrate as Kentridge applies an eraser to his charcoal forms, reducing them to a smear. It is, in fact, the palimpsestic technique of erasure and redrawing that gives rise to the continual metamorphosis and regeneration of objects and scenes. This —rather than any narrative logic—establishes interconnections between bodies and events: everything flows from something else.

Kentridge made *History of the Main Complaint* at the time of the Truth and Reconciliation Commission (TRC) in South Africa, and he describes the work as embodying the kind of questions over individual and

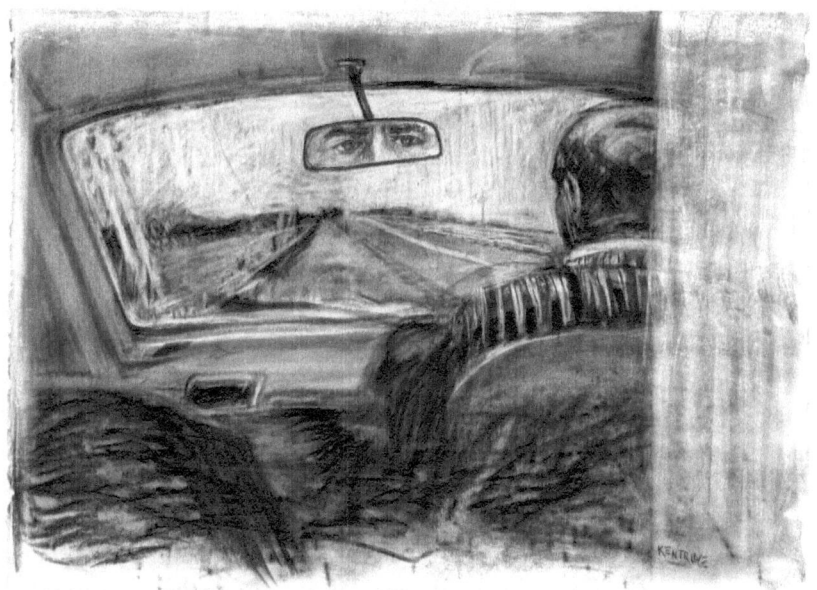

FIGURE 7. William Kentridge, untitled drawing for the film *History of the Main Complaint* (1996). Charcoal on paper, 1,200 x 1,600 mm. Courtesy the artist.

collective responsibility that were in the air at the time.[6] The various medical imaging technologies referenced in the film function as metaphors for an examination of the hidden realm of conscience—and for Kentridge's idea that "[w]e desperately hang on to the surfaces of things, particularly the surfaces of our bodies."[7] Here, this desire to avoid probing too deeply into ourselves—but also into the truth of the human rights abuses revealed at the TRC—is countered by machines plotting the lesions in bodies, objects, landscapes. In this sense, the injured Soho, is, as Godby suggests, the injured body politic, whose wounds are exposed to scrutiny; the troop of doctors, dressed, like Soho, in pin-striped suits, are, if not a metaphor for the TRC itself, a more subtle indication of a state turning its gaze upon itself. Soho's conscience is awakened by the accident—although we are, of course, left wondering if his sudden recovery means business as usual.

In his discussion of the film, Godby argues that linear narrative is rejected by Kentridge in favor of a more postmodern focus on the competing micronarratives of history—and that time itself is fractured in ways that disrupt a coherent chronological flow. At the same time, there is a kind of overlaying of narrative. Kentridge's technique of erasure and substitution inclines us to interpret each element as allegory; so many parts map onto so many others—the body of the victim is the body of the state, is Soho's body. The fragments of memory, unfolding through the body of Soho, effectively become part of a collective memory, so that Soho's "car journey is South Africa's recent past."[8]

But how does such allegorical interpretation engage us affectively? If Soho's car journey is South Africa's journey, how is the audience implicated in this journey? It is plain that established models of cinematic identification do not operate in such a context; we are not interpellated through any form of character identification, for example. Yet there is a sense in which we might identify with Soho at the wheel of his car. And to the extent that we do this, the car journey serves not merely to establish a historical time frame, but to situate us in a specific bodily, social, and political relation to South Africa's recent past. This past is not located in a space from which we have departed but is figured as the environing world that shapes Soho's experience. To grasp the implications of this distinction, we need to understand the process of metaphorization, not in semantic terms, but in terms of what José Gil calls "the mechanics of the space of the body" or the relationship between things and the body.[9]

The kind of identification facilitated here does not presuppose a body unified under a single coherent image, but rather a body that acts in multifarious spatial relationships: a body that impresses its form in space, and that is simultaneously penetrated and invested by space and time. These interactions within space give rise to the "space of the body"—a realm that is neither subjective nor objective but a space of intermediation.[10] It is by virtue of its multiple operations in space—and specifically the way that it folds into space—that the body can act as what Gil calls a "decoder": "The exfoliations of the space of the body, as abstract forms, integrate the information coming from a perceivable body and make possible its translation into a different object belonging to a different sensual sphere."[11]

Simple kinesthetic metaphors work through just such translation. Shock or disappointment, for example, can be registered through metaphors of proprioceptive or other embodied experience ("hit by a ton of bricks" or "a bolt from the blue") that exhibit similar flows or lines of force, and produce similar disorienting effects (a loss of balance, a loss of grasp). Gil suggests that these images trigger a "reversal" of "affective investment," entailed in loss or disappointment where the sudden disappearance of an object means that a set of anticipated actions ceases to be present in the field of possible bodily space.[12] It is this bodily investment in the metaphor that underpins the symbolic operations of *History of the Main Complaint*. Simply to describe or illustrate South Africa's past as a journey would be a banality, but Kentridge exploits the capacity of the affective body to translate metaphor; hence, semiotic decoding cannot illuminate the purchase of the work.

Soho's journey unfolds largely from the space within the car. We see the road ahead, the figures dashing in front of the car, through the windshield—and at one point, we see a pair of eyes in the driver's mirror, as a back-seat passenger might. This interior space is a place that we understand, not simply through our familiarity with the operations of driving, but in terms of the bodily security that it yields—and in relation to the sense of passing through open space at high speed, avoiding any corporeal engagement with the outside.

In a car accident, outside events literally impinge upon the space of the body, modeled according to the space of the car interior, and on the time of the body, keyed to the speed of the car. In this respect, the car accident—mediated through bodily understanding—provides a potent metaphor for the sense of exposure that results when a protective enclosure is ruptured. But the theme of driving in South Africa implies a particular mode of what Casey calls "implacement"—the location of the body within a social or lived space. For many people in South Africa, the enclosed environment of the car offers a sense of security in areas where one would hesitate to walk, and where one routinely locks doors and windows and drives quickly to guard against carjacking. It may, correspondingly, engender a particular fear of outsides, so that the barrier offered by the car body is invested with extra significance. There are, then, two dimensions to the affective impact of the crash: first, the penetration of the interior car space—the violent encounter with a feared outside—and, second, the realization of a loss of control. One moment Soho is driving along, simply following the line of the road—and the next, an accident has occurred. The accident appears to happen *to* Soho, and yet, as the driver of the vehicle, he must be responsible in some way. The nexus between driving and responsibility is not elucidated; in simply moving from the road to the hospital, from the driver to the patient without explanation, Kentridge constitutes a gap—an ellipsis in which the body undergoes a transformation that is not initially subject to understanding or narrative description, echoing the structure of traumatic memory.

In doing this, Kentridge seeks to engender a confrontation with unwitting or unacknowledged collusion: "[T]here may not be blame but there is responsibility," he argues.[13] The metaphor of the journey might thus be understood not simply as dramatizing this responsibility but as evoking the disjunctive relationship between being "at the wheel" and being a disinterested observer. The accident means something to us because we are able to understand the bodily implications of it, but as Soho is unwittingly implicated in a larger politics of place, so we are confronted with the possibility that our comfort zone, or "space of the body," can likewise locate us within this larger sociopolitical domain.

If the car as a kind of extended body space represents a particular mode of inhabitation of the South African landscape—one that proffers a sense of security by reinforcing tangible boundaries that protect one from the terrors of what lies outside—it might also be understood, in part, as a "block" to translation and, hence, to affective encounter. If, as Gil suggests, the body's capacity to translate depends on a process of exfoliation in which it constitutes itself as it folds out into space, and enfolds what is, in some sense, outside, then it may at any point impose limits on these transactions—both physical and metaphorical. Or, indeed, limits of translation might suddenly become apparent when a boundary or limit point reveals itself to be in play. Here—and in some of the works I discuss below—the car is realized as just such a boundary, constituting its inhabitants as somehow separate from its outside.

The figure of the traumatized body of Soho, however, impels the flows of translation across this boundary. Lying in a hospital bed, Soho's body is revisited by the trauma of an accident *in spite of itself.* This "repetition" of a trauma is analogized in the flow of images linking Soho's body to the body of the accident victim; insides to outsides. Trauma itself, then, serves as a trope for revealing unacknowledged connections or responsibilities. The accident precipitates this flow, much as the loss of a house does in Solzhenitsyn's story "Matriona's House," of which Gisela Pankow says: "As soon as the house disintegrates, space is 'unfolded' and time, 'folded' into the protective envelope that the house represents, also unfolds, and allows a hidden dynamic in space to appear."[14]

Soho is, in effect, *a body sustaining sensation,* and insofar as he is a trigger for, or embodiment of, "conscience," he is not a sign for an introspection of the self-contained mind. Rather, he is envisioned by Kentridge as operating in the alternate field of what Casey terms "the exteroception of the environing place-world and . . . the intermediation of the body."[15] It is by virtue of such operations that Soho's journey is an affective and corporeal metaphor—a metaphor that, in and of itself, prompts an examination of conditions of perception.

Journeys: 2

In the video installation *At the End of the Day* (1994), the Northern Irish artist Willie Doherty exploits a familiar feature of the geopolitical landscape of Northern Ireland—the roadblock—in conjunction with the rhetoric of the peace process, in a manner that seems to ironize the use of clichéd directional metaphors of journeys and end points. The piece consists of a sequence shot through the windshield of a car driving along a border road. The car goes round a bend and suddenly comes to a halt in front of a concrete roadblock. This short sequence is repeated over and over, and each time the vehicle comes to its abrupt stop, a voice recites a short phrase. The phrases are succinct but portentous, playing conspicuously upon the overt symbolism of the car, roadblock, and dead end:

At the end of the day there's no going back
We're all in this together
The only way is forward
We have to forget the past and look to the future
We're entering a new phase
Nothing can last forever
Let's not lose sight of the road ahead
There's no future in the past
At the end of the day
It's a new beginning
Let's not repeat the mistakes of the past.

If *At the End of the Day* subverts—or, perhaps, frustrates—a tendency to invest metaphor, a tendency grounded in the body's capacity to assimilate such imagery to its own sense of spatiotemporal unfolding, then another of Doherty's works of this period more explicitly explores the resurfacing of affect through the body's propensity to engage in such translations. *The Only Good One Is a Dead One* (1993) consists of two video sequences, projected simultaneously and accompanied by a monologue (fig. 8). Each video is shot through the windscreen of a separate car, using fixed point-of-view shots that have the effect of locating the viewer in the space within the cars. One of the cars is parked in an urban street at night, the camera static. The other car moves along a country road, also at night. A hand-held camera records the road, traffic signs, distant lights—but since these repeat over and over, we have the impression of a car going nowhere, traveling in circles.

The voice on the soundtrack suggests that the car's occupants are engaged in surveillance, but it alternates between the bravado of a perpetrator confidently planning an ambush, and the paranoia of someone who feels "conspicuous"—like a victim. The car is both surveillance vehicle and getaway car, experienced both as an intimate space of reflection and concealment and as an exposed site that makes one vulnerable; that can be penetrated by a bullet, and that can suddenly veer out of control:

I worry about driving the same route everyday . . . Maybe I should try out different roads . . . alternate my journey. That way I could keep them guessing.

I don't remember when I started to feel conspicuous . . . . a legitimate target.

I've been watching him for a few weeks now. He does the same things everyday . . . Sadly predictable, I suppose. The fucker deserves it.

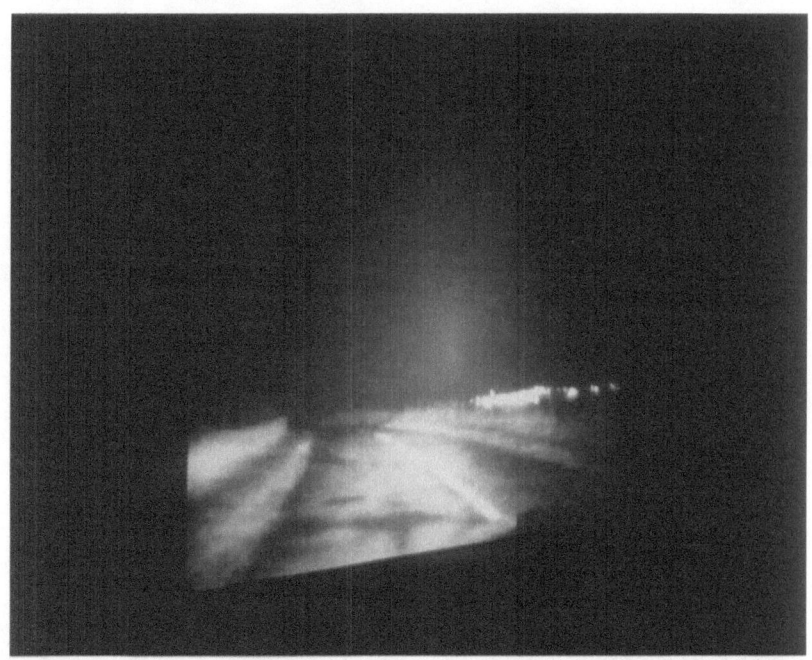

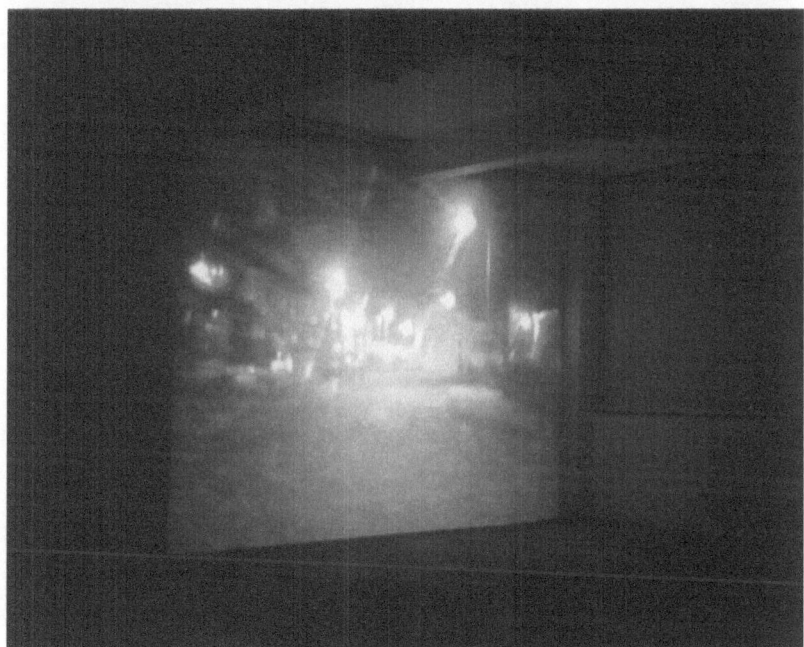

FIGURE 8. Willie Doherty, *The Only Good One Is a Dead One* (1993). Video installation. Matt's Gallery, London; and Alexander and Bonin, New York. Courtesy the artist.

We've known about him for a long time but we've been waiting for the right moment. Waiting for him to make a move.

I keep thinking about this guy who was shot . . . I remember his brother said. "We were sitting having a cup of tea watching the TV when I heard this loud bang at the front door . . . We both jumped up to see what it was, he was nearer the door than me and got into the hall first . . . But by that time the gunman was also in the hall and fired three of four shots directly at him . . . point-blank range . . . I'm a lucky man because then he panicked and ran out to the street, where a car was waiting for him."

Sometimes I feel like I'm wearing a big sign . . . "SHOOT ME".

As far as I'm concerned he's a legitimate target.

The only good one is a dead one.

If I'd had the shooter earlier I could have had him a dozen times. Dead easy! . . . I've walked right up behind him, looked straight at the back of his head . . . He was wearing a checked shirt and faded jeans . . . He didn't even notice me, and I walked straight past him.

I'm certain that my phone's bugged and that someone is listening to my conversations . . . Every time I lift the receiver to answer a call I hear a loud click . . . as if someone else is lifting the phone at the same time . . . I'm not imagining it because some of my friends also hear this strange noise when they call me . . . My anxiety increases when my phone rings occasionally in the middle of the night. This is totally inexplicable as no-one would want to ring me at three or four in the morning. . . . It scares the hell out of me . . . I think that my killer is ringing to check if I'm at home.

He reminds me of someone . . . Maybe someone I went to school with.

I feel like I know this fucker . . . I know where he lives, his neighbours, his car . . . I'm sick of looking at him.

I saw a funeral on TV last night. Some man who was shot in Belfast. A young woman and three children standing crying at the side of a grave . . . Heartbreaking.

One morning, just before I left home at half six, I heard a news report about a particularly savage and random murder . . . That's how I imagine I will be shot . . . as I drive alone in the dark I visualise myself falling into an ambush or being stopped by a group of masked gunmen . . . I see these horrific events unfold like a scene from a movie . . . I was very relieved when dawn broke and the sky brightened to reveal a beautiful clear winter morning.

He drives the same road every day, buys petrol at the same garage . . . It'll be easy. No sweat!

I can't stop thinking about the awful fear and terror he must have felt . . . Maybe it was so quick he didn't know a thing.

I can almost see myself waiting for him along the road . . . It's fairly quiet so it should be safe to hide the car and wait for him as he slows down at the corner . . . A couple of good clean shots should do the job.

This particular part of the road is very shaded. Tall oak trees form a luxuriant canopy of cool green foliage . . . The road twists gently and disappears at every leafy bend.

As my assassin jumps out in front of me everything starts to happen in slow motion. I can see him raise his gun and I can't do a thing. I see the same scene shot from different angles. I see a sequence of fast edits as the car swerves to avoid him and he starts shooting. The windscreen explodes around me. I see a clump of dark green bushes in front of me, illuminated by the car headlights. The car crashes out of control and I feel a deep burning sensation in my chest.

In the early morning, the roads are really quiet . . . You can drive for ages without passing another car . . . the landscape is completely undisturbed and passes by like some strange detached film.

It might be just as easy on the street . . . I could wait until he's coming out of the house or I could just walk up to the door, ring the bell and when he answers . . . BANG BANG! . . . Let the fucker have it.

It should be an easy job with a car waiting at the end of the street . . . I've seen it so many times I could write the script.

In the past year I've had some really irrational panic attacks . . . There's no reason for this but I think that I'm a victim.

I worry about driving the same route everyday . . . Maybe I should try out different roads . . . alternate my journey. That way I could keep them guessing.

I don't remember now when I started feeling conspicuous . . . A legitimate target.[16]

As is often noted, Doherty, in this and other works, draws on the vocabulary of 1940s and 1950s film noir to imbue his scenes with a certain psychological tension.[17] The use of the point-of-view shots and of foreboding shadow play create a sense of a confining space: even when moving forward, we are committed to a particular track that (in this case) seems to lead nowhere but round in circles. And if we read these spaces as conveying a psychological terror, our familiarity with the conventions of Hollywood noir murder mysteries serves only to reinforce the notion that these are premonitions of disaster. So, as much as Doherty lays bare the production of affect in his self-conscious quotation of a stylized cinematic form, he exploits our bodily investment in the image, our propensity to feel affect as we read the space of the body.

But it is in light of Chapter 3's discussion of the failure of affect that this work becomes particularly interesting. Previously, I discussed artists' strategies for revivifying affective encounters in a manner that can promote empathy. Within drama therapy, imagery is used to similar ends to enable violent criminals to understand the impact of their acts. Murray Cox, for example, describes a Shakespeare production in the English secure psychiatric hospital Broadmoor that provoked the following response from one inmate: "When you picked up the skull it really got to me; hit me right in the stomach; I've killed a person and I've done a lot of work on how the relatives must feel . . . but it never crossed my mind until now that there is a corpse somewhere of the person I killed."[18] The effect, in that instance, is achieved through promoting the shock of recognition, so that one feels not simply a disinterested kind of pity-at-a-distance, but rather a jolting realization of one's own connection to a death. This is, in essence, a nonvolitional identification that may engender, but is not prompted by, empathy. Indeed, one could say that it induces a kind of unwilled empathy—what Rosalyn Diprose calls the "nonvolitional generosity of intercorporeality."[19]

Doherty's narrative concerns the operations of conscience as it arises from the body's propensity to analogical identification, to translate through the body. Thus, the planning of an ambush, the identification of a space of physical exposure, induces in the perpetrator a feeling of conspicuousness—so that being in one's car no longer yields a feeling of security. The tracing of an analogue reminds us that no space is self-contained; space shaped by the body's movements in a particular temporal unfolding can at any time be ruptured by rhythms dictated by the outside—by the speed of a bullet penetrating the windshield, which can suddenly bring time to an abrupt end. The dark, portentous spaces of noir cinema are thus deployed to suggest not just the inevitability of death but the intersection of two different narrative tracks. The micronarratives that constitute storytelling after postmodernism are not just discrete events, in this case, but events that overlap and envelop each other.

Fear, trepidation, the feeling of conspicuousness, are not, however, simply psychological projections onto a landscape or urban setting. The conventional logic of expressionism presumes that affect flows from insides to outsides, that scenes are tinged by the mood of inhabitants. But, in Doherty's work, affects arise in places through the exteroceptive operations of the body in lived space. These bodily operations are revealed, through specific contingent placements, as a kind of "hidden dynamic in space." Conscience—or empathy—in this sense arises from the "decoding body," which is sympathetic in spite of itself. In Doherty's work—as in Kentridge's—characters are not agents precipitating action. They do not drive narrative but simply emerge as nodal points. Subjectivities irrupt from the convergence of affective flows, the identities of victims and perpetrators sustained only by the intensification of affect and a kind of unregulated contagion. In this regard, the inhabitation of space—of a political place—is seen to give rise to specific psychological effects. In Chapter 3, I discussed the work of several women artists who slowed down the process of apprehension as a means of both establishing productive affective connections and reflecting upon the way in which one is compromised by a culture of violence. Doherty, in contrast, achieves similar ends by locating us within the confining space of the present—a slab of time that loops and repeats, allowing no interlude for sustained reflection. *The Only Good One* is, in essence, a study of the way in which time and distance collapse as one is caught—rendered conspicuous—in a present from which there is no escape.

Journeys 3: End of Time

Jo Ractliffe's *End of Time* (1999) is a work conceived and partly located on a stretch of highway near Nieu-Bethesda in South Africa's Great Karoo (fig. 9). When first presented, it took the form of images of donkeys (originally constructed from pinhole images) erected on large roadside billboards.[20] In 1996, Ractliffe was making an inventory of a 1,400-kilometer passage of the landscape in this area: "a seemingly endless blandness."[21] Her aim was to document a journey by uncovering ways in which "registers of nothingness" are intersected by events that may go unnoticed by the car driver. One such incident involved the death of three donkeys, which Ractliffe found shot by the side of the N1. This area is traversed by a community of itinerants, the Karretjie Mense (Little-Cart People) who travel with their donkey carts from farm to farm, looking for work. Ractliffe scoured the area for forensic clues, trying to determine what had gone on but found nothing.

Not only was there a complete absence of evidence, so far as she could tell, but more interesting to her as an artist, there was a failure to witness.

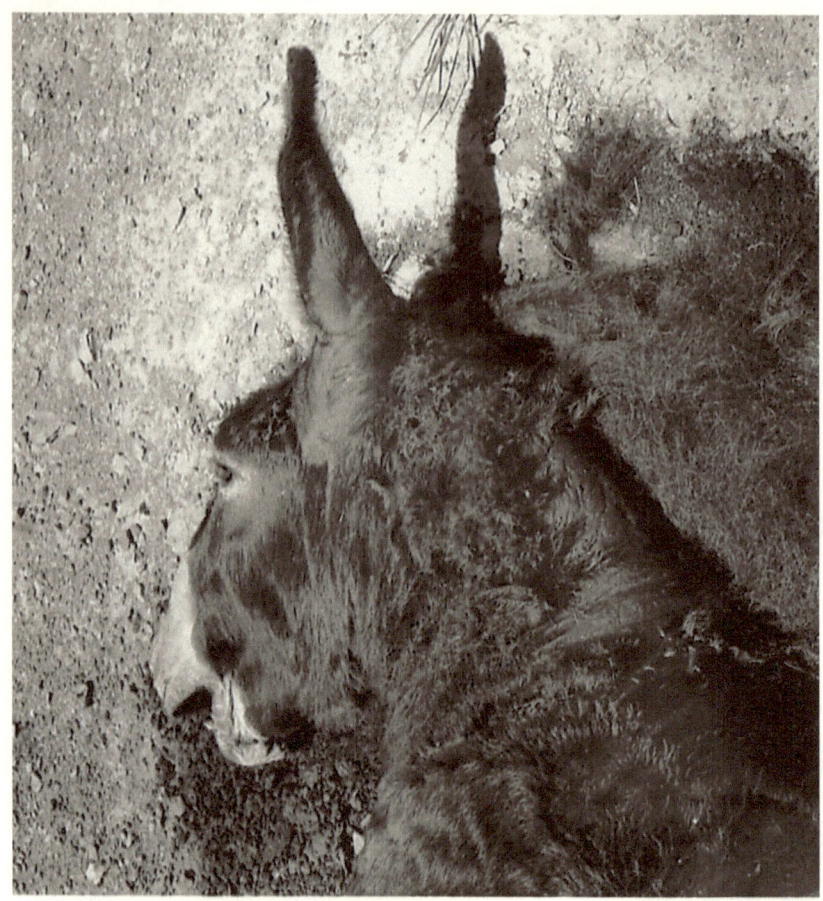

FIGURE 9. Jo Ractliffe, *End of Time* (1999). Silver print, 1 x 1 m. Used with permission.

Driving this route, one simply had this impression of an infinite void. Brenda Atkinson in writing about *End of Time*, describes the road to Nieu-Bethesda as a "non-place"—a term coined by Marc Augé to describe the bland, international spaces of airports and freeways, which don't appear to be subject to idiographic processes of inhabitation.[22] Such places are pre-dominantly *passed through* rather than made over by inhabitants.

Casey reminds us, however, that place is not simply characterized by flow, but is essentially heterogeneous; that is, heterotopic and heterochronic. Even a place that is subject to being traveled rather than inhabited is lived at different speeds and through different modalities. One could argue then, that "nonplaceness" merely describes the spatiotemporal experience of the fastest traveler—the executive transiting through an airport, which, to him or her is bland, uniform, boring, but is a place of work, or even partial dwelling, for certain locals—or the driver on the road to Nieu-Bethesda passing by at 100 kilometers an hour, with no regard for the slower traffic. Insofar as space is modeled by the body and its movements, the nonplace is effectively the nontranslatable place: the point at which one's car operates as a block to translation, and to the infolding and outfolding of space, to the encounter with an outside. Ractliffe's project sets out to uncover place as heterogeneous, as subject to different modes of inhabitation—but rather than revealing or reconstituting other trajectories through this place, she addresses the perceptual domain of the car traveler through her billboards, counterposing the speed of donkey travel, the speed of a bullet, and the sudden end of time, with the pace of a car journey. Here, as in Kentridge's *History of the Main Complaint,* we are confronted with the notion that the car inures us to the image and reality of death; in this regard, it is a kind of time capsule.

The aim of *End of Time* is not to produce "other" histories of place, to reveal what the First World traveler might hitherto have missed. Like the work of Kentridge and Doherty, it is rather an exploration of conditions of perception; what Paul Virilio calls an "endotic" rather than "exotic" mode of enquiry, distinguished on the following basis: "Seeing that which had previously been invisible becomes an activity that renews the exoticism of territorial conquests of the past. But seeing that which is not really seen becomes an activity that exists for itself. This activity is not exotic but *endotic,* because it renews the very conditions of perception."[23] Whereas the prefix *endo-,* "within," might at first appear to imply the opposite of *exo-,* "without," and thus a reorientation toward the self, Virilio's intent is, as Victor Burgin has pointed out, to identify a "between" condition in which one sees simultaneously from within and without (Virilio is inspired by the experience of seeing both dusk and dawn simultaneously while flying over Greenland).[24] *End of Time,* in this vein, does not presume to offer us the "exotic" viewpoint of the Karretjie Mense, but to explore differential modes of being in place as a means of evoking an incommensurability that challenges any singular set of perceptual conditions.

Ractliffe's investigation of perception and affect moves beyond simple understandings of stimulus-response to extend a corporeal metaphor of the postcolonial state (in similar fashion to Kentridge) that in turn elaborates a concept of embodied perception. If Ractliffe's billboards present the donkey as an abstraction or part-object standing for the political force of apartheid, this image is not amenable to iconic decoding. It is an attempt to address emplacement or the perception of space itself.

The work is, in this sense, a metaphoric account of a form of what Casey calls "double tracking"—or engaging perception in different registers. This double tracking occurs within a postcolonial place—a domain that can be demarcated in both political and aesthetic terms as an intercultural "between" space in which new encounters might be negotiated. But here I want to make a larger claim, not just for Ractliffe but also for other "post-apartheid" artists (and by this I mean not simply those of this epoch but those that directly address the psychology of transition). The political force of Ractliffe's work, it seems to me, lies in its conceptualization of the *failure* of many encounters that take place within a notional postcolonial (and more specifically, post-apartheid) space. In realizing an intercultural space as place, Ractliffe invites us to consider our bodily relationship to it, thereby isolating a fundamental political question: on what terms are we here? This is not a strategy to delimit further encounters, but to renegotiate the terms of encounter at a deeper level; that is, through a critical consideration of conditions of perception.

Ractliffe's work thus effectively challenges the ready assumption that we are on new ground—as well as the management of memory that is effected through the construction of a new beginning. Within post-apartheid South Africa, the TRC process has, of course, impelled an investment in such a new beginning, but not without some cost (the work of Henri and Grunebaum, discussed below, demonstrates that certain memories get lost in the process of transition). Moreover, it might be said to have given rise to a certain form of exoticism insofar as spectators may partake of a rhetoric of revelation. The notion that brutal truths were hidden under apartheid can clearly be overextended to the point where "seeing" for white South Africans becomes a function simply of uncovering truths that were occluded under apartheid (suddenly whites see what blacks could always see; vision that was previously impaired is restored to full functionality). But in the work of the more sophisticated post-apartheid artists, we find that this interest in the deeper questions of perception—of conditions of viewing—overrides and complicates a simple notion of unveiling as a corrective that always begs the question of how vision itself is politically compromised.

Journeys 4: Moving Across a Minefield

I am suggesting that this kind of exploration of perception becomes something akin to a *postcolonial method*—particularly in relation to inter-cultural space. It is a function of *what art itself does*, proceeding from the particular capacity of the medium for enacting modes of embodied perception, but it is also a political strategy. In the following example from the collaborative, international exhibition project *Memorias intimas marcas* (Intimate Memory Traces), we see this method effectively employed as a means of guiding a journey by an artist into an explicitly contested place.

Originally conceived by the Angolan artist Fernando Alvim, the aim of *Memorias* was to revisit Angola in the aftermath of war. The project began as a research trip to Angola in 1997, involving three artists—Alvim, the South African Gavin Younge, and the Cuban Carlos Garaicoia—each representing one of the nations involved in the conflict in Angola in the 1970s and 1980s.[25] Alvim suggests the cartographic aspects of the project in a piece depicting a map of the minefields of Cuito Cuanavale, superimposed with the figure of a human kidney—but the cartographic process is extended into what is effectively a "chronographic" mapping of space in time, most explicitly in the work of Younge, which pays close attention to the dynamics of the journey into "foreign" territory in the wake of previous South African incursions.[26]

Forces Favourites, Younge's video installation for *Memorias*, does not foreground the South African experience, even though it makes some reference to its country of origin (the title, for example, refers to a radio program for South African troops aired during the Angolan conflict) (fig. 10). The piece comprises a circle of sturdy-looking South African Post Office bikes, each with a video monitor strapped onto the carrying basket. These monitors run footage shot by Younge during his research trip to Angola. The soundtrack, which incorporates the signature tune to *Forces Favourites*, gives a sense of the terrain covered in a journey through Angola—from the rural outback where a woman tends her animals to the sound of wind-chimes, to the noise of downtown traffic, from a panting runner at the start, to the sounds of airplane engines on the tarmac of a military landing strip.[27] Part of the video is shot from the back of a truck and reveals the wrecks of military vehicles strewn along the roadside, but Younge's presence in this place (he is never seen or heard on camera) is most emphatically marked by his bike, which cuts a path through the city, countryside, and minefields.

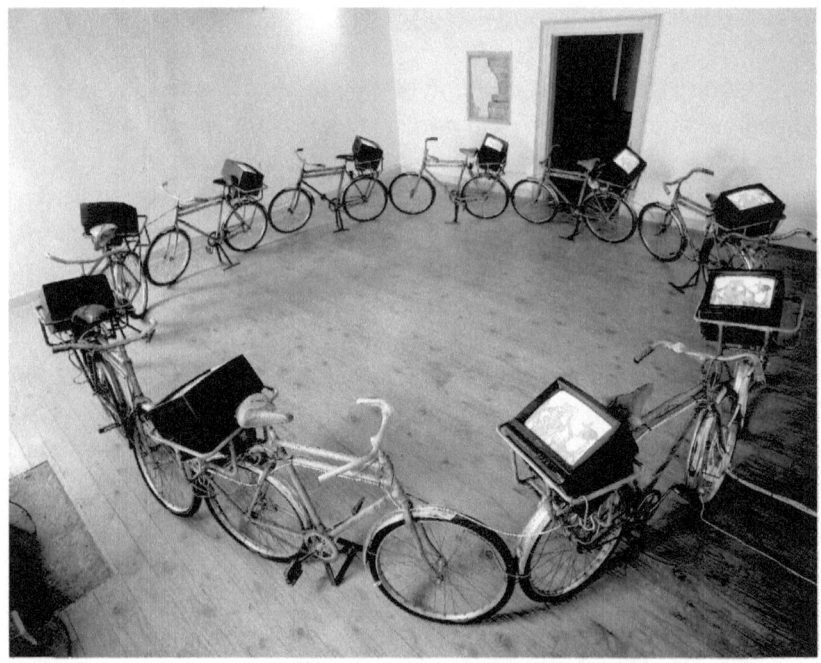

FIGURE 10. Gavin Younge, *Forces Favourites* (1997). Installation view. Bicycles, vellum, video installation. Photo by Geoff Grunlingh. Used with permission.

Adults never ride bikes in Angola, so Younge imported one of the Post Office bikes that are a common mode of transportation for men in South Africa, strapping a video camera at the back so that he could shoot footage as he rode—a setup that inevitably marked out the artist as an outsider. The footage shot from the bike is a rather haphazard recording of the flow of events along a very particular mono-track. The camera, of course, does not penetrate in the manner of ethnographic or documentary film. It simply records the evidence of life unfolding along the course navigated—somewhat arbitrarily and inexpertly—by the artist. Events are not interpreted; we are offered no privileged insider knowledge.

Younge's work, much like Salcedo's, is concerned with traces and with the transformation of places and things. It is sometimes noticeably people-free: a circle of bikes without riders, abandoned military vehicles on video monitor screens. But at other moments, the video registers a flurry of human activity. The material evidence of devastation is thus offset against images of inhabitation, very often of children playing. Frequently, Younge shoots objects, animals, and bugs in place of human subjects.[28]

The different diurnal rhythms and speeds of travel he registers point to the diversity of activities and the different kinds of journeys undertaken in this place—to the essential heterochronism of place. But as the morass of activity unfolds, the camera focuses on only a portion of this (a detail of the riverbank is scrutinized, while the noise of the ambient space suggests an array of activity going on elsewhere; we follow the single track of the bike, pursued by children as it cuts a path through a city center or a mine-field). Younge thus generates a sense of the macro and micro never quite meeting; small details are at once arbitrary and replete with significance— the impression is that a million other details are there and could have been chosen. These details are, in fact, distractions, somewhat obstructive inas-much as they prevent us from seeing the bigger picture, insisting on a my-opic focus on a single, apparently inconsequential track. This technique, however, might be interpreted as one that works against a tendency to rev-elation by closing in and refusing panoramic, scene-setting shots.

Unlike Doherty's *The Only Good One*, which thematizes visibility and exposure through revealing certain hidden connections, Younge's sense of the divergent paths and limitations of different tracks, traversing the same ground emphasizes the failure of encounters. But, as in Ractliffe's work, this failure does not signify a lack of presence or connectivity; rather it is a cue to examine the effects of the body's occupation of space—and to investigate the specificities of its inclusion in a field.[29]

There is a clear distinction to be made between such work that ad-dresses perception in the present—both as psychological and political phe-nomenon—and work that is fundamentally historiographical (that is, geared toward uncovering the truth of the past). A particularly problematic exam-ple of the latter is provided by an element in Pippa Skotnes's exhibition *Miscast: Negotiating Khoisan History and Material Culture* (1996), consisting of a linoleum floor covering depicting images of Khoisan people subjected to colonial violence. By walking on this linoleum, the audience reenacts— and thereby confronts—the "trampling" of the Khoisan by colonials.[30] Such works, although "politically correct" in their didactic message, are clearly limited by their implicit address to the white liberal conscience (and body) and staggering in their failure to allow subjects figured as "others" to occupy space on their own terms. Not surprisingly, Khoisan people found the piece abhorrent, the site of whites trampling "Bushman" images re-invoking historical trauma and reenacting their humiliation.[31] As Ernst van Alphen has argued, the lesson here is that we don't all see, feel, and apprehend the world from the same perspective, but also that restaging the traumatic event may simply retrigger its memory in those already affected by it.[32]

Prima facie, *Miscast* would seem to concern itself with the issue of "implacement"—both politically and through its terms of engagement. The installation exploits awareness of body space as a means of questioning historical encounters within a particular place. But rather than promoting new encounters within place, Skotnes treats installation space as a didactic arena, effectively isolated from lived place. In its attempt to awaken consciousness by reenacting the incursions of a white body, Skotnes's *Miscast* privileges self-exploration at the expense of tracing the topography of memory. *Miscast*, then, offers a moral lesson premised on an encounter, not with living people, but with a historical spectacle, in which the white spectator is inscribed as an agent, while the Khoisan are reduced to ciphers of oppression.

The notional white spectator is caught in the act—rendered conspicuous—through consumption of this work. But whereas Doherty's work examines the affective experience of being rendered conspicuous, here the shock of recognition is induced for pedagogic ends. This instrumental use of art once again raises the question of how an affective engagement might promote critical thought. *Miscast* may confirm the liberal white viewer in his or her distaste for apartheid (and we would surely assume that the audience for such an artwork *is* a priori "liberal"). But the problem is that the basic lesson has already been learned by this audience. Skotnes is no doubt right in her intuition that, in order to be properly understood, it needs to be inscribed onto the body (understood through wounds, in the Kafkaesque or Nietzschean sense). But as we saw in the earlier discussion of the *encountered sign*, what counts is where the image takes us, what affect propels us into. Art cannot simply give us the answer—which would, of course, merely short-circuit critical thought. It needs, in a sense, to relinquish the moral position in order to enable ethical inquiry.

In other words, the affect of shame cannot be an objective, except insofar as it promotes a form of *seeing oneself seeing*. Virilio's account of this latter kind of examination identifies the experience of inhabiting a kind of "between space" as the key to revealing conditions of perception. In very different ways, Doherty, Kentridge, Ractliffe, and Younge each address the between space that not only relativizes modes of perception but does so by inviting us to inhabit an inside and an outside, as it were, at the same time.

In the corrective strategy of Skotnes, however, there is no between space. This is partly because the work has none of the moral equivocation of Doherty's—but it is principally because it constructs a clear distinction between the mobile agent and the static representation, fixed in place.

The privileged white subject travels into history in *Miscast*, whereas the Khoisan subjects remain anchored in colonial representations. This sets up an uncomfortable distinction, echoing Zygmunt Bauman's characterization of a First World in which residents live in time—"space does not matter for them, since spanning every distance is instantaneous"—and an "opposite" world whose citizens live in—and are in fact tied to—space.[33] It is not surprising, then, that postcolonial critics (such as Sara Ahmed) have focused on the hubris of First World nomads and argued that one of the ways in which otherness has traditionally been configured is by fixing subjects in a topography of time and place.[34] In an art historical context, Okwui Enwezor has been critical of the tendency of white liberal art (like *Miscast*) to represent black bodies as fixed according to colonial markers, even as representations are produced in the spirit of critique.[35] What we might learn from this manner of critique—and from the critically engaged work of certain artists—is that place itself has to be treated as the locus and product of dynamic interaction, but also, in a sense, *turned back into space*, metaphorized as a locus in which bodily perception can be destabilized.

Younge's work, like Ractliffe's, is topographical in its modus operandi, proposing the journey as a means of renegotiating place as fluid and heterogeneous locus. But it is also exemplary of a postcolonial art form that seeks to disable—but not forget—the ways in which appellations have fixed subjects in place. Ahmed demonstrates that the concept of the stranger often serves as a fetish that is mobilized to define the borders and boundaries of given communities.[36] The construction of a national border has certain ironic resonance in the context of South Africa's so-called border war, fought in Angola, a country with which it shares no natural border.[37] In a sense then, Younge's project is one of remembering the encounters that are already implicated in the names "stranger," "foreigner," and so on.[38] *Forces Favourites* stages a reencounter with a place and a culture marked by colonial violence—but the nature of that encounter is compromised by a focus on the conditions of perception itself. It provides, in effect, a collage of embodied experience: an image of what it is like to ride through the bush on the back of a truck, to scramble up a riverbank, to peddle a bike through a minefield, to sit inside a school—and to come across the inhabitants of this place in each of those modes. None of these offers a fully satisfactory encounter or perspective, but each sets up a "space of the body." As we traverse this politically charged land, Younge seems to take us back into space—to paraphrase Casey—as a means of critically questioning the ways in which we are taken into place.

Forces Favourites incorporates one short oral testimony. This is recounted as the camera pans the body of a man, identified as "E.M.," lying on a stretcher alone in a very dilapidated hospital in Cuito Cuanavale, devoid of beds, staff, and medicine. The scene is somewhat unexpected, following immediately on from footage of relaxed-looking Angolan soldiers disembarking from a plane on a military airfield. As we cut to the hospital, a man opens the door and leads us to the single patient lying in a corner. The patient's blanket is peeled back to reveal a bloodied leg, the foot and bottom part missing. He says: "I was cutting wood there . . . cutting wood to make fire. After I arrived there I was trapped in a minefield on the land-mines. Until now it will be 4 days without any medicine." Younge allows us only a fleeting encounter with E.M., who looks into the camera for a moment while his statement is being played.[39] Then the camera moves across the room and cuts away sharply to scenes on the river, and subsequently to a beetle scurrying across the riverbank. The effect of this brisk editing is to emphasize constant movement, perpetual regeneration, and the continuation of life on different levels—much of which passes us by in a way that eludes understanding. If the face-to-face encounter eliminates —momentarily—the distance between the spectator and E.M. as an Angolan "subject," the fact that the encounter is cut short serves only to frustrate us. A certain form of witnessing seems to be required here—but we are denied the opportunity to engage with the image.

The incongruity of the scene—as much as its brevity—reduces it to what could literally be termed a micronarrative, abutted by disconnected scenes that evoke quite different modes of inhabitation. The leitmotif of this work is transportation; E.M. has been stopped in his tracks. He is simply waiting but nothing arrives. And so we move on.

This sequence, we must remember, unfolds on monitors, balanced in the baskets of rather cumbersome bicycles. The closed circle of bikes, recalls, as David Bunn points out, the defensive formation assumed by Voortrekker wagons.[40] The inertia of the scene is an effect of this arrangement but also of the makeshift and antiquated nature of these bizarre bike constructions, combining to form an abandoned monolith, echoing the images of burnt-out vehicles on the Angolan roadside, no longer serving a designed purpose but subject to overgrowth and renewal. The only way to see this work—this place, through the monitors—is to approach alongside one of the bikes, as if one were going to ride it. From this position, we read the caption: "until now it will be four days without medicine."

Hearing and reading this statement in this manner curtails our response. E.M. cannot be "reached." He is going nowhere; we are going nowhere; only these bikes, anchored to their circular track, take us into place. There is plenty of to-ing and fro-ing in the video, but nothing is really delivered.

Younge's is not an exoticizing representation—a revelation of that which had been previously occluded. His work does not indulge in the fiction of revelation that pretends we were once unable to conceive of another's pain. It is rather about the problems of negotiating vision itself. We encounter faces—the face of a landmine victim in constant pain, the faces of children playing in minefields—but not in ways that can easily be apprehended. These are not the faces of Third World poverty and suffering, fetishized for a Western audience, which, as Slavoj Žižek points out, can easily consume such images, thereby renewing the sense of superiority that First World humanitarianism affords (it's not as if we can respond to his call and get E.M. out of there).[41] Inasmuch as they reveal something of the suffering and the wounds of war, they refuse to let us share memories.[42] They point, instead, to the gap that postcolonial societies must address; a gap that, I suggest, spans the distance between a form of sense memory and that of common or collective memory.

Place and Site

In speaking about his film *Felix in Exile* (1994) and his approach to the South African landscape, William Kentridge has noted the absence of markers at certain sites of death, violence, devastation, and massacre: there is no memorial at Sharpeville, for example.[43] Willie Doherty has directly addressed the massacre of Bloody Sunday through the work *30 January 1972* (1993) in which an image of the events that occurred on that date is projected back-to-back with an image of the same location in Derry in 1993.[44] A live sound recording of the shootings is played, along with extracts of contemporary interviews with residents who either witnessed the massacre directly or remembered it from media accounts. The installation could thus be seen as a kind of temporary "living" memorial, constituting a form of community remembrance, related to this specific site. But clearly, insofar as Doherty's work invokes the ways in which the people of Derry live the memory of Bloody Sunday now, and the way in which the events of January 30, 1972, have shaped life in that city, it operates in the realm of—and according the dimensions of—place. Like Kentridge's work, it operates in a temporal gap that calls for more memory work, although not necessarily one that could be more appropriately filled with a memorial.

Place-names such as Sharpeville or Derry have become loaded terms by association with violent events, but the places themselves—precisely because they are subject to the temporal overlay of reinhabitation—often manifest a failure to signify. This failure is something that emerges repeatedly in Jo Ractliffe's work. Ractliffe's *Vlakplaas: 2 June 1999* (*Drive-by-Shooting*), for example, is a video and photo installation comprised of still photos, shot surreptitiously from the road, of the former South African government death squad training camp, Vlakplaas. Formerly under the command of the notorious Eugene de Kock, nicknamed "Prime Evil" (now serving multiple life sentences for murder), Vlakplaas signifies a dark period in the country's history; and, indeed, since its operatives have been implicated in countless killings, it potentially constitutes a site at which "evil" might be located. It is now, however, a farm garden, devoid of clues that might reveal its former function. It is the ordinariness of place that emerges in *Drive-by-Shooting*, which again plays on the security and danger associated with the car.

These same themes characterize the *Sectarian Murder* photo series (1988) by the Belfast-born artist Paul Seawright, which traces the journeys of murder victims some fifteen or sixteen years after their deaths (fig. 11). Citing a date as a title in each case, Seawright provides a short text for each photograph, explaining how and where the bodies of murder victims were found at the locations photographed. For example:

Tuesday 30th January 1973

The car traveled to a deserted tourist spot known as the Giant's Ring. The 14 year-old boy was made to kneel on a grass verge, his anorak was pulled over his head, then he was shot at close range, dying instantly.

These journeys pass through "ordinary" places—streets, playgrounds, parks, waste grounds, tourist spots, the shores of Belfast Lough—in which there can be no permanent markers, memorials, or reminders. The recon-

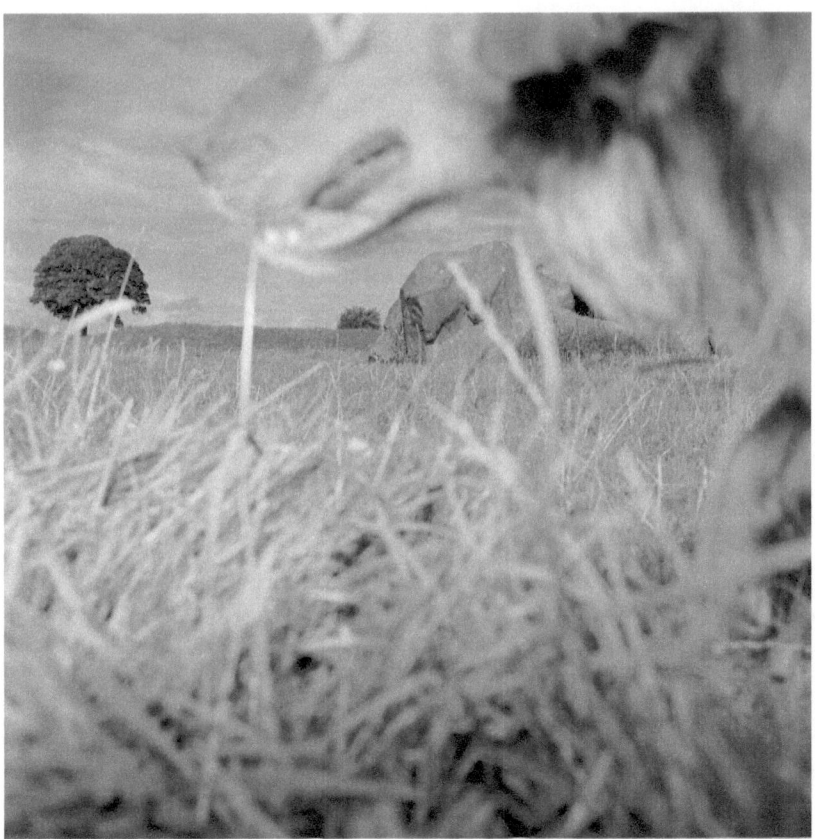

FIGURE 11. Paul Seawright, from *Sectarian Murder* series (1998). Type C print with text, 75 x 100 cm. Courtesy Paul Seawright, University of Wales, Newport.

stitution of the path of an abduction that took place in 1973 seems to suggest a forensic dimension, as with Ractliffe's *End of Time*. But Seawright is interested principally in the movement that occurs through and within a place, rather than in an examination of a static site, read forensically for clues. As the artist documents the site at which a body is found, he simultaneously records the presence of other occupants, traversing the same area for whatever purpose: a walker in the park, a dog at the Giant's Ring beauty spot, some indistinguishable figures on the horizon, a man pushing a child on a swing in a park, people driving or walking to the shops. It is the "snapshot" of these that captures the temporality of place, overlaid with discrete micronarratives.

When we make a journey, we invariably engage in "double tracking":

As I journey from place to place in the everyday life-world, two parallel and simultaneous processes are likely to occur without premeditation. On the one hand, I find myself attending to the immediate perceptual environs, the "near sphere" or "focal field." . . . I notice *this* looming person or *that* on-coming car in my path. On the other hand, I am also aware of a more encompassing circumambient field within which the focal field itself is set. Although this larger field is mappable (it would constitute a district or region on a map), I do not take it as metrically determinate or even as laid out in a regular way. Instead, I grasp it as a diversely configurated, multidimensional environment with its own inherent directionality.[45]

Heeding both information coming in from the focal field and from the circumambient world, one not only "keeps track" of the journey, but "double tracks." Younge, Kentridge, Doherty, and Ractliffe might each be understood as double tracking insofar as they register perception in relation to these different fields, moving between the detail (of the riverbank, roadside, landscape) and indices of the far sphere. In Kentridge's case, these two spheres frequently dissolve into each other (there is a famous case in his film *Mine* where a coffee plunger becomes a mine shaft). In Doherty's *30 January 1972*, we stand before an image of the street while one of the speakers remembering the massacre recalls seeing a set of eyelashes stuck to a wall. In his photo series, however, Seawright freeze-frames the perceptual field in such a way as to contrast the near detail and the far. His is, in this sense, not a traditional narrative style of photography (although ostensibly it has a story) but an exploration of the relationship of micronarrative to place and of the way in which this unfolds through bodily perception. Place is revealed as a multidimensional field in which narratives intersect— embodied narratives that enter our perceptual domain through visual encounter. But here the banality or ordinariness of the everyday journey across a park, or down a street, rubs against the extraordinariness of the traumatic narrative—the story of abduction and murder that can be situated within this landscape. This is not to say that such traumatic narratives are exceptional in such a context; indeed, they are not. Seawright disperses the narrative of trauma within the everyday life place in such a way that we understand that narrative as co-existing within, rather than characterizing, a visual field.

I have been drawing thus far on Casey's notion of a journey as it links with his conception of place. It is useful to emphasize how the conception of place functions in contradistinction to "site" in order to tease out the implications for an understanding of commemorative work. Journeys, Casey argues, are not just "travels in time or across space":

they engage ineluctably in place—often in many places (and not just in succession but also all-at-once . . .). But we can say just as well that places engage us in journeys. This is so to the extent that there is nothing like a completely static place, a place involving no movement, no change, no transiency. If places introduce permanency into journeys—since they are where we can *remain* as we move about—journeys bring out what is impermanent and continuously changing when we are in place itself. To be in a place is to be somewhere in which movement in the local landscape and thus journeying in that landscape becomes possible. In a site, by contrast, we are stuck in space (as well as frozen in time) . . . In this circumstance site stasis sets in, and journeys become mere travels or trips. In contrast being-in-place brings with it actualities and virtualities of motion that have little if anything to do with speed and everything to do with exploration and inhabitation, with depth instead of distance, horizon rather than border, arc and not perimeter.[46]

This notion of the place itself, engendering and supporting continual movement through it, might also be understood to underpin the analysis of Salcedo's work proposed in Chapter 3, in which I argued that the space of installation enacts Das's conceptualization of traumatic memory as a process of remaking the world. As soon as one envisages the place of inhabitation, one is effectively moving through it, so that the stasis—or at least, repetition—implied in the acting out of trauma is potentially overcome. Moreover, the ineluctability of place mitigates against the notion that trauma effects a removal from the social world, and the assumption that, following a decathexis from the lost object, one returns to the world as one left it prior to the trauma. Place is not just a destination—a site to which one returns (characterized, as Casey would say, by its "thereness" rather than "hereness").

In the work of Younge or Seawright, trauma is revealed through a journey in place where it is coextensive with other kinds of event. Thus, for example, one can inhabit a site of death and perceive, at once, the presence of children playing and the evidence of war damage—or the dog in the field and the memory of a murder that occurred there. The uneasy juxtapositions simultaneously track the divergent paths of different inhabitants, past and present, *and* the different dimensions that shape memory in a single subject. As I argued in Chapter 2, trauma (as a subjective experience) cannot be registered as a past event in separation from other present experiences (or under the sign of the "victim" that expropriates all experience beyond that of having once been a victim); rather, the negotiation of sense memory also entails a negotiation of common memory: a form of double tracking.

These are more than bizarre juxtapositions, however. Rather than simply being set next to each other, Casey suggests that objects in place—and here I am linking these to the "journey narratives" associated with them—are subject to overlap or envelopment. The intertwining of objects and narratives is what constitutes (in the terms of both Casey and Merleau-Ponty), a depth relationship.[47] In this light, I want to suggest that work like Seawright's should not be understood as deploying a technique of estrangement—that is, of drawing attention to objects by rendering them strange by association. Like Kentridge or Ractliffe, Seawright entwines the ordinary and the extraordinary (in terms of the traumatic, the obscenely violent) in such a way that binds them in place, and often thereby to a "space of the body," which, in turn, allows them to unfold at a deeper level.

Such work takes us into place in a way that the memorial monument cannot. Moreover, it is able to address precisely the issue of differential experience—of memory as an encounter between an inside and an outside—that is so problematic for the more static memorial, particularly in situations where a memorial must confront a shared history of oppression or state-sponsored violence. James Young, in particular, has elucidated the limitations of the memorial site in his study of postwar Germany and Austria, in which he argues for a new kind of "counter-monument" that engages more dynamically with an audience.[48] The impossible demands placed on the public memorial are especially apparent from Young's discussion of the Berlin Monument for the Murdered Jews of Europe and its failure to satisfy the quite distinct needs of different stakeholders. That monument's function was overdetermined from the outset, mired in a debate over Germany's desire both to "move on" and to honor the wishes of those wanting to commemorate lost family and community, or simply to acknowledge the terrible wrongs of the past. Thus, Young suggests, the singular monument must always be, in some sense, a marker of insufficiency.

Commemorative work certainly must exceed that which occurs at the single site (notwithstanding the needs of specific families and communities for a monument), and works by Kentridge, Doherty, Ractliffe, Younge, and Seawright point to the value of conceiving of memorial practices and art in relation to a more expansive concept of place. They also operate within a kind of "interim space," opened up by the often volatile relationship between common memory and sense memory.

Journeys 5: The Commemorative Tour

Interim space, in this context, may be understood as the contingent place that emerges in the wake of loss and conflict, particularly as the memory of place is inscribed within a postcolonial history. As processes of reconciliation (in places such as South Africa or Australia) subsume memories of violence and loss, effectively urging the completion of processes of mourning as a society enters a new postcolonial phase, so the gap between sense memory and common memory manifests as a rift in time. The shape and feeling of this rift, or space between, is mapped within the works I have discussed; moreover, the artists we have considered—who are each "post-conflict" or postcolonial in some explicit way—manifest such space as a locus for present and future encounters.

The memory work undertaken by this kind of art is not akin to that of the monument or memorial but to that of a newer and more radical form of commemorative project, epitomized by the South African enterprise known as the Western Cape Action Tour (WECAT). Such a project operates quite explicitly in the spaces opened up by debates over commemoration and the insufficiency of conventional memorials, and in the gap between the tourist trip and the deeper encounter within inhabited place. For visitors to, and inhabitants of Cape Town, WECAT functions as an "alternative" tourism, running tours through the townships of the Cape Flats—the part of Cape Town that most holidaymakers never see. As a cultural intervention, it constitutes an active engagement with the inhabitation of place in the wake of the devastating violence of apartheid, addressing many of the questions canvassed in the artwork I have discussed.

The WECAT project was formed by eight former members of Umkhonto we Sizwe (MK), the military wing of the African National Congress. Yazir Henri, the project co-ordinator, describes its aims in terms of working through trauma and also promoting listening and interaction.[49] "Through people encountered and places visited, the stories that are recalled during a day spent with these former soldiers embrace the many, many aspects of life under apartheid that are not included in the TRC's brief and that do not always fit the . . . narrative of transcendence, triumph, redemption and reconciliation," WECAT director Heidi Grunebaum notes.[50]

Much as the Berlin Monument for the Murdered Jews of Europe is felt by many Germans to run counter to the forward-looking impulse of a city that refuses to be "held hostage to mourning," so Grunebaum points out, the TRC has effectively foreclosed upon the possibility for reflecting upon—and perhaps continuing to mourn—the losses of the past. WECAT, however, provides us a means to "encounter the living pastness and ever-changingness of everyday sites that are transformed and become imbued with multiple meanings as stories are told in, about and through them." Moreover, as with Paul Seawright's work, there is a blurring of "memorial spaces and the ordinariness of everyday places" when we encounter sites of massacre—quite ordinary places—as they are inhabited now.

As an outsider visiting Cape Town for the first time and taking a WECAT tour, I was initially struck by the ordinariness of the locations we visited; the more so because the experience of traveling in a small van with three local tour guides lends a certain air of expectation: one expects to pull up at a monument or spectacular vista—at least, at something self-evidently important. But the experience of a WECAT tour is quite unlike this. Each time our small group left the van, we were unsure of what we should be looking at—what might be important in the landscape or part of the township at which we had arrived. And clearly part of the function of the tour was to work upon such expectations; this was not a place that was to be delivered up to us in a series of snapshots. At the same time, our guides did reveal to us the importance of key sites. Our tour stopped in front of the police station in Athlone, one of the "Coloured" townships of the Cape Flats, where Nkululeko Booysen spoke of his experience of arrest and torture. Then we moved on to a public toilet where in 1989, Booysen told us, the bodies of two MK operatives, Robert Waterwitch and Coline Williams, had been found. Our guides explained that official versions of the events surrounding their death were contradicted by their intelligence, which suggested the operatives had been blown up and dumped behind the toilets by security police, although the TRC investigators had not been able to establish conclusively what had happened.[51]

After telling this story, Booysen invited us to take photographs. While one member of our party chatted further to the guides and the other two returned to the van, happy with a couple of snaps of the site, I wandered around wondering what and how to photograph. This was, of course, the conundrum of Ractliffe's *Drive-by-Shooting*, her work on the banality of the site of Vlakplaas—and of Seawright's *Sectarian Murder* series. How does one encapsulate the history of a locale that today is traversed by so many inhabitants going about their daily business? More precisely, how can this past and this present be interwoven in some form of memory image? In Seawright's or Ractliffe's work, a formal solution is proposed to this problem—one that enables us to see more clearly the relationship of place to memory, the competing temporal dimensions of place and the manner in which these shape perception.

WECAT, similarly, takes us *into place*, and lets us decide what to photograph. Outside the toilets in Athlone, Booysen pointed out to me a tiny black and red ribbon attached to the tree—something in the immediate focal field to animate a photograph, but so small as to be barely noticeable. He explained that his group had adopted this as a kind of memorial signifier. They had placed these ribbons at each site of remembrance—sites where death had occurred and where, in most cases, a formal monument was lacking. Remembrance, he explained occurred in the discussion on the tour, in our introduction to the place and in the interactions that this precipitated with members of the local community.

After Athlone, we visited the township of Guguletu—a place I "knew" through a film that is the subject of the next chapter. Booysen took us to the intersection of NY1 and NY111—the place where in 1986, seven young men had been gunned down by security police in what was claimed to be a legitimate anti-terrorist operation. Again, Booysen pointed out the ribbon on the tree at the intersection. This time, he said, the tree was especially significant. The mothers of the murdered young men—whom Booysen represents, and who often join the WECAT groups—had been pushing for a memorial after the TRC investigation finally established that government security forces had been responsible for the deaths. They hadn't got the memorial they wanted, so the tree had become symbolic of their ongoing struggle. But the tree itself had been threatened. There was a move by the council to cut it down, so the community had been fighting to keep it.

These locations were potentially memorial sites in the limited sense of the term that Casey proposes. Yet—in the absence of memorials—we experienced them as places at which we might meet local people, some of whom expressed views on the subject of memorials, some of whom had known the murdered men. As we went back to the van from this stop, I asked Booysen again why there was no more permanent memorial to the Guguletu Seven here. He had previously emphasized—and subsequently demonstrated—that this tour was a form of memorial that exceeded the limitations of a stone monument. But then he told me that in fact there *was* a monument a little way down the street, about which he had misgivings. He said that the mothers of the murdered men regarded it as inadequate.

For Booysen, the tree itself served as a focus for remembrance, but, he conceded, the mothers had envisaged something approaching the scale and grandeur of the equestrian statue of Louis Botha outside the parliament building in the city center. What they really wanted, he explained, was the *dignity* of the Botha monument. This was not, then, an argument about the form of a monument, but about a certain lack of respect, a failure to acknowledge. A rather low-budget concrete monument had, it seems, been hurriedly erected at the mayor's instigation, without consultation with the families, in what appeared to be a politically expedient concession to community wishes, rather than a genuine attempt to honor the memory of the victims and their families. What Booysen and his WECAT colleagues demonstrate is that there is a gap here that a memorial can't fill, because it requires an engagement with those who have suffered. Indeed, it may be precisely the temporal dimension of the encounter that cannot be fulfilled by the singular negotiation, the singular monument, because what is called for is a renegotiation of relationships over time, a process that the monument threatens to cut short.

As Veena Das reminds us, the task of historiography is not simply to break silences and to uncover hidden truths; sometimes, it is to recognize that pain *seeks acknowledgment* in different ways. In their theoretical writing, the WECAT directors Grunebaum and Henri reference Delbo's concept of sense memory to evoke the personal suffering that is "displaced by the nation-building discourse that mediates . . . TRC testimonies."[52] It is clear that the task of giving memory a home, of placing it within the visible domain, cannot, then, rest solely with the publication of testimony (with hearings such as those of the TRC), nor with the monument, since the former is often simply a beginning point and the latter is only one limited kind of acknowledgement. As sense memory is subsumed into common memory (as through the publication of testimony), it is necessary to guard against its colonization. This is not an argument for resisting change or anchoring personal memory in a specific past; rather it affirms the need to recognize the contingencies of memory politics. In this, it points to the need for art that creates a space for sense memory *outside* that of common memory—or, at least, that continues to track the spaces *between*.

5

Face-to-Face Encounters

> [People] confound themselves with their role; they become victims of
> their own "good performance"; they themselves have forgotten how
> much accidents, moods, and caprice disposed of them when the question
> of their "vocation" was decided—and how many other roles they might
> have been able to play; for now it is too late. Considered more deeply
> the role has actually become character; and art, nature.
>
> —Friedrich Nietzsche, *The Gay Science*

By identifying the means by which we are "taken into place," the
artists discussed in the last chapter reveal some of the "accidental" features
that determine character. In Willie Doherty's *The Only Good One*, a character oscillates between the roles of victim and perpetrator. Fear and anxiety are the affects that dispose him to make particular identifications. He
has already become a certain kind of person in this case, but his character
remains the result of caprice, teetering on the verge of something quite different, another path that he might so easily have pursued.

As far as the spectator of an artwork is concerned, affective identifications, mediated through bodily perception are of a different order from
those identifications that proceed from an affinity or emotional sympathy
with character. Emotions may be understood to arise from playing a role:
method actors get into character in order to generate feeling; drama thera-
pists use characterization to induce empathy. But if emotions are affects organized by a set of subjective or interpersonal relationships, overcoded by
social or moral considerations, what of the affects that might undercut the

boundaries of character; the same affects that might—through art—take us outside of character and toward a form of critical thinking? I am proposing a somewhat schematic distinction here, not to obscure the complex relationship between affect and emotion, about which there is much more to be said,[1] but rather to find a means of articulating the role of affectivity in political art. Brecht determines the ground of this inquiry in ruling out emotionalism, or sentimental identification, as a viable political response. For him, "We are all actors and . . . acting is an inescapable dimension of social and everyday life."[2] Thus the spectacle should *reveal* rather than *conceal* the act of acting; it should expose the mechanisms of identification rather than allowing us to fall victim to our own good performance. But the question remains of how affectivity in art might operate *even as* the act of acting and the creation of character is revealed—a question that reduces to the problematic of Deleuze's *encountered sign*: how might affect itself lead to a critical understanding that undercuts rather than affirms the bounds of subjectivity, thereby taking us beyond ourselves?

To pursue this question, I return to South Africa in its era of transition. Specifically, I shall focus on the responses of some key artists and filmmakers to the highly charged spectacle of the Truth and Reconciliation Commission—an event that raises issues concerning the manner in which testimony is both *performed* by perpetrators and witnesses and received by an audience that plays its own role in the unfolding drama.

Many observers—among them the artist William Kentridge—have commented on the theatrical aspects of the TRC, at which witnesses gave testimony before a live audience, often on the stages of public halls, filmed for screening on nightly television.[3] This very public mediation of testimony distinguishes the TRC and its representations from a number of other large-scale testimonial projects, the best known of these being the Yale-based project for the archiving of Holocaust testimony, founded in 1979. One of the founders of that project, Geoffrey Hartman, has recently reflected upon its video-visual aspects, noting that in the early days, the desire to create conditions conducive to uninterrupted personal recollection, and to embody the voices of those giving testimony, led to the decision to film speakers as talking heads.[4] The camera, Hartman observes, invariably focused entirely on the witnesses—often zooming in for "Bergmanesque close-ups"—effectively effacing the interviewer. Nothing indicated the discursive context of the testimonial act, not even an initial verification shot. This approach Hartman now questions, since it failed to acknowledge what he calls the "testimonial alliance" between interviewer and interviewee—in other words, the importance of the interviewer as facilitator and listener, as one who is "representative of a potentially larger community, one that does not turn away from but recognizes the historical catastrophe and the personal trauma undergone."[5]

One could argue that such an awareness of both historical catastrophe and personal suffering is a fundamental underpinning of the TRC; the need for testimony to be *received* within the new South Africa is perceived to be at least as important as the utterance itself. Giving testimony is thus the occasion for a face-to-face encounter in the sense evoked by Gayatri Spivak (and elaborated on by her commentator Sara Ahmed) when she argues that what is important in the politics of resistance or liberation is not simply the act of speaking but the possibility of being heard.[6] Collective activism for Spivak must involve a politics of listening, predicated on the listener's willingness to enter into such an encounter with another. Through encounters, the difference between the one who testifies and the listener is not necessarily eradicated, although it may be reduced; it is, more precisely, inhabited. Thus Spivak points to the possibility of a mode of ethical listening—and seeing—that can support and tolerate difference, rather than either repudiating it or assimilating the experience of the other to the self.

More than the Yale archive for Holocaust testimony, the TRC structures into its self-representation a politics of encounter in which responses to testimony are not only visible but sought and measured. The expressive idiom of the Yale video testimonies could never capture the dynamics of such a project, with its focus on the reception of the speech act. Hence, with the TRC, we find a shift away from framing testimony as private individual expression and toward a tendency to see it as an affective event that induces a range of responses.

This shift is embodied by the internationally acclaimed U.S.-made documentary film *Long Night's Journey into Day* (Deborah Hoffman and Francis Reid, 2000). Constituted as a series of vignettes featuring four distinct cases, the film documents the testimony of both victims and perpetrators, exploring the reception of testimony in meetings and interviews beyond the TRC hearings themselves. The testimonies are thus seen not primarily as monologic reflections, issuing from the individual, but as setting in train a series of face-to-face encounters. Within this framework, the film manages the emotional responses of a broader audience.

One of the vignettes tells the story of the 1997 hearings, linked to the assassinations in 1986 of the so-called Guguletu Seven—seven young men killed in the Cape Town township of Guguletu in what an obfuscatory official inquest deemed to be a "legitimate anti-terrorist operation." The segment is introduced by a national news bulletin aired at the time of the shootings. The news reader cautions at the outset that the images about to be shown may prove disturbing to sensitive viewers. But the voice-over describing the bodies as those of terrorists, shot by police as they attempted an ambush, clearly works to diffuse the distress of a significant section of the viewing audience. What we witness is not simply misreporting at a factual level, but the manner in which images are, in an instant, stripped of affect to the extent that the sight of a young man, lying dead, bound by a rope, with which he is yanked into view of the camera, does not incite appropriate affect.

This systematic abjection of the victims is countered immediately in *Long Night's Journey* by shots of the mothers at their homes. Whereas the South African film *Guguletu Seven* (dir. Lindy Wilson, 2001) gives some sense of the men's identity as individuals, throughout *Long Night's Journey*, they are cast exclusively as sons, mediated through testimony of the bereaved mothers. We subsequently hear the mothers tell of how they first encountered this news footage, articulating the pain of seeing a child dragged by a rope, of finding out about the death of a son from a television report. During their testimony the camera cuts to various members of the audience at the hearing, visibly weeping at what they witness. Several of the commissioners, including Archbishop Tutu who presides over the proceedings, articulate the difficulty of witnessing the mothers' pain.

This reorientation of the Guguletu Seven tragedy in terms of familial identity clearly builds on and promotes a generalized identification with the mothers, grounded in a readily translatable horror at the thought of the loss of a child. However, it also plays on a sin of omission. In the news footage, we are confronted with the workings of crude devices that can deaden or heighten affect in the blink of an eye. What Hartman has called "the guilt or shame accompanying [the] sight" of testimony is not only at its sharpest in this scenario, but a guilt born of complicity seems to fuel the depth of sentiment that characterizes the audience response to the mothers' testimony. We are touched by the grief of the mothers, but also by horror: a shock of recognition.

The true horror of this encounter for many is not that we didn't see the full extent of this tragedy until the hearings made it public—but precisely that it *was* publicly seen, that it was not hidden from view but received without the affect that we now feel to be generalizable as we are touched by each mother's loss.

In perhaps the most disturbing sequence of the Guguletu segment, we see the mothers themselves as part of the audience at the hearing, viewing videotapes of their dead children made by the police in the aftermath of the shootings. Several of them are overcome by emotion and the screening is brought to a halt as they are led from the room. If the previous scenes of the hearings worked to suggest that an audience might share, in part, some of the pain of the witnesses, this possibility is now shattered. It is at this point that the gap is widest between the mothers, who perform their grief through expansive gestures that elude the grasp of those who meekly try to support them, and the onlookers, who, for the most part, remain impassive, stunned into silence.

The Guguletu Seven segment culminates, however, with the encounter between the mothers of the victims and Thapelo Mbelo, one of the police officers involved in the shootings. Mbelo figures as the catalyst for this encounter, since it is he who requests a meeting with the mothers, and as the subject of a personal transformation. A former member of a secret government death squad, Mbelo testifies that he shot one of the seven in the act of surrender. *Long Night's Journey* supplements footage of this testimony with images of Mbelo talking to camera about his former work. He explains how killing was, for members of his squad, "just a day's work," executed without feeling. After participating in an official cover-up for so long (he confesses that at the inquest, and also at the trial of a journalist who had challenged official accounts of the case, "[W]e all lied"), Mbelo says he now wants to bring things into the open. The narrative of his redemption is underscored by contrast with the figure of the white security policeman, Sergeant Bellingan, the only other one of over twenty-five police involved to apply for amnesty in this case. Bellingan, whose testimony is intercut with Mbelo's, gives a very different account of events, with the clear implication that his amnesty application is evidence neither of a sense of remorse nor of commitment to the process of reconciliation.

If remorse is seen to be generated in Mbelo through the testimonial process, it is conspicuously absent in Bellingan, who remains emblematic of a failure to encounter those perceived as other—and perhaps, in this respect, of the limitations of the TRC itself. As the commissioner points out in footage of the hearing incorporated into *Long Night's Journey*, Bellingan hedges his bets, announcing that he will seek amnesty only *if* he is found guilty of an offense. Correspondingly, no expression of sympathy is offered unconditionally; emotion, in this context, is produced in measured quantities, as quid pro quo. Moreover, Bellingan's encounter with the victims is effectively finite; Mbelo, who must face his accusers daily, observes with some bitterness that Bellingan can at least retreat to the haven of his white community. It is this sliding away from an encounter—rather than any lack of emotive pleading—that marks the absence of remorse; for if Mbelo willingly entered into the face-to-face encounter and looked into the faces of the women he has wronged, this is something that Bellingan and others have demonstrably failed to do.

Long Night's Journey thus counters the absence of affect (in Bellingan, in the Mbelo of the shootings, in the news footage), not with a display of sentiment, but through the staged encounter itself. The meeting between Mbelo and the mothers takes place on camera, under the supervision of a TRC member, who briefs the mothers on what to expect and how best to handle the meeting. For the mothers, the occasion provides an opportunity to question Mbelo, to express their anger and sorrow, and to negotiate the issue of forgiveness. One of them is motivated by her Christian faith to offer forgiveness; by allowing God to be the judge, she suggests, "we . . . get rid of the burden we carry inside." Another of the mothers articulates a resolve to withhold her forgiveness. She confronts Mbelo with a face animated by contempt. The reverse-shot frames the less expressive, but clearly perturbed visage of Mbelo. A subtitle, translating from Xhosa, reads: "Your face is something I will never forget. I have no forgiveness."

This captioning of Mbelo's face has a marked visual impact, functioning as a kind of stigma—a mark that forces us to bear witness, not to the affect expressed, but to the affective impact of the face. It informs us that this face is seen in a particular way by the mothers. Although we cannot see through their eyes, we scrutinize Mbelo's countenance, assessing his response to these words. Mbelo gropes for words that might adequately convey his newfound contrition and sympathy: "Mama, I don't know what to say. We have hurt you . . . I am ashamed to look you in the face." The camera lingers, waiting for the expression of remorse to emerge, but what could such an expression consist in? Can there be a look of remorse?

Mbelo effectively describes a shift from the affectless state of killer working for a government death squad to the shame of being branded a traitor and murderer by his own community. Shame, however, manifests itself as a look of discomfort, a failure to respond adequately to a question. As the psychologist Silvan Tomkins argues in his work on affect, shame reduces facial communication.[7] The shame response, particularly as it involves self-confrontation, "calls a halt to looking at another person, and to the other person's looking at him, particularly at his face."[8] Remorse, however, entails reflection, moving beyond the autonomic response that consists of this retreat. More than pure affect, it is a self-conscious gesture, directed at another. It is not performed or expressed unilaterally, for it is not simply an indulgence of one's guilt, but is enacted in the tension of the face-to-face encounter.

In what might be understood as a gesture of remorse, Mbelo submits to the mothers' accusatory gazes, asking for forgiveness, apparently without expectation. There is something compelling about this display, even in the absence of emotional expression. All Mbelo can do is stand before those he has wronged and simply accept the burden of their grief. Because of what he has done, because of how these women have suffered, we feel he should offer more. The affect of the guilty party is necessarily insufficient in this context, the more so as it induces an excess of affect in the victims. But this is where remorse must be understood as comprising more than the affects of shame and sorrow. Its motivating sentiments—shame, pity, empathy— must be somewhere in evidence, but as an ethical gesture it requires more than the performance of these; indeed, at a certain point, it calls upon the actor *not* to share his own feelings but to witness the pain of another. "Whatever he feels about what he did is his business," says one of the mothers. But when they meet Mbelo, they have to ask him, "How do you feel?" knowing precisely that what he feels is insufficient, irrelevant. "I feel bad" is all he can offer.

The film's focus on the personal face-to-face as the scene of an ethical transaction might be understood as underscoring the philosophy of the TRC as this is elaborated by its president, Desmond Tutu. In the name of what he terms "restorative" (as opposed to retributive) justice, Tutu introduced the vocabulary of repentance and forgiveness to the amnesty hearings—a move that has provoked a critical response, largely from within South Africa but also from Jacques Derrida. Derrida argues that there is a fundamental confusion between the logic of forgiveness (a nonpenal, nonreparative logic) and that of justice. Moreover, this extends to a confusion between the collective or state responsibility to deliberate on claims for amnesty and to dispense that amnesty, and the individual right to bestow or withhold forgiveness.[9] In other words, witnesses induced to express forgiveness are, in effect, doing the state's bidding.

Wedded to TRC ideology, *Long Night's Journey* arguably compromises its witnesses in this respect. But if, on one level, the film actively and somewhat optimistically promotes the redemptive value of the encounter, it also moves beyond the sphere of the juridical to trace what Derrida terms "the enigma of the forgiveness of the unforgivable"—the affective state that the juridico-political cannot approach, much less appropriate.[10]

Whether a victim of terrorism says "I forgive" or "I do not forgive," this "zone of experience remains inaccessible," Derrida argues, and we must "respect its secret."[11] We cannot properly understand what it is to be asked to forgive under such conditions, and ultimately such experience is inaccessible to law, to politics, even to morals. But what is important in the encounter is the sharing of language: "Even if I say 'I do not forgive you' to someone who asks my forgiveness, but whom I understand and who understands me, then a process of reconciliation has begun."[12] Thus, *Long Night's Journey* documents the beginning of a process of reconciliation, even as it lays bare the problems inherent in encounters that require such different and difficult things from perpetrators and victims.

Long Night's Journey is in many ways a film about the failure of evidence. One of the commissioners herself confesses that she would find it hard if Bellingan were to receive amnesty, because she needs palpable evidence of remorse: a sign that he is not a monster but a human being, capable of feeling. Mbelo, who figures as the vehicle for transformation, clearly comes closer to manifesting remorse, but in the end this does not turn on the performance of emotion. The narrative end of the film is signaled when one mother says, "Yes, I forgive you." But here her affect undercuts the script. She forgives in a spirit of anger, because at this point it is best for her, because she is a Christian, and because Mbelo is there facing her.[13]

Long Night's Journey thus presents a story of maternal grief, focused on the mothers' entry into a formal process of reconciliation. It is both hindered and helped along by its ideological commitment to reconciliation as this is structured and promoted through the TRC. If personal experience is sutured into a narrative of transformation, this in turn facilitates the realization of a space of encounter in which the limits of empathy are manifest, and in which affect reveals itself to be essentially feral, unconstrained by the rhetoric of forgiveness.

The ethical issue here is whether, within this space, the mothers' "secret," in Derrida's terms, can be respected; whether the wider audience encounters the witnesses in a way that acknowledges the distinct nature of their experience, and the extent to which this cannot be shared. *Long Night's Journey* at times invokes devices that foster emotional identifications and promote what Brecht called "crude empathy," defined as the tendency to abstract from the specifics of the life depicted and identify with a single emotion or affect; to respond by thinking "I wonder what I would be like if that happened to me."[14] What is wrong with that kind of empathy is, of course, that another's experience—in this case, a profoundly alienating and fundamentally secret one—is assimilated to the self in the most simplistic and sentimental way; anything beyond the audience's immediate experience remains beyond comprehension. Hartman identifies this moral problematic as central to the empathetic relationship: "the pathos of the testimonial moment loses its specific context precisely because it arouses a widespread anxiety"—in other words, the very basis for empathy mitigates against the Spivakian encounter because in overidentifying "in the very name of morality" with those who testify, we fail to "respect the difference between their suffering and our own."[15]

Yazir Henri has described exactly this process occurring through the TRC.[16] Henri, whose insights derive from his own experience of testifying before the TRC, suggests that telling one's story is the beginning of a process in which one must find a way of "owning memory." Once testimony enters the public domain, however, it is regarded as common property. As a result, control of speech is effectively wrested from the witness as testimonies are unwittingly appropriated into self-aggrandizing, "white-liberal" or redemptive narratives. Hearing testimony becomes a means of indulging "white guilt" insofar as it allows an audience to act out an emotional response. Caught up in the emotion of the occasion, we become "victims of our own good performance" if we allow testimony to become about us (our guilt, our sadness), rather than the witnesses. For Henri, the failure to respect another's ownership of testimony—and the fact that it cannot be shared—betrays what amounts to a failure of encounter. This in turn has the potential to compound the suffering of the witness.

But herein lies a dilemma for artists and filmmakers seeking to respond to the TRC in some way. Against the backdrop of apartheid, which engendered a form of desensitization that effectively blocked empathy, there is compelling reason to re-present tragedies such as that of the Guguletu Seven as human dramas, through which a broad audience can make an identification with core emotions. Such a strategy at least counters the lack of affect in those who—like Bellingan—embody the brutality of the apartheid regime. If we are to challenge the role of uncritical emotional identifications, we need, therefore, to distinguish the importance of affect in the structuring of social relations and empathy, and also to open up the issue of how we negotiate the affective and emotional impact of testimony.

To pursue this, I shall look now at *Ubu and the Truth Commission*, a project that explores not emotion per se but the intensities of affect as it flows in and out of character—a project that has perhaps gone further than any other in the domain of theater and visual art in critically examining the reception of testimony (figs. 12–16). *Ubu and the Truth Commission*, a stage play written by Jane Taylor and directed by William Kentridge, which featured puppetry by the Handspring Puppet Company and projections of animation by Kentridge, confronts the central tension of the TRC—the jarring of differently motivated, quite differently charged forms of testimony—by adopting a structure that reflects that of the TRC with its double focus on both victim and perpetrator testimony.

The world of the white security policeman, testifying at the TRC under duress and for purely self-serving reasons, is evoked in the live action in a burlesque narrative featuring Alfred Jarry's character Père Ubu, originally a power-hungry pretender to the throne of Poland, brought to life in the play *Ubu Roi* in 1896. The figure of Ubu, traditionally a bombastic character who acts without regard for the consequences of his actions, is shown in the grips of a paranoia, attempting to wriggle free of the demands of justice. Guilty of violent crimes committed in the name of the state, he gradually comes undone as the Commission closes in on him, demanding accountability and eventually securing the incriminating testimony of his wife.

In co-opting Ubu as a satirical device, Taylor and Kentridge reference an established tradition. Jarry's original play—although not itself conceived as political satire—has frequently been interpreted as a vehicle for debunking the activities of imperialist or totalitarian nations and despots.[17] Essentially a loose parody of *Macbeth*, *Ubu Roi* reduces heroic subject matter to burlesque. In the spirit of the *guignol* or Punchinello tradition that Jarry much admired, the characters are two-dimensional caricatures, given to rampant violence without pause for thought.[18] Typically in *Ubu Roi*, the actors themselves take on the character of marionettes, although puppets are often incorporated into productions.[19]

In *Ubu and the Truth Commission*, however, puppets are used both to evoke a monstrous state apparatus (Ubu's dogs of war, the crocodile paper-shredder) and to portray the witnesses who have suffered its consequences. In the midst of a drama centered around the manic hysteria of Pa and Ma Ubu, the witness puppets emerge, paradoxically, as the most human entities on stage, displaying precisely the kind of affect lacking in the central characters. This is not only an inversion of an aspect of the Ubu tradition, but a means of reorienting a text that, as satire, focuses exclusively on its political targets—on the perpetrators of violence—rather than on the victims of this violence.

The *guignol* excesses are, nevertheless, in abundant evidence in this production, displaced in part onto the animation.[20] As Ubu is seen in the live action contemplating his future under threat of exposure from the TRC, the projected animation ties him to a past that contains acts of unspeakable violence, incriminating him in the actions he now repudiates.

Kentridge draws Pa Ubu with the attributes Jarry himself invented in a series of prints and drawings: notably the triangular head, sometimes featuring a stylized moustache and the umbilical spiral that also becomes the symbol of Ubu in abstraction (fig. 12).[21] Whereas Jarry's Ubu usually carries a walking stick tucked into his pocket, however, Kentridge gives him a menacing prong, which forms the leg of a tripod into which Ubu himself is prone to morph. The tripod is sometimes just a tripod, providing support for a camera—and occasionally also a cat, an eyeball, and a radio set—but it also functions as an instrument of torture, so that no clear distinction is drawn between devices that record violent events and those that collude, and even intervene, in them.

In one sequence, the tripod shoots a man, explodes his body into fragments, heaps these fragments together, and reignites them until they disintegrate into a galaxy of tiny specks in which the spiral of Ubu emerges. The manic attempts of the tripod to eradicate the body read in relation to a cartoon tradition in which the body, infinitely prone to metamorphosis and regeneration, is an indestructible entity. But, in this case, the sequence is inspired by the South African police's policy of blowing up bodies as a means of destroying evidence. The codes of animation are thus co-opted—in somewhat surreal fashion—to reference the real event: real bodies, lacking the durability of cartoon figures.

The explosion is one part of larger animation sequence, providing a backdrop to a scene in which Ma discovers evidence of her husband's misdeeds. As Ma reads from documents detailing his activities, Pa Ubu echoes

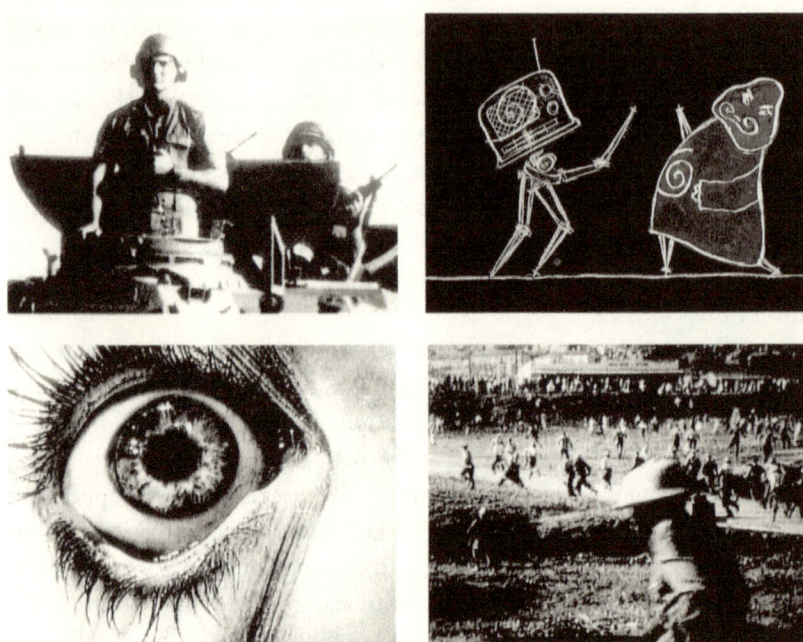

FIGURE 12. William Kentridge, scene from *Ubu and the Truth Commission* (1997). Used with permission.

her words in Afrikaans, speaking as if giving testimony. He describes the practice of "tubing" (a form of torture in which an inner tube is used to suffocate the victim) and of beating detainees to death and then burning their bodies. The human body, he explains, takes around seven hours to burn, leaving ample time for a *braai* (barbecue). Animated images flood the stage during this "testimony," so that they read as an extension of the documentary evidence Ma has uncovered. In the midst of the animation, the specter of actual violence and death irrupts in the form of documentary footage (this includes archival images of police with whips lashing a crowd in Cato Manor in 1960 and storming a group of students at Wits University, and footage of the Soweto uprising of 1976) (figs. 12, 13). As this documentary imagery is run against cartoon violence, otherwise comic characters emerge as sadistic egos motivating violence, which has material consequences.

Kentridge's is not an expressive account of the suffering engendered by political violence. Repetition and manic multiplication convey the nature of violence rather than any registration of the pain it causes. These are schematic, hastily drawn, anonymous figures as Kentridge acknowledges

("It is far easier to draw a crowd of thousands than to show a flicker of doubt passing over one person's face") and, indeed, their effect is cumulative.[22] In this respect, the animation might be understood to embody the spirit of the cultural sadist who acts without regard for the consequences of his actions. In aesthetic terms, it is a "sadistic text" in the technical sense, suggested by Bataille when he notes that because the sadist does not speak the language of the victim, he cannot tell us what it is like to hurt.[23] The sadist's pathology entails a total repudiation of the other; the sadist acts upon others regardless of—indeed, in spite of—their feelings. Constructed from such a perspective, the "sadistic text" is simply a catalogue of torture and barbarism. It is distinguished not by pacing but by speed, repetition,

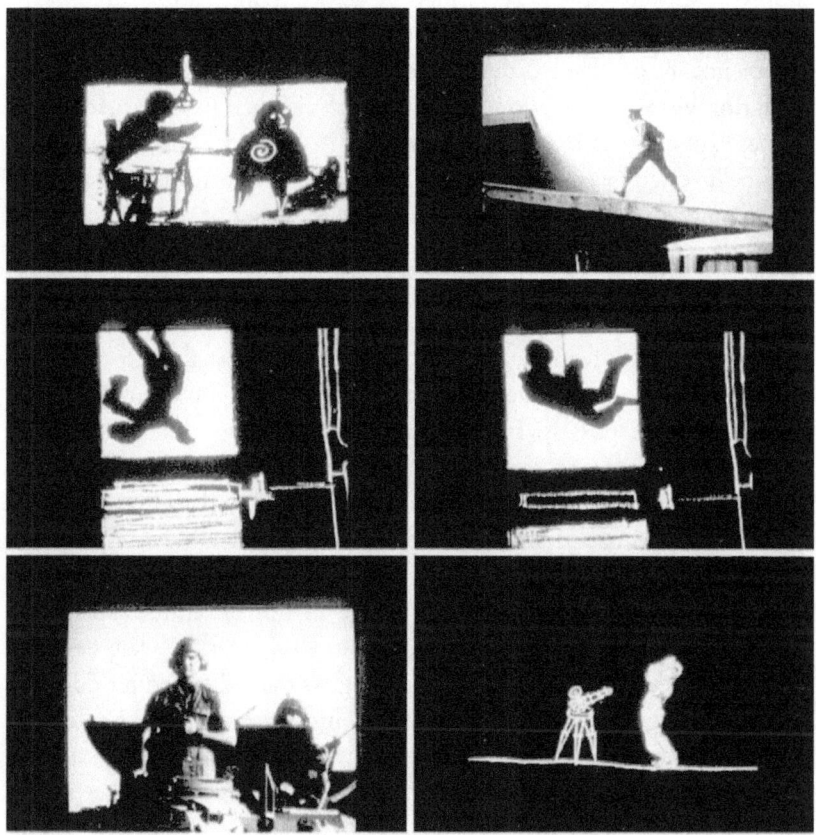

FIGURE 13. William Kentridge, scene from *Ubu and the Truth Commission* (1997). Used with permission.

and multiplication, becoming increasingly frenetic as the actions of the sadist are repeated *ad nauseam*: here the tripod and the cat race around causing devastation, their actions multiplying exponentially until we see a torture sequence going on in every window of an enormous skyscraper. It proceeds very quickly to the bombastic, hyperbolic, and ridiculously extreme—to acts of apparent insanity.

Deleuze has pointed out that such features conspire against the development of "artistry" in the form of the novel.[24] Cinematically, the sadistic text has even less direct appeal, since its descent into the abject is notoriously hard to witness (consider the controversy provoked by Pasolini's film *Salò*, an interpretation of Sade's 120 Days of Sodom). By contrast, the medium of animation can accommodate extremes of barbarism that would simply be unwatchable if performed by actors. While capitalizing on the capacity of the medium to simultaneously elaborate and deaden the effects of violence, Kentridge has developed a particular range of techniques for rendering visible the institutionalization of violence in apartheid South Africa, exploring, as Rosalind Krauss puts it, "how the formal might indeed be invested by the political."[25] Charcoal lines flow from showerheads, light fittings, and microphones, plunging into scenes of torture where the line itself appears to pierce a body, to damage it in some way. Graphic lines are, at once, lines of connection and lines of flight, suggesting the irrepressible flows of violence. Here Kentridge's trademark practice of modifying his charcoal drawing with an eraser provides an analogy for what he calls the "battle between the paper shredders and the photostat machines" —a sense of the post-apartheid struggle between the officials intent on shredding documentary evidence and those copying documents to keep as insurance against future prosecutions.[26] Not only drawings but their grounds disappear as paper is torn up and re-collaged: a blown-up body is rendered simply as so much confetti.

If the sadistic world of Ubu is evoked in animation, the sadistic pathology is enacted on stage. The character of Ubu speaks the language Bataille associates with the sadist when he argues that "the torturer does not use the language of the violence exerted by him in the name of established authority; he uses the language of authority, and that gives him what looks like an excuse, a lofty justification. The violent man is willing to keep quiet and connives at cheating."[27]

Pa's final testimony predictably extols the virtues of soldiering and of loyalty to one's country ("no longer fashionable, except in some smaller countries") and is grounded in denial: "I stand before you with neither shame nor arrogance. I am not a monster. I am an honest citizen, and would never break the law . . . these vile stories, they sicken me. When I am told what happened here, I can't believe it. These things, they were done by those above me; those below me; those beside me. I too have been betrayed! I knew nothing."

For Pa, giving testimony is a performance. As he sets off for the TRC, he tells his dogs, "[W]e're going into show business." His speech is rehearsed, carefully crafted in front of the mirror in an earlier scene, but when delivered at the end of the play, it has been transformed into a poignant, emotive plea. His best line, perfected with a toilet brush for a microphone, is: "There's only one thing I will have to live with until the day I die—it's the corpses . . . of the people I have killed. Remorse. I can assure you, a lot, a hell of a lot" (fig. 14).

Pa has no trouble performing remorse. But remorse, we realize, means nothing as a monologic diatribe crafted in the mirror; it is not a question of expressing sentiment convincingly or with passion. Rather, remorse as an ethical act is activated only in the true face-to-face encounter. The play's dialogue as well as its structure tells us that such an encounter is impossible for the character of Ubu.

If the *Ubu* text is a sadistic one, reflecting the consciousness of the perpetrator, not the victim, then it cannot be modified to include the victim's story (the sadist does not speak the language of the victim; if he properly understood that language, he would not be a sadist according to the Bataillean logic). Thus, the blending of witness testimony with the Ubu play is far from seamless. A tension is maintained between the grotesque self-absorption of Ubu and the affective intensity of the witness statements. Neither text speaks to the other; they are enacted within distinct realms. But we are reminded at every turn that each is an effect of the other; that Ubu exists through the abjection of his victims.

In animation, Kentridge draws literal lines connecting Ubu and a panoply of perpetrators to the consequences of their acts. On stage these invisible lines of connection are established when puppets and actors occupy the same space, as, for example, in the scene at the Ubus' dinner table. Behind the table stands the owner of a *spaza* shop (a small shop located in a house) whose merchandise is plundered by the Ubus for dinner. The puppet must attend to his shop each time the Ubus' actions cause disarray, but neither he nor the Ubus acknowledge the other's presence.

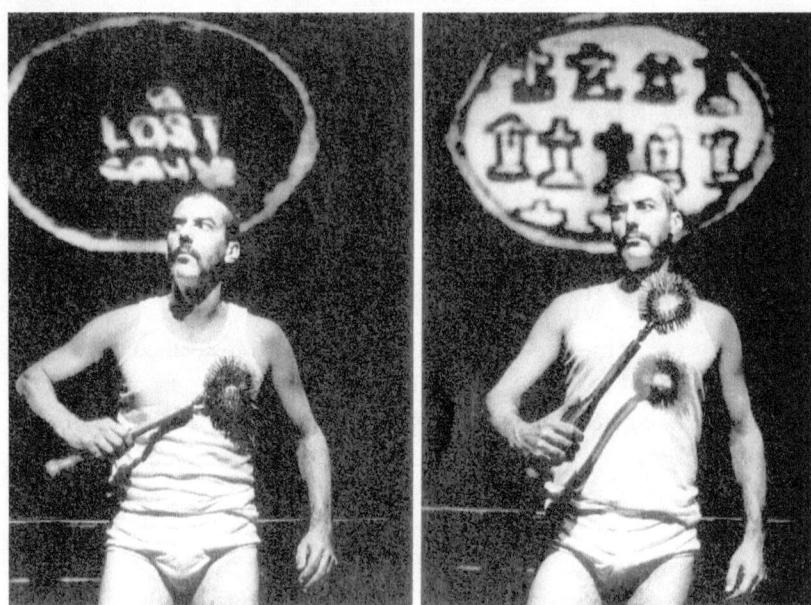

FIGURE 14. William Kentridge, scene from *Ubu and the Truth Commission* (1997). Used with permission.

Although there are various points at which the witness puppets seem to enter the imaginative world of Ubu, as specters haunting him in his sleep and so forth, their giving testimony takes place in a space beyond the mise-en-scène of his living space, and even his dream world. Pa Ubu is oblivious to the content of their testimony; he cannot hear them speak and when he does catch words, they are invariably misheard. Pa Ubu, then, sometimes hears but never really listens. The witnesses' voices enter his consciousness simply as problems that threaten his security and way of life, giving the lie to the language of authority that he persists in speaking.

Distinct languages are spoken here—the various African languages of the witnesses and the Afrikaans and English of the Ubus. They are spoken in a dialogical fashion, not in the sense of constituting a dialogue, but in Bakhtin's sense, employing the notion of dialogue as "double-voicedness." Voices intersect; they do not converse, but the exposure of one language to another has a corrosive effect. Ubu has no relationship with the witnesses (to quote Bataille: "If he bothers with his fellow men at all, he talks the language of the State to them").[28] The language of the sadist cannot withstand the victim's testimony; moreover, as Bataille said of Sade's writing, it "repudiates any relationship between speaker and audience."[29]

The witnesses' testimony quite palpably cuts across the text, which makes no affective connection with its audience. When the first witness emerges, a disembodied voice is heard addressing the witness puppet from the darkness on stage: "Can you hear my voice clearly, can you hear the translator?"—the same voice that orients the witnesses at the TRC hearing in *Long Night's Journey*. When one of the Guguletu mothers testifies in the latter, there is a moment of laughter when she cannot figure out where the commissioner is speaking from; a similar dislocation is apparent here, because the witnesses seem to speak from an isolated place, addressing figures and spaces of which they are hardly aware—an amorphous audience for whom their words will have consequences.

The stories of the witness puppets, based on actual TRC testimony, are disturbing and moving. Their performance, however, is constrained by a Brechtian commitment to revealing the act of acting. Generally, the puppets are supported by two puppeteers, always in evidence on stage. They are the real actors in this case; one delivers the testimony, focusing on voice inflection and imbuing speech with an expressive intensity that invariably writes itself across the face of the speaker; another is concerned with puppet movement and gesture. These two manipulators stand on either side of the witness puppet in a manner that suggests the actions of people who comfort and support witnesses during TRC hearings (fig. 15). But it is their expressions and their gestures that infuse the ensemble with an affective intensity. As the light catches the deeply hewn wood of the puppet faces, we read into them a kind of pathos.[30] But every gesture, every turn of the head or motion of the arm, is acted first by the puppeteer, whose body shadows the puppet, literally choreographing and enacting a rhythmic flow to complement the sound of the voice. The effect is that of an ensemble in which puppets and puppeteers move together in a dance, slow enough for us to observe the detail and significance of every action.[31]

The presence of manipulators in no way impedes the production of affect. Here it is necessary to distinguish between an expressive idiom that privileges the subject as the source of emotion and a language of affect in which affect is seen to be generated between bodies. By engaging in expressive facial gestures, the puppeteers encourage us to read emotions across bodies, imputing those produced by the manipulators to the puppets themselves. But at the same time, the Brechtian "separation of elements," by

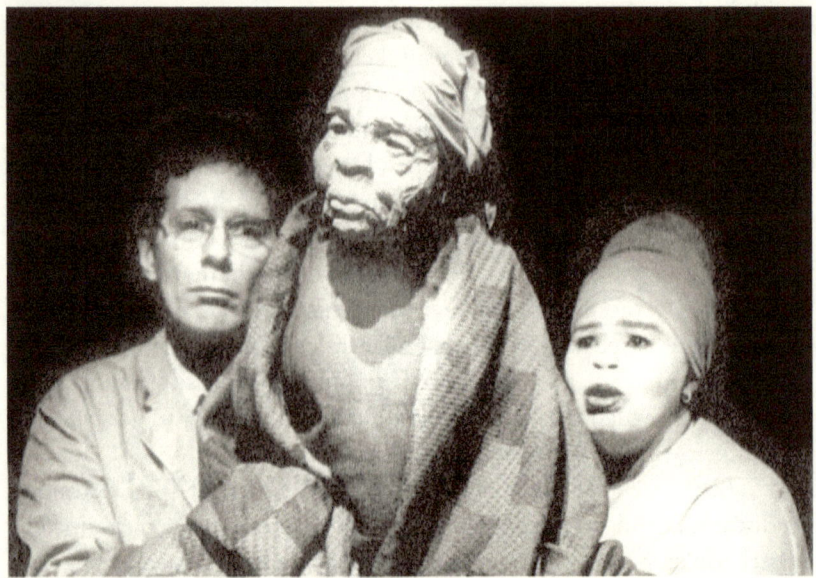

FIGURE 15. William Kentridge, scene from *Ubu and the Truth Commission* (1997). Used with permission.

which voice and gesture are distinguished as the products of separate manipulations, works to break down the illusion of character.[32] We literally see the flow across bodies as different elements and actors conspire to create this singular force. And it is to this physical process of infusion that our bodies respond.

The puppeteers deliver their testimony in African languages. It resonates across the stage like an incantation, the words, embodied momentarily but then disembodied, belonging not exclusively to the puppets, puppeteers, translators, or audience, but circulating between these groups. By the time the testimony is translated, it is drained of its expressive potency; the emotional cadences are lost—remaining, as it were, in the bodies of the other performers. There is a kind of uniformity to the translated phrase. The translators can never own the words they speak. It is difficult—but also strictly unprofessional—for a translator to imbue another's words with expressivity.[33] The translator thus tends to flatten out each sentence, but also, because she is unsure of what is coming next, retains a rising inflection. If this registers anything, it is a certain sense of surprise as the words flow through her body—as she is inhabited by speech.

The manner in which the testimony floats and permeates the space on stage serves to break what Bataille calls the "sly silence" of the torturer, the "dishevelled denial, putting an end to any possibility of speech."[34] The language of the state no longer holds court (as it did, for example, at the time of the original Guguletu inquest, conducted entirely in Afrikaans, never translated for the victims' families). Silence is ruptured by the emergence of African speech, never fully accessible to the nonspeaker, and by the act of translation itself.

Spivak has spoken of translation as essential to an encounter with the other, not simply because it renders the experience of the other transparent—it cannot, in fact, achieve this—but because it forces an awareness of difference. Translation is an act that enlivens a text, but in doing so, it fails to grasp something of the original as it is transformed for a new audience. Here the act of translation figures as one part of a mediating chain in which voices flow from puppeteers to puppets to translators.[35] Each of these figures lays bare the labor of acting; that is to say, rather than laying

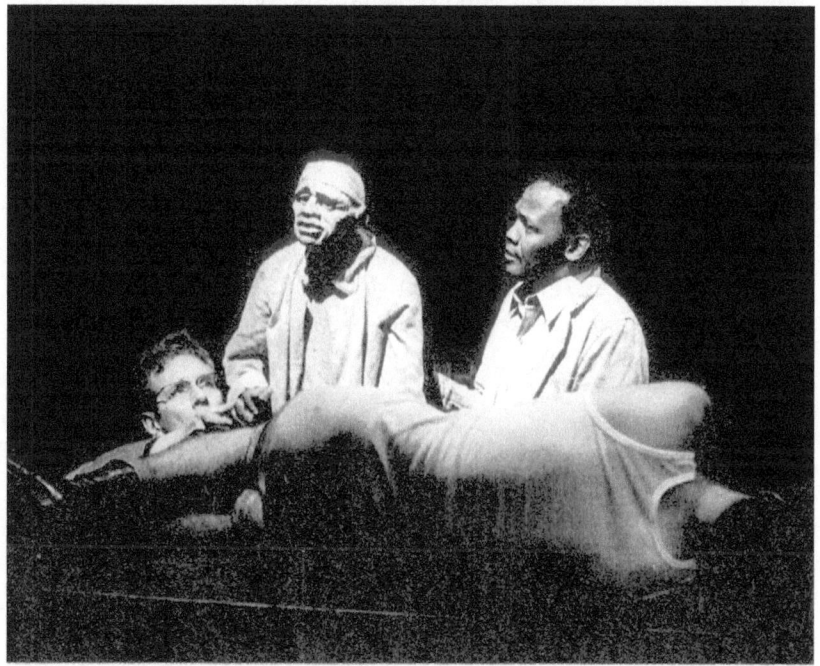

FIGURE 16. William Kentrige, scene from *Ubu and the Truth Commission* (1997). Used with permission.

claim to the words they speak, they evince something of the loss entailed in translation and refuse both the appropriation of testimony and the presumption of identification. But at the same time, translating itself—the receiving of speech—becomes an act of incorporation, of bodily perception and encounter.

Busi Zokufa, playing the animator of a puppet who describes the "necklacing" of her son, voices one of the most disturbing testimonies of the play, commencing with the chilling words, "[S]omeone came and told me they are burning your son." She tells of arriving at the scene of her son's death to find him doused in petrol, of being offered a match to throw at him, and finally witnessing his body burn. Zokufa "acts" this role, imbuing her performance of the words with emotion so that she appears to embody the voice of the puppet. So absorbed is she in this affecting account that she seems to overstep the role of the animator, but the effect of her performance is immediately checked by the deadening impact of a rather flat English translation.

On another occasion, a puppeteer is animating a puppet with testimony concerning the identification of children's bodies. Voicing the shocking words "they didn't have eyes," he suddenly lets the puppet fall. It looks dead. The puppeteer himself is pointing to parts of the puppet's body, saying, "he had this bit . . . that bit . . . no skull . . . they haven't got hands. They haven't got legs."[36] He has taken over the speech, let the puppet die, as it were. Once the symbiotic relationship between puppet and manipulator is broken, the scene becomes a clinical display, reminiscent of an autopsy, with the puppeteer pontificating over the corpse. He is now acting like an expert witness, giving testimony on his findings. In this exchange, in which we are brought up short by the devastating content of the testimony but also spared the pathos of its enactment, it is as if we are party to the company's consideration of the question of how one might "act" or bring to life such testimony. In this instance, testimony is presented to us as unactable: beyond the reach of actors, beyond even the scope of the witness puppets. At the same time, the radical distinction between the corpse (the generic "terrorist" presented in a dispassionate news bulletin) and the mother (whose grief turns this death into a human tragedy) is, quite literally, collapsed.

The catch in this staging of an empathic encounter might be understood to lie at the point at which affects cohere as emotions, configured as the property of individual characters. *Ubu*, however, is not merely con-

cerned to demonstrate the role of chance—of accident, mood, and caprice—in the production of character. Nor, strictly speaking, does it rest
on the production of an alienation effect. We are affected by the performance of the witness testimony—sometimes moved, shocked, horrified—
but at a formal level, we are continually seduced, drawn into an identification with the actor-animators through our embodied perception of their
motion and carefully crafted expression. This identification is focused essentially on the witness-puppet ensemble and its supporting elements (the
voices of translators and so forth). Insofar as it alights from time to time on
a singular body, it fixes on the endeavor to enliven a puppet as this is enacted by the puppeteers. Thus one is subsumed by the performance, affected by it, even as the illusion of character breaks down.

The emotions of the witnesses are themselves part of the production
in this case, broken into discrete elements (a hand gesture, a nod, a speech
inflection) that each appear to require the labor of a manipulator. The elements of this performance, separated and subjected to a redistribution of
affect, allow us to bring to life a puppet-witness as easily as drain her of life,
to feel not just the emotional impact of testimony but the effects of caprice
on character and disposition. Even as we *feel into* the body of the witness,
we cannot indulge in an identification with character, except insofar as we
experience these tiny elements of character performance in isolation.

Ubu, then, draws us into a spectacle in which emotions are abundant
and contagious; simultaneously faked and deeply felt. Operating in the region below the narrative organization of emotion, it engages affect, not as a
stimulus to promote an emotional response, but as a far more diffuse mech-
anism, playing on the bodily perception of aesthetic operations. In doing so,
it adds a critical dimension to a body of testimonial media and art (including *Long Night's Journey*) that has identified the face-to-face encounter as a
key domain in the politics of testimony and reconciliation. In this domain,
art no longer claims to take us into the place of a witness but constitutes
this space of encounter as one in which empathy is, in part, the product of
being touched by another and, in part, an effect of *seeing oneself feeling*,
catching oneself in the act of acting. Insofar as *Ubu* is, itself, a political intervention, it demonstrates how visual art and theater can advance strategies
for the "management of empathy" that Hartman calls for: an empathy that
comes into play when, as Spivak says, we inhabit the space—the difference—between ourselves and others.

Global Interconnections

Some months after September 11, 2001, the Australian artist Gordon
Bennett exhibited a series of paintings under the title *Notes to Basquiat: 911*,
in which a miscellany of motifs drawn from paintings by the late New York
City artist Jean-Michel Basquiat combine to evoke the New York City of
the terrorist attacks (figs. 17–21).[1] Dramatic, Basquiat-inspired cityscapes of
tower blocks and skyscrapers are surmounted by a Shamsa pattern (like
that found on the inside cover of the Koran), superimposed in places with
Arabic text, saying "in the name of Allah, the beneficent, the merciful," its
characters rising like flames above the skyline. Under this portentous sky,
Basquiat's cartoon planes hover, along with U.S. fighters and passenger
planes, potentially signifying the vehicles of suicide attackers (fig. 22).[2]
Like the planes, the word MORTE, inscribed above a cross at the foot of a
tall tower, as it appears in Basquiat's *Portrait of the Artist as a Young Derelict*
(1982), takes on an ominous association, although none of these elements
specifically denote the time and place of the terrorist attacks, with the ex-
ception of a VCR in *Notes to Basquait (CNN)* registering the time as 08:48.
It is in a formal rather than narrative register that an apocalyptic breakdown of structure is suggested. Chipped fragments of the Shamsa design
float around on their ground as various other areas of pattern transmogrify:
boxlike windows on flat walls become jagged fragments, subsiding into a
surface pattern that begins to resemble the monumental fragment of steel
skeleton that survived the meltdown of the World Trade Center, the shad-
owy form of which recurs at various points in the series. Elsewhere the

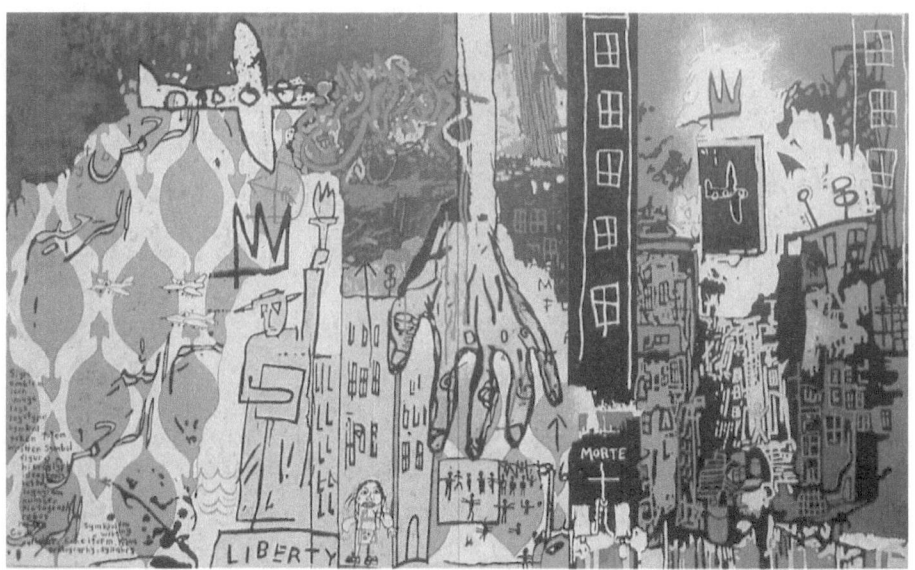

FIGURE 17. Gordon Bennett, *Notes to Basquiat (911)* (2001). Acrylic on linen, 182.5 x 304 cm. Photo by Richard Stringer. Used with permission. Gordon Bennett is represented by Bellas Gallery, Brisbane; Sutton Gallery, Melbourne; Sherman Galleries, Sydney; and Greenaway Art Gallery, Adelaide.

cityscape gives way to a riotous, Pollock-inspired swirl of color that derives, in this instance, from media footage of the explosion and fire at the World Trade Center (fig. 18).

The immense sweep of these works, their subject matter, but also the references to a history of art, suggest that this is a form of history painting: the painting of tragedy rather than trauma. Bennett has, in fact, described himself as a modern-day history painter, concerned with the legacy of Australia's colonial past.[3] But is the tragedy of September 11 really the subject matter of these paintings, or did historic events simply overtake Bennett as he worked through his ongoing relationship with Basquiat? Bennett initiated his public "dialogue" with the New York artist in 1998 with the first *Notes to Basquiat* series, which already incorporates some of the images reworked for the 911 paintings.[4] This is, then, a project begun long before September 2001. Unlike traditional history paintings, these have been transformed by events that occurred during their production, so that they bear the imprint of history as it unfolds.[5]

Part of what is implied in the now rather outmoded term "history

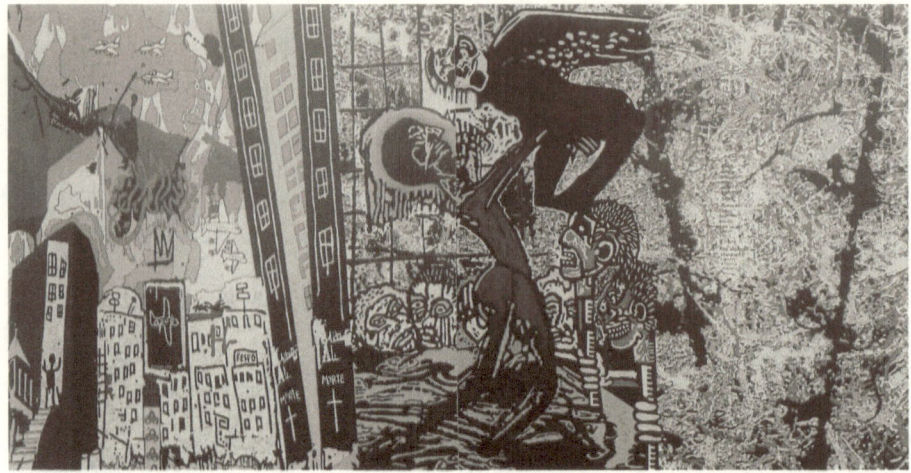

FIGURE 18. Gordon Bennett, *Notes to Basquiat (Jackson Pollock and His Other)* (2001). Acrylic on linen, 152 x 304 cm. Photo by John O'Brien. Used with permission. Gordon Bennett is represented by Bellas Gallery, Brisbane; Sutton Gallery, Melbourne; Sherman Galleries, Sydney; and Greenaway Art Gallery, Adelaide.

painting" is a certain distance, a perspective on the event (the art of common memory as opposed to sense memory). If Bennett has no temporal distance from the event, he might be understood to have a certain cultural and geographic distance from its epicenter by virtue of being an Australian artist. And there is a sense in which, in these works, the boundary that separates inside from outside is perpetually referenced and realized in various forms. In using the term "9/11," or the contraction "911," Bennett is, self-consciously, "speaking American" (Australians abbreviate dates the British way: day first, then month; and 911 does not have the added significance of being the emergency services number in Australia).[6] To talk American is one way of manifesting (ironic) distance from, yet fascination with and connection to, the cultural and economic center of New York. Yet at the same time, the affective intensity of these works does not seem to admit of an outside; these are absorbing rather than exotic spaces, populated by cultural hybrids, like Big Shoes—who is, as Ian McLean suggests, a melange of Basquiat's character of that name and echoes of Mayan, Oenpelli, and Native North American body images (fig. 19).[7]

The phenomenon of 9/11 itself, in its scale and impact, might be regarded as changing the terms of engagement with history to some degree.

The attacks seemed to shatter the notion of distanced perception, coming closer than any event in recent memory to constituting a genuinely global tragedy, from which geographic distance no longer guarantees isolation. If the trauma of 9/11 was geographically centered in the United States, it clearly was not contained within national boundaries. The immediate shock of 9/11 was felt viscerally across the globe—even though it may not have been experienced identically by citizens of New York City, London, and Pakistan; but, by the same token, the nature of one's affective or empathetic response was not necessarily a function of belonging to a nation.

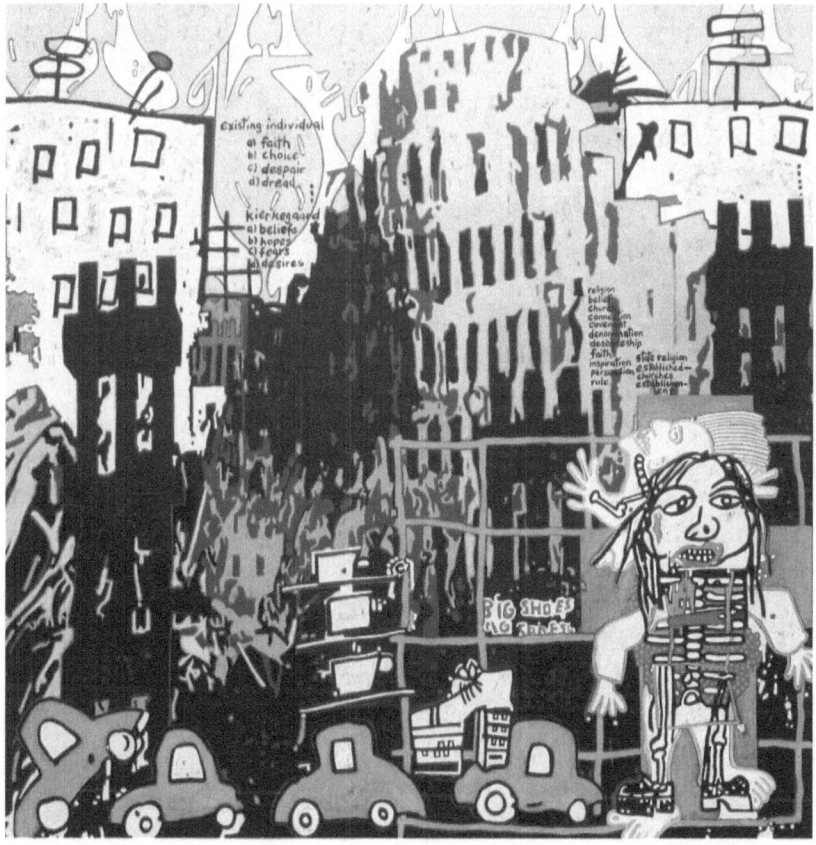

FIGURE 19. Gordon Bennett, *Notes to Basquiat (Big Shoes)* (2001). Acrylic on linen, 122 x 122 cm. Photo by John O'Brien. Used with permission. Gordon Bennett is represented by Bellas Gallery, Brisbane; Sutton Gallery, Melbourne; Sherman Galleries, Sydney; and Greenaway Art Gallery, Adelaide.

There were bereaved families in Asia and Europe, for example, who were more traumatized than many Americans who weren't directly affected by the tragedy; and there are asylum seekers in Australian detention centers who might be regarded as suffering greater hardship than the average U.S. citizen as a direct result of the events of September 11.[8]

These global interconnections are, of course, deemphasized in the wave of nationalism that accompanied and fueled the U.S.-led "war on terror." It thus becomes a key political task to the trace the transnational flows that place many apparent "outsiders" at the center of this global event: to represent the site that signifies the tragedy of 9/11, not as a place commensurate with the borders of a city or state, but as a lived space, characterized by an enfolding that puts "outsides and "outsiders" at the heart of this conception of a damaged or traumatized place.

By the same token, if we may be drawn into Bennett's New York City from different points on the globe, so this imagined *dystopos* may be localized elsewhere; it may well be Australia or Baghdad, as much as it is New York City. It is an alienating space, but not one we can necessarily escape: a place that is in some ways close to home.

In *Notes to Basquiat (Mirror)*, a flamingo pink masklike face confronts, in a mirroring pool, the black head of one of Bennett's muses, the "angel of history" (fig. 20).[9] An eye from each head combines to form a separate face in the keyhole form in the center, confronting us directly in a manner that is distinctly Basquiat, but that also recalls the comment by Dick Hebdige that the latter's work provokes "the feeling that we are being watched by the object, that the crowds of skulls, cartoon characters, masks, and disembodied eyes that stare and peek out from the picture plane are all looking back directly at us, not over us or round us—from a place that is not our place but in which we are nonetheless thoroughly enmeshed and implicated (though we never feel 'at home' there)."[10]

Bennett's notional New York City has much the same feel to it. The viewer may not feel at home there, but there is a familiarity to this dis-ease that may yet remind us of home. If part of Bennett's intent was to register a sense of alienation, he does not internalize—or even embody—this feeling but, like Salcedo, gives it extension within the place world. Affect is not merely encoded into a subject body but dispersed throughout the landscape in a manner that creates the possibility for its communalization. The work thus operates transpersonally to register, at once, a kind of affect (the anxiety of not feeling at home in the place in which one finds oneself) and

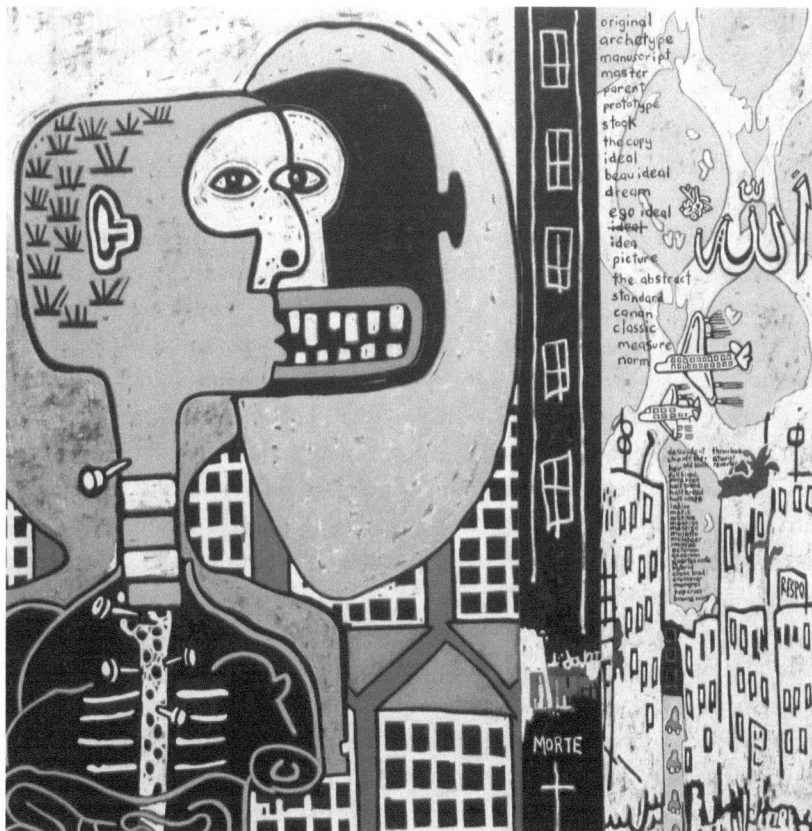

FIGURE 20. Gordon Bennett, *Notes to Basquiat (Mirror)* (2001). Acrylic on linen, 122 x 122 cm. Photo by John O'Brien. Used with permission. Gordon Bennett is represented by Bellas Gallery, Brisbane; Sutton Gallery, Melbourne; Sherman Galleries, Sydney; and Greenaway Art Gallery, Adelaide.

a sociality (it realizes a place where this condition of not being at home can be articulated and, in a certain sense, shared, or at least compared).

The roots of this connection may be found in Bennett's own affective response to Basquiat's works, in which the condition of unhomeliness is neither wholly owned by the artist nor confined to the viewer response, but is potentially transferable or shared: an inclusive rather than exclusive outsiderness. As Hebdige argues, it is not that this is Basquiat's place and we are somehow on the outside: "Basquiat always looked back at himself—as well as us—from the place of the Other."[11] He was, says Hebdige, both a privileged insider and an outsider by virtue of his position as "American mod-

ernism's first (and last?) officially appointed black savior," so that the painting itself is testimony to "the high existential price paid by some of those
who strive to live without certainly between the categories."[12] A number of
critics have noted that it is not only the forms themselves in Basquiat's work,
but the edges and intervals that signify: the spaces in between forms. For
Hebdige, Basquiat is present in these empty intervals as much as in the
panoply of voices emerging through his forms: "Basquiat came (from) everywhere at once . . . but he still stands there at the crossroads . . . stares back at
us from his work as we peer in at him . . . it was . . . never clear who was
most smitten ('beaten,' 'infatuated,' 'polluted') by what or by whom—him
or the masterpiece tradition, him or his admirers, friends, critics, lovers."[13]

Basquiat, who deployed so many visual, verbal, and cultural languages
with an extraordinary fluency, was never merely an appropriation artist in
the postmodern sense. Rather than assimilating imagery to the self, or constructing a self out of an array of available languages, Basquiat's glossolalia—his construction of a language-like idiom out of a mix of semantic
elements taken out of their original linguistic context—does not so much
serve to create a single, livable, hybridized identity as a space of interrela-
tions. Glossolalia, of course, does not "make sense" to those who hear it
spoken. It is put together from sounds familiar to the speaker, but once
these sounds are incorporated into this idiosyncratic tongue, their meaning
is lost. Even though there is a linguistic source for the sounds, there is no
interpretative community for the speech that emerges. Yet forms of glossolaliac speech—such as speaking in tongues—do not depend on translation
to convey affective intensity.

Rukmini Bhaya Nair has invoked the phenomenon of glossolalia to
suggest the postmodern anxiety over meaning and truth, produced by the
rapid transformation and hybridization of language in the global cultural
economy.[14] Can we ever know what a hybrid language—a postmodern
painting, for that matter—really means? This problematic returns us to
Deleuze's injunction to ask not what it *means* but what it *does*. In this case,
the work's capacity to incite affect may in fact be a *function of* its embodiment of this uncertainty over meaning, of its ability to play upon one's tenuous grasp of the significance of any given symbol. We feel that we only
ever "get the picture" contingently, when elements resonate with each other,
fleetingly, before their meaning is further confused by the introduction of
still more random signs. Texts on Basquiat cite his commonly used sources
(Henry Dreyfuss's *Symbol Sourcebook: An Authoritative Guide to Interna-*

tional Graphic Symbols; Burchard Brentjes's *African Rock Art*, etc.), but information of this kind really tells us less about meaning than about working practice; it simply evidences a process of composition.[15]

How is it, then, that we see the artist "looking back at us" from this place he has created? Basquiat is known principally as a neoexpressionist in spite of the fact that he copies and borrows as much as any postmodern appropriation artist. This is largely, of course, a description of a certain gestural style—but also, I think, because of the manner in which he operates at the intersection of sense memory and the representational economy. In dwelling at this point of intersection or emergence, he instantiates a relational space in which he comes into view as the artist, seen by others, witnessed by us—but also as a person who acts out a series of relationships: Basquiat "smitten" with an art world smitten by him; smitten with his idols, such as the African-American baseball player Hank Aaron or Charlie "Bird" Parker, for whom he named or inscribed a number of works.[16]

Is Gordon Bennett similarly "smitten" with Basquiat? In his copious quotation and adoption of the style of Basquiat, he pays a generous homage. But the *dialogic form* of this homage is always in evidence; these are notes *to* Basquiat—a kind of open letter, by which Bennett establishes a certain empathic connection with Basquiat. Bennett is, in effect, entering the interstitial meeting place that Basquiat opens up. In doing so, he does not simply imitate or *act as* Basquiat, nor does he insert himself into a frame or picture of Basquiat's making. Combining with Basquiat is, for Bennett, a way of doing history and politics, and of examining the foundations of identity and experience. If Basquiat invents a certain painterly method, Bennett does not simply "borrow" this in order to elaborate his own concerns. He is interested in how Basquiat's work might be encountered from a *different* place, and in what happens when different accounts of history and experience are registered simultaneously within a given frame. Like Sandra Johnston, he explores the heightening of affect that occurs through combination, deriving a new *form* for his work out of an empathic connection felt for another.

Basquiat too is something of a history painter; think of his *Untitled: History of Black People* or the tracing of connections from Africa via the slave ships to the bluesmen of the Mississippi Delta in *Undiscovered Genius*. These vast transnational, cultural genealogies, entailing the assimilation of multiple languages and sign systems, do not so much anchor identity in history or uncover a prefabricated or timeless African subject; rather, they reveal what Stuart Hall refers to as "the continuous play of history, culture and power" in the present.[17] Through such works Basquiat articulates a creolized subjectivity that is always in some tension with the postmodern identity constructed in the marketplace. Whereas the latter often reduces to a choice of brand-names, Basquiat's shopping around entails a continual negotiation of an inside and an outside, a being between categories (what some commentators identify as a postcolonial identity)—but also an engagement with what Paul Gilroy refers to as the "vital memories of the slave past."[18] History, in his regard, can never be distanced. For the memories of past subjects to be made vital—that is "living"—in the full sense, they must in some way be inherited, opened up to empathic connection through their reembodiment in present imagination. But at the same time, it is impossible for a New York City artist in the 1980s to occupy the "inside" of a sense memory of slavery.

There are resonances here not just with Bennett's approach to the colonial history of Australia, but with his experience of growing up in Queensland. Bennett's Aboriginal mother grew up in a mission after being orphaned at a very young age.[19] The apparatus of an official assimilationist policy, the missions generally functioned—as Bennett puts it—as "a type of 'holding camp' in which Aborigines were placed after being forcibly removed from their land."[20] After securing the permit needed to leave the mission, she found domestic work with a wealthy white family in the town of Monto, where she met and married an Englishman and raised her family as Euro-Australian. The process of assimilation was, Bennett explains, "completed" by his mother and "inherited" by him.[21] Bennett thus grew up with no sense of his Aboriginal heritage, first learning about Aborigines in social studies classes at school. It was not until the age of eleven that he became aware of his own Aboriginal background—something that created "a rift" in his sense of identity. Bennett effectively saw Aboriginal culture and Aborigines from the "outside," from within the European-Australian colonial culture from which, in turn, he became increasingly alienated. While experiencing an exclusion from European-Australian culture, he "could find nothing with which to identify with Aborigines or Aboriginal culture."[22] Rather than enabling him to "find" his Aboriginality, art school education gave Bennett the means to reject essentialist constructions of Aboriginality as something "waiting to be found" (he cites Hall) and the notion of Aboriginal culture as static and homogeneous.

If Bennett found in his painting a *place to be*, through this position-

ing, he was able to shift, somewhat, the ground of colonial relationships—
to attempt to undo the fixity of identity by staging new relationships within
place. His New York City series entails a representational journey out of
place, but the vehicle for this is his relationship to Basquiat. It is in this relationship that Bennett has been able to *be Aboriginal*, in a sense; that is, to
be in a manner that escapes the bounds of fixed colonial definitions and
that derives from his own experience of what it is to be an Aborigine. For
Bennett, there is no fixed set of characteristics that define or determine Aboriginality; rather, it is something that must be known through experience:
"I was told by many Aboriginal people that Aboriginality is in the heart. I
interpreted this as an underlying 'truth' that cannot be verbalized, save to
say that it is an essence of shared experience of pain and loss and the struggle to maintain human dignity in the face of a colonial onslaught."[23]

This radically dessentialized notion of Aboriginality should not be
understood as a reactive or negative definition. It eludes the fixity that Bennett criticizes, promoting instead an acknowledgement of a shared, contingent experience; thus, Aboriginality is not something one finds in the
past, but something that emerges through a negotiation of memories of
pain and loss in the present.

Bennett's overt construction of a transnational identification with Basquiat seems to evoke the possibility of a sharing of experience, or at least
giving voice to a particular, localized experience, through the language of
another who does not share an identity with the artist—through, as Ian
McLean puts it, an "imaginative migration" to a foreign place. This imaginative migration has analogies in popular culture. David McNeill has argued that the Australian Aboriginal boxer Anthony Mundine's brash Amer-
ican-style persona might be understood as constituted in a kind of global
"ebonics" that offers a way to affirm a mode of black identity that sometimes carries with it an aggressive oppositional politics.[24] In a faint echo of
Muhammad Ali's legendary repudiation of U.S. involvement in Vietnam,
and in the midst of a wave of post 9/11 patriotism, the would-be super-
middleweight champ expressed opposition to the U.S. war in Afghanistan
—a move that antagonized the U.S. boxing community and also embar-
rassed patriots at home, exacerbating the distance between Mundine and
Middle Australia, which had never accepted his flirtation with U.S. black
style. As McNeill notes, a prominent sports journalist once remarked that
Mundine's bravado would be okay if he did it "in an Australian accent."
But, it can be argued, American black style clearly links Mundine into a

collective identity—and offers him a speaking position—that registers a disjuncture with mainstream Australian values. Is something similar going on—albeit in a more reflective vein—in Bennett's work? Does Bennett's painting any longer have a marked Australian accent, or is its idiom now a globalized art world ebonics?

In rejecting an essentialized notion of Aboriginality, Bennett explicitly intended to eschew the kind of Aboriginal identity that would simply provide "a foil for anyone to affirm that colonial identity I myself had rejected."[25] In other words, he refuses to live out a preconstructed Aboriginal identity, preferring instead to explore the ways in which otherness has been configured by fixing subjects in a topography of time and place. To that end, we might question what it means for Bennett to speak or paint with a non- (or even *un*-) Australian accent—although this question must ultimately turn back on our cultural assumptions about the nature of accent as a marker of identity and belonging to place.

Arjun Appadurai has asked how it is that in anthropology we have not simply located subjects within particular places but have effectively "incarcerated" people in places.[26] Anthropology, he argues, ascribes a condition of physical immobility to the subjects it studies. These subjects are regarded as fixed in place, whereas observers (explorers, missionaries, and eventually anthropologists) are regarded as quintessentially mobile. In Chapter 4, we considered this issue of fixing in place and its relationship to a politics of moving through place as a means of redefining intercultural encounters. Gavin Younge's *Forces Favourites* attempts to undermine the structural relationship between the traveling observer, and the less mobile, less privileged, Angolan local through a focus on movement itself. In this light, Bennett's transnational negotiation of a local politics of indigeneity is an important strategy of reorientation. And it is an unexpected one, inasmuch as one of the central struggles in Australian indigenous politics is the ongoing fight for land rights and acknowledgment of Aboriginal ownership.[27] Notwithstanding the continuing need to establish the fundamental connection to place that underpins the land-rights claim, Bennett seeks to affirm that not all aspects of Aboriginal people derive from an identity fixed in place. This move is perhaps all the more radical given that the transnationalism of Gilroy's *The Black Atlantic* doesn't have the same purchase in the Australian context as it does in relation to the African diaspora, where slave routes literally ensured the dispersal across national boundaries of African culture.[28] Bennett's work has always been concerned with forms of internationalism, and with the intersection of colonial and indigenous history. But the kinds of connections drawn here don't seem to follow genealogical lines of descent; his empathic identifications, insofar as they are cultural, are constituted in encounters in the present.

Appadurai's anti-essentialist rejection of defining characteristics amounts to an extreme version of the argument that the relationship between an idea or identity and a place is always contingent. He holds that "ideas that claim to represent the 'essences' of particular places reflect the temporary *localization* of ideas from *many* places"—hence, nothing is strictly "native."[29] The danger of slipping into a form of essentialism is that it gives rise to a tendency to exoticize, to make differences between self and other the sole criteria for comparison. Moreover, it legitimizes a process of fixing in place, so that one might then be judged according to whether one stays in one's place (acts in a predictable way, talks with an appropriate accent and so on).

By moving away from the ground one is expected to occupy as an Aboriginal Australian, Bennett strategically avoids affirming Aboriginal identity; he refuses to become "a foil." But this movement that counters the stasis of colonial relationships is not merely a fleeing *from* (this would, of course, simply reinscribe the power relations of colonialism). Bennett does not leave intact the notion of a static homeland from which one departs. The act of speaking with an African-American accent—in this case, with Basquiat's "voice"—is a *talking back* into Australia; the speaking from New York City is, in part, a strategic undermining of the ground of Australian identity, a demonstration of its temporary localization, of the disjuncture between place and identity. It counters fixity with an investigation of polythetic resemblance: that is, "family resemblances between places involving overlaps between not one but many characteristics of their ideologies."[30]

Rather than envisioning places as encapsulated by single "diacritics" (essences or marks of distinction), and then comparing them to other distinct places, Appadurai suggests that a polythetic approach allows us to recognize multifarious configurations of resemblance and contrast, to identify "multiple chains of family resemblance between places [that] would blur any single set of cultural boundaries between them."[31]

Decoupling the idea that to be Aboriginal means to be Australian in any one particular sense, Bennett shows us the dimension in which to be Aboriginal can for him be enacted in his relationship with Basquiat, who, in turn, enacts a particular kind of relationship to New York City. In this sense, New York is not appropriated as metaphor for a quintessentially Australian condition; rather, in the localization of a particular idea or thematic, Bennett finds a "home" in the milieu of Basquiat.

What does it mean to find a home in this sense—and how does this differ from constructing an identity from aspects of another place "brought home," as it were? Home, for Bennett, is a crucial mediating term in the conjunction of Aboriginality and Australia—a term that cannot be treated as a given but must be understood in relation to an experiential reality. In the Australian vernacular, "home" is a peculiarly concrete term; real estate agents use the word to refer to the actual edifice of a house (a freestanding family-sized dwelling is a home; an apartment is not) as well as to signify the value-added concept of a house made over by its inhabitation. Bennett has, indeed, offered critical comment on the "home in the suburbs" ethos, shifting the notion of home toward an experiential definition that not only moves beyond the materialist concept of home as house but, more important, away from cultural or nationalistic inscriptions.

In a 1993–94 series of watercolors accompanied by handwritten "open-letters," titled *Home Sweet Home*, Bennett expressed the tension he experienced trying to set up home in the suburbs:

Please excuse me, I don't mean to offend. I was just reflecting on the "great Australian dream." Leanne and I own our own house in the outer northern suburbs of Brisbane. We saved like crazy to pay it off. . . . We put a lot of time and effort into it—but for what? So I could go to the backyard Barbie with the neighbours, have a sense of community, have children, get drunk, watch tv. I think it was the barbeques that got to me in the end. The party talk both at home and at work and around the neighbourhood. The subject of Aborigines always came up. It was then that I felt an outsider. I could not fit in. The bloody boongs, the fucking coons, abo's, niggers—put them in a house and the first thing they do is burn it down. Try and imagine what it is like, sitting quietly. Listening to this shit while your stomach turns in knots—try to fit in, keep the peace, after all you live right next door, right? Who needs to be a target for all that bullshit—life's tough enough as it is. So, there I sit, in a quiet rage, hoping no-one will notice my tan, my nose, my lips, my profile, because if I start trouble by disagreeing, then that would be typical of a damn coon wouldn't it?
  G. Bennett 10.45am

McLean argues that Bennett is one of the few Australian artists to "frame the condition of centerlessness in terms that are specific to the Australian experience of colonialism"; in effect, to detail a politics of the feeling of "homelessness."[32] As McLean suggests, there is neither a "nostalgia for home" nor an idealization of the "freedom of a post-modern in-be-tweenness" in Bennett's work. If the project of "finding identity" is a prob-lematic one for Bennett, so too is the uncritical yearning for home; because home—as Sara Ahmed has pointed out—is now less certain even than identity.[33] Is home the place where I was born, the place my ancestors came from, the place where I live now? As Bennett shows, home for him was none of these; and even the apparently axiomatic linkage of indigeneity and locale did not for him produce a sense of belonging to a particular place. We might, then, understand Bennett as echoing Ahmed's notion that home must ultimately derive from sense of "feeling at home"—a re-sult of the interactions of the body in place. Thus, "home" is not a utopian site but a condition dependent on a set of relationships in which one lo-cates a self; in other words, a relational space.

If *Home Sweet Home* draws attention to the disjunctive relationship between home and Australia, in the 911 series, Bennett raises the possibil-ity of finding "home" elsewhere through an imagined community that is not coextensive with nation. Nations, Benedict Anderson has noted, are nothing other than imagined communities, uniting within a defined set of borders people who neither know one another nor share common experi-ences, and they have, as Paul Gilroy argues in *The Black Atlantic*, tended to promote the "unthinking assumption that cultures will always flow into patterns congruent with the[ir] borders."[34] For Bennett, the place marked as the New York City of September 2001 is neither utopic nor apocalyptic in the traditional sense; as McLean points out, it is not the end point of a journey, a coming home, or a judgment upon.[35] Rather, a certain sense of being at home is made possible through the polythetic investigation of re-lationships that unite places—or, more specifically, that unite people by virtue of their lived experience of place. One can feel at home in this process inasmuch as it counters a certain alienation and promotes an em-pathic encounter in which one can see oneself (at home) in another place.

In one painting from the 911 series, *Notes to Basquiat (Death of Irony)*, Bennett does conjoin Australia and New York City on September 11, trans-planting a Captain Cook figure familiar from an earlier work, *Prologue: They Sailed Slowly Nearer* (1988) (fig. 21). *Prologue* was a response to the bi-centennial celebrations of the arrival of the First [European] Fleet in 1788 —and the commencement of what European Australian history benignly terms "settlement," but what indigenous groups increasingly call "inva-

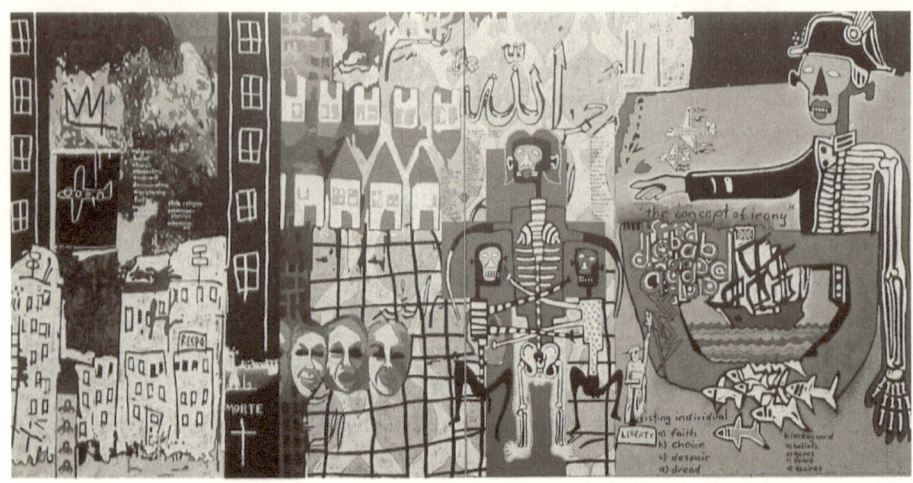

FIGURE 21. Gordon Bennett, *Notes to Basquiat (Death of Irony)* (2001). Acrylic on linen. Photo by John O'Brien. Used with permission. Gordon Bennett is represented by Bellas Gallery, Brisbane; Sutton Gallery, Melbourne; Sherman Galleries, Sydney; and Greenaway Art Gallery, Adelaide.

sion." In the earlier work, Cook points toward the Sydney shoreline (a speech bubble contains the words "It's a bay—and a good one"); now with ghoulish pink, masklike face and a partially skeletalized body, he points from the ocean toward the New York skyline, two passenger planes hovering above his arm. Between ship and shore is a cluster of houses with red pitched roofs, like those that appear in *Home Sweet Home*, where they signify suburban Brisbane. Of course, at one level, "irony" is everywhere in these dramatic evocations of the relationship between "civilization" and death. Cook's ship now seems destined for the tower inscribed as death / *morte*, his course identical to that of the two passenger planes. In *Notes to Basquiat (Jackson Pollock and His Other)* and *Notes to Basquiat (the Coming of the Light)*, the towers once again create a division, reminiscent of those medieval conventions for suggesting the relationship between one world and another. Beyond the edge of New York City, in both cases, lies a kind of hellish underworld.[36] But rather than being hierarchized, like a Last Judgment, in which one descends into the reaches of hell, these paintings suggest an endless global panorama in which images recur and flow into other vistas. "Civilization," hell, suburbia, art, faith, enlightenment, home are all moot in this densely tangled mass.

The kinds of connections Bennett draws with Basquiat's New York

City life are not necessarily historical connections—or even cultural connections in any firm genealogical sense of the term. They are, however, social and political connections, forged in the moment of transcultural encounter, since polythetic resemblances may have no grounding (cultural, ethnic, racial) except in the experiential, which must be traced and voiced to be realized.

What then are the methods for tracing, representing, realizing transnational cultures of this nature? Ulf Hannerz has argued that the flow of cultural forms through the world is echoed in "differentially cultivated competences for symbolic codes." He asks: "Could there be affinities which allow us, for example, to appreciate what Nigerians or Indonesians do as they sing or dance even as what they say when they speak sounds to us as only gibberish? Perhaps we have to draw different boundaries of intelligibility for each symbolic mode; if that is the case the notion of the boundaries of 'a culture' as a self-evident package deal, with definite spatial location, become suspect."[37]

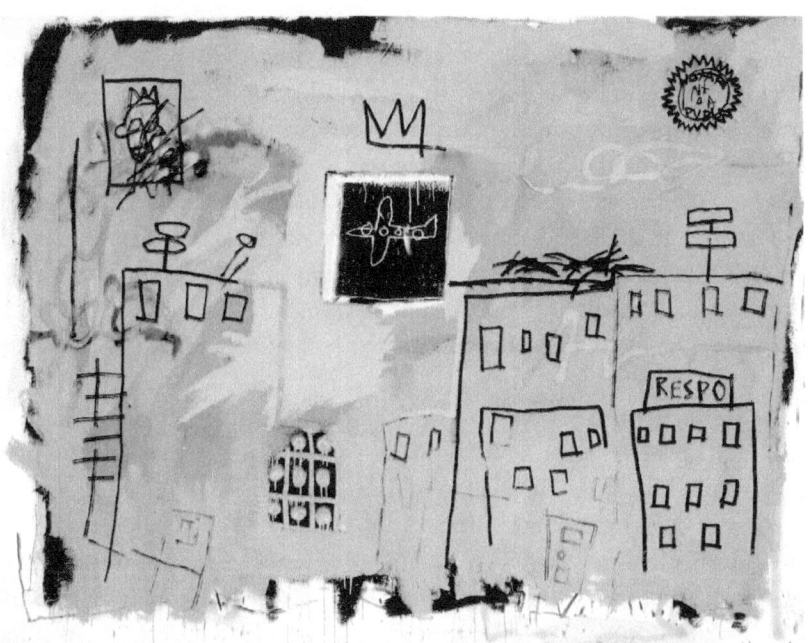

FIGURE 22. Jean-Michel Basquiat, *Untitled* (1981). Acrylic, oil paintstick, and spray paint on canvas, 218.4 x 264.2 cm. © Jean-Michel Basquiat. Licensed to VISCOPY, Australia, 2003.

A whole range of interpretative skills that allow us to "appreciate" cultural forms originating elsewhere become second nature in the sense that they flow from our participation in a global market, or from the "McDonaldization" of culture. When the Japanese artist Masato Nakamura exhibited neon golden arches in the form of the MacDonald's M in the Third Asia-Pacific Triennial in Brisbane (1999), universal brand-name marketing made for easy translation. But Bennett does not merely engage the naturalized everyday "reading" skills that equip us to deal with cultural forms that are always already globalized; nor does he simply follow the flows of global cultural exchange. Rather, he traces a set of new connections—polythetic relationships that themselves constitute transnational links that are variously manifested—sometimes unseen, invisible, partially realized, tenuous.

Moreover, his intervention is, as we have seen, underpinned by a critique of identity that in some ways moves further than the pop and postmodernist focus on the fabricated self. The radical de-essentializing of the subject that occurs in the work of quintessential postmodernists such as Cindy Sherman, Yasumasa Morimura, and Sylvie Fleury might be regarded ultimately as reinscribing a narcissistic project of self-creation at its center: *I shop, therefore I am.* Bennett not only delves deeper into genealogy or history but resists material reconstitutions of identity. What Bennett's work does in rejecting essentialized identity ("I am Aboriginal") is engage in a relational project that entails a journey out of place. Not "America is me," but I am (contingently at this point) in America; I am *in conversation* with Basquiat. But the real distinction is that Bennett—although he in some sense "finds himself" in the exercise of painting and citation of Basquiat—does not make himself the subject of his work. He is, rather, concerned with generic possibilities of becoming; with creating a place to be and, by extension, a place of empathy.

But how do we discern the boundaries of intelligibility in relation to the link between Bennett and Basquiat—or the connections between Australian postcolonial political sensibilities and those deriving from a U.S. politics of race, for example? If these works are, to some degree, constitutive—rather than reflective—of polythetic resemblances, then it is through the work that empathic connection is engendered. If Bennett is in some ways a skilled interpreter of Basquiat—as he is of Pollock, and as Basquiat is of many of his sources—is there a sense in which he can effect a cultural translation? Can he interpret for others languages that inspire affective responses but that to the broader audience are largely gibberish?

I am not suggesting here that the bulk of Basquiat's overseas audience cannot understand his idiom (although, as I have already indicated, it is not clear that it can have any stable "meaning" as such); rather, I am suggesting that Bennett may in fact be able to generalize a particular affective or empathic reading of Basquiat for his audience. But Hannerz's question concerning the possibility of a transcultural, extralinguistic "understanding" of foreign symbolic forms is also provocative because it returns us again to the essence of empathy. There may be certain preverbal affective skills that enable us to be touched by certain images—although it would be absurdly idealistic to suggest that universal sympathies cut across cultural boundaries unassisted. Just as Hannerz suggests that extralinguistic "understandings" follow particular cultural flows that in some sense constitute an extension of an interpretative community via the spread of interpretative skills, so affective capabilities require some structural underpinning. As Johnston's work demonstrates, we don't automatically deploy these skills each time we are faced with a moving or traumatic image.

Perhaps, then, Bennett's interpretative skills have to do with recognizing the process involved in Basquiat's work; he sees what a Basquiat painting *does* rather than what it means. And he may see this because, (a) like Basquiat, he is a skilled painter and polyglot—or even glossolaliac, and (b) he possesses what Janneke Lam terms "affective skills."[38] As we noted in Chapter 3, a loss of affective skill is manifested in trauma through the process of "psychic numbing." Drawing on Winnicottian psychoanalysis, Lam argues that the incapacitation resulting from this loss must be not only given a sign but enabled to signify through the creation of a relational or potential space. This argument follows the structure of Laub's call for a witnessing of testimony, but cast in spatializing terms, it is useful for identifying the nature of an artistic relationship within a particular representational frame. Furthermore, I take Lam's emphasis on the acquired skill to highlight not only the affective skill required for empathic understanding but also the tenuous nature of our grasp over such skills. For Bennett, Basquiat himself is a sign embodying the affect (anxiety) of living as a stranger on the inside: of being a black artist in a white art world, of being the "invisible" Aborigine in white suburbia. Basquiat's painting (particularly as it embodies this condition of being at a crossroads, of inhabiting not only forms but also the spaces in between) provides, in effect, the possibility of an interaction with semiotic objects that allow one to play, to "turn feelings into narratives of emotionally defined experience."[39] But, as in the case of Johnston, it is the artist's capacity to transform images through an elaboration of psychic material that is significant: specifically, to open up a space for empathic encounter for others to inhabit.

Bennett is, in this regard, a skilled, sensitive or empathetic reader. His skills, however, emerge not from a special endowment but out of the experience of living through loss—loss of affect, loss of affective skills. As he explains, his Aboriginal heritage was, in effect, lost to him before he was born. His family's assimilation—that is, the erasure of their Aboriginality—was completed in his mother, to be inherited by Bennett himself. Thus the loss was not even mourned by Bennett. Its inheritance is, however, lived in the condition described in *Home Sweet Home*—of being the invisible Aborigine looking in on a scene in which one plays a role in an inhospitable suburban narrative. The excruciating moments described in the texts of *Home Sweet Home* are moments in which the experiences of inhabiting an inside and an outside combine to register the vital memories of past losses, and the loss of affective connection itself.

By *feeling into* Basquiat, Bennett uses shared affect as the basis for elaborating an emotional experience of place. This place is both New York City and the suburbs of Brisbane, united through the temporary "localization" of an idea. But in his empathic reading of Basquiat, Bennett is also engendering the kind of sociality that Appadurai sees as the quintessential globalized cultural formation. If we take seriously the notion that we may, in some respects, have more in common with people on the other side of the world than with our neighbors, then—since we might never encounter those people in daily life—there is a role for art and other cultural forms in tracing connections in a way that can engender contact and actualize and expand the interpretative community, or "community of sentiment." The flows that are traced, then, might in fact be invisible, allowing "a hidden dynamic in space to appear."[40]

This hidden dynamic might be understood primarily in terms of the empathic connection (potentially) linking people by virtue of an experience of loss or trauma. But it might also—as Appadurai suggests—approximate Diana Crane's notion of "invisible colleges" (of scientists working in discrete pockets around the world).[41] In our case, then, the invisible college would unite artists working on resonating themes. Such a concept has been enacted in the context of an international art exhibition through the curator Okwui Enwezor's *Documenta 11* (Kassel, Germany, 2002).

Documenta 11 perhaps went further than any previous art exhibition in not only tracing global interconnections but promoting a form of glob-alized cultural politics in which transnational social alliances could be so-lidified through the bringing together of work in the exhibition—and, specifically, through the manner of its installation, which emphasized the juxtaposition of works responding to the experience of conflict, racism, and oppression in different regions. So, for example, relationships were es-tablished through the proximal installation of the Palestinian-born Mona Hatoum's *Homebound*—in which furniture and kitchen utensils located behind a wire fence are connected to a circuit by electrified wires—and images of Auschwitz and Robben Island by the South African photogra-pher Santu Mofokeng. When it works well, this kind of installation facili-tates the carryover of an affective response from one piece to another; Ha-toum's incarcerative space engenders a certain bodily response that leads one into Mofokeng's initially austere Robben Island images (which may be less affective to the non–South African eye), so that one is effectively as-sisted in a process of embodied perception.

But such a curatorial strategy risks the accusation of didacticism when its affective operations are deadened—that is, when an audience is unable to make an empathic connection. This was the case with *Documenta 11*. If the commentator/viewer did not experience an affective resonance between works, and thus took their juxtaposition simply to "mean"—literally to sig-nify historical instances of oppression that don't affect us—it was perceived as a lesson: "joyless" and "good for you."[42]

In Bennett's case, however, the work already embodies the affective response; that is to say, a kind of corporeal generosity that makes empathy possible. A process of interconnection is internal to the work—and this process can be tracked through a series of expropriative encounters. Bas-quiat's imagery is enveloped into Bennett's work. But there are also signs that Bennett's own history is folded into this body of work. Significantly, some of Bennett's more affective work (that is, work that falls more obvi-ously into the domain of *sense memory*) finds its way into the earlier *Notes to Basquait* of 1999. In two paintings, in particular—*Notes to Basquiat: Ideal* and *Notes to Basquiat: Hand of God*—Bennett's own *Welt* paintings are referenced (fig. 23). The *Welt* series began as an overpainting of a Pol-lock drip-style painting on a black ground. This created a surface that, for Bennett, evokes the scarified back of an African slave. In these works, he also made reference to Kazimir Malevich's black square and cross forma-tions, and to Lucio Fontana's cut canvases, so that abstract forms are made

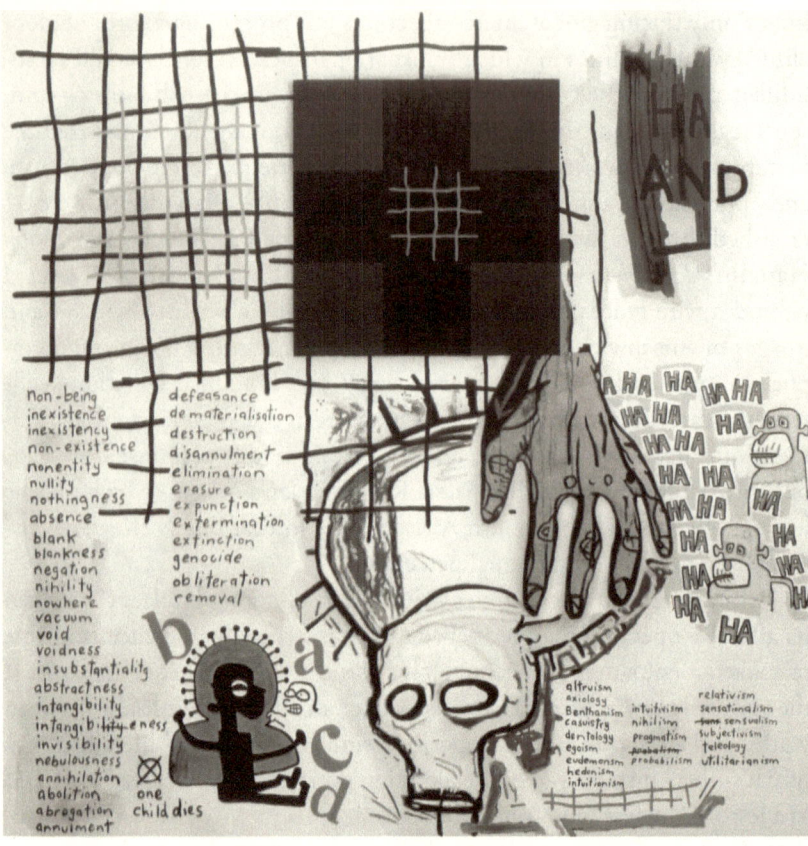

FIGURE 23. Gordon Bennett, *Notes to Basquiat: Hand of God* (1999). Acrylic on linen, 182.5 x 182.5 cm. Used with permission. Gordon Bennett is represented by Bellas Gallery, Brisbane; Sutton Gallery, Melbourne; Sherman Galleries, Sydney; and Greenaway Art Gallery, Adelaide.

to bear stigmata: blood red cuts in their skinlike surfaces. In these two images, however, the dark cruciform image is inscribed with a blood red grid: no longer the regular geometric grid that Bennett incorporated into earlier works, but the shakily hand-drawn grid that appears in certain of Basquiat's paintings. In the 911 works, the welts are no longer there, but the same grid reemerges, framing a form that we might interpret as part of the World Trade Center wreckage.

The recycling of motifs—especially of those scarification images—allows memory of a wounding process to flow across distinct bodies, into different spaces of representation, where they often recede from view. Bennett's welts have disappeared at Ground Zero—but a kind of invisible history links him to this site. Rather than an assimilation of Basquiat, or a constitution of self through appropriation, the process here is one of dispossession of self. Roslyn Diprose defines this as the essence of corporeal generosity:

Generosity . . . is not reducible to an economy of exchange between sovereign individuals. Rather it is an openness to others that not only precedes and establishes communal relations but constitutes the self as open to otherness. Primordially, generosity is not the expenditure of one's possessions but the dispossession of oneself, the being-given to others that undercuts any self-contained ego, that undercuts self-possession. . . . Generosity is being given to others without deliberation in a field of intercorporeality, a being given that constitutes the self as affective and being affected, that constitutes social relations and that which is given in relation.[43]

Whereas the dynamic of appropriation suggests a unidirectional pull toward a core self, Diprose's model of generosity describes not simply the reverse of this—an exchange between two poles—but a porosity of boundaries that allows for a freer flow across bodies and borders: borders that constitute the boundaries of self, but also the imagined boundaries of cultures and nations. I want to suggest that this is the essence both of Bennett's working process and his politics.

The term "appropriation" never accurately describes the thrust of Bennett's working process, inasmuch as it posits a core self as owner (*proprius*)—a self is that is fundamentally singular even when composed of multifarious sources. But how do we move from this toward a notion of self as inter-, or even trans-, subjective? One can complicate the picture by talking about postcolonial identity and the interstitial space at the "'crossroads'" of culture. But this might yet understate the productive aspects of a description of an in-between condition. Bennett's painting, I suggest, moves beyond the diagnostic, and also the expressive (in the conventional art historical sense), to engender something of the "new language of community" that critics such as Rukmini Bhaya Nair and Gayatri Spivak have promoted as succeeding postcolonialism.[44]

If Bennett's painting encodes a corporeal generosity in its expansive style, this promotes an empathic connectivity between people and places. Yet empathy, as we have seen, entails more than an affective or prereflective connection; it implies an acknowledgment of difference. For Bennett, difference is encountered as a form of loss—through the inaccessibility of identities constructed around characteristics of race. His failure to fully inhabit categories of identity gives rise to an awareness of difference, but, at the same time, it is an effect of what Marianne Hirsch calls a "postmemory" of trauma: the inheritance of traumatic family and community history that marks one intergenerationally, not through primary experience of trauma, but through the burden that falls on survivors, or survivor's children, who are not the ones who suffered the primary loss.[45] Transgenerational trauma necessitates empathy in the sense that one cannot relive the losses of previous generations or share their memories, but one is compelled to negotiate a shared memory in which the sense memory of others touches the communal memory of those outside. Of course, the experience of this gap and the secondary experience of losses can in itself be traumatic, but there is a sense in which—through inheritance—one is perpetually aware of a separation. One can never fully inhabit the sense memory of others.

The theoretical impulse of Bennett's work could thus be seen to lie in the transformation of affective memory into empathic encounter as a modality of doing history. Just as Gilroy calls for "a redemptive critique of the present in the light of the vital memories of the slave past," Bennett responds to the vital memories of the colonial past, not just in his more overtly genealogical works that deal explicitly with colonial history, but in redemptive critiques of the present, as in the 911 works. His history paintings are, in this regard, memoryscapes that register sense memory in the moment, relocalizing it in a contemporary configuration of a landscape like that of New York City.

What makes Bennett's work "redemptive," in Gilroy's sense, rather than simply commemorative, is that it opens up a new set of empathic relationships, creating what Appadurai calls new "landscapes of group identity" or "ethnoscapes" that enable genealogy and history to confront each other: new "imagined communities" for people who are, to use Gilroy's words, "external to and estranged from the 'imagined community' of the dominant culture."[46] Bennett reveals to us a set of connections between home and elsewhere; that is, between himself and Basquiat, but also—as the notion of tragedy and trauma gets localized and "owned" by New York City—between the city and its others.

In relation to 9/11, the issue of interconnectivity is a fraught one. In the United States, in the immediate aftermath of the attacks, there was a huge investment in denying potential connections between events lest this mitigate the culpability of terrorists.[47] On another level, the very real sense in which the trauma of refugees flows from the attacks and related political maneuvers is often underplayed. When we speak of the trauma of 9/11, for example, we think instantly—and unsurprisingly—of those who suffered at the World Trade Center, or of those who lost loved ones there, but we don't think automatically of the Afghan refugees in Australian detention centers. We may think of isolated examples of racial abuse flowing directly from the attacks (Muslim children abused on a bus in Brisbane, a Sikh attacked in the New York City subway) but we don't necessarily think in terms of the networks of social relations by which subjects and bodies are inscribed with racial and colonial identities that become fixed in places overtime. Thus, the 911 series may be understood as enacting a politics that renders connections visible.

In these images, the trauma and terror of 9/11 does not seem to proceed from the attacks of that day. It is always already in place. Literally, these images come from elsewhere: a silhouetted figure in the darkened doorway of a building comes from Basquiat's *Prayer* (1984) (where, appropriately enough, it appears in relation to a piece of Australiana: the Kangaroo woman that makes the rain); the Statue of Liberty is a quotation from *Undiscovered Genius*, Basquiat's own evocation of the slave past. So this New York City is remade out of images in which genealogies are already embedded. Nothing here really *means* New York City; this place is simply the description and the locus of the Bennett/Basquiat relationship, one that owes its inspiration to Bennett's description of what it is to be Aboriginal.

Bennett and Basquiat (as mediated by Bennett) are, in essence, two narratives that intertwine to become bound to place, to forge a landscape that is at once an ethnoscape, bearing the marks of its own generation and genealogy, and a memoryscape in which bodies bear the marks of history. It is a terrain upon which Bennett's own pain can "find a home" in Das's sense. But this does not mean that Basquiat's experience—or 9/11, for that matter—is simply a metaphor for Bennett's own experience. One trauma is not privileged over another in this arena. The notion of metaphor—understood as a figurative representation of an underlying event or experience—is problematic in this sense. It has, in fact, proved contentious in the context of trauma imagery precisely because it implies the appropriation of another's, quite distinct experience.[48]

Bennett envisages a 9/11 that is not only frightening for the death and destruction wrought on that day but is simply the conditions in which so many other lives have been lost or destroyed. The terror of 911 is neither the threat of al Qaeda terrorism nor that of Bush reprisals; these are indistinguishable on this ground. It is, however, all that flows from this kind of force: the terror and trauma of victims of terrorism everywhere, of refugees, of Islamic children abused in the United States or Australia. The experience of dispossession—like the evocation of power and authority—is not located in a single figure or source. It is, rather, enacted as multifarious strands coming into a confluence in this work.

If Bennett's earlier work dealt with dominant cartographies, colonial mappings of space, the 911 series is concerned not with a recognizable or existing cartography of New York City but with the space of intervals that Basquiat describes. In this sense, it is to form rather than content that we must attend. In the passages between figures, in the relation of pattern to ground, or in the confluence of Arabic script and sky, politics and form converge in what Deleuze might describe as flow of intensity.

Grounds give way, sky caves in, large structures implode. Yet this is not narrative painting that tells a story of a day that terrorist planes hit the twin towers. The planes are there, but these are the same planes that Basquiat painted. And this is not the momentary triumph of Islamic militancy over U.S. trade; the large patterning that evokes Islamic culture fragments in concert with the buildings. Amid this molar chaos, figures like Big Shoes remain, but Big Shoes is now a hybrid amalgam from everywhere.

Bennett's painting combines what Nair terms "eutopos or the nowhere glory of an ideal utopia and dystopos"—a dystopia that is by definition, the site of dislocation or unhomeliness.[49] The location of dystopia, Nair argues, can never be identified, although its territory can be claimed. Yet it is the claiming of a territory that enables the formation of communities and, as Nair suggests, a way out of the postcolonial moment. By the same token, it may also constitute a way out of the *traumatic moment*, conceived of both as a repetition in memory and as the current moment of "trauma culture" in the arts.

Afterword: Beyond Trauma Culture

In recent years, issues relating to post-9/11 global politics, trauma, and the postcolonial have made a mark on the contemporary art world. But there is a certain inevitability about the way in which such phenomena, cast as thematics, pass into and out of fashion, particularly in the domain of international biennials. There have been important exhibitions exploring these issues, yet the perpetual pursuit of new themes means that "trauma culture" will soon become passé, and global politics, the topic of last year's biennial or *Documenta*. In this light, the question "What comes after trauma culture?" can only elicit a trivial kind of speculation about the next trend to emerge in art and popular culture. The politics of trauma is here reduced to a matter of content that may engage art momentarily but will not endure as a formative concern.

Theoretical analysis must, however, move beyond any such separation of content and form if it is to account for the sustained development of a contemporary *political* in art. It is certainly possible to raise the question "What comes after the postcolonial?" in a much deeper vein than that suggested above. Insofar as the postcolonial can be understood to stand for a body of theory or knowledge, this question signals an inquiry into the progression of political thinking. It does not imply relinquishing the postcolonial for another fleeting fancy but, rather, the evolution of thought beyond its postcolonial phase. Postcolonial theory, in this respect, is accorded a generative status. Clearly, it can be argued that visual art has its own evolutionary momentum—that it pursues a set of depth concerns, particular to its own suite of disciplines. But to the extent that we now consider cognate areas like postcolonial studies or trauma studies to be properly interdisciplinary, it is time to ask how visual arts disciplines might be understood as *constitutive* theoretical discourses.

This idea that art might produce thought may be distinguished from the notion of art partaking of a body of theory engendered elsewhere. Of course, artists and art theorists may still look to philosophy for a certain manifestation of an idea or argument, but it is nevertheless possible to demonstrate that art is engaged in a synchronous development of theory. Whereas once disciplinary definitions might have allowed us to circumscribe the nature of art's core activity, limiting it to a set of aesthetic concerns, in the new interdisciplinary dispensation, we cannot so readily cede the domain of thought to philosophers. Literary theorists, after all, have been the major drivers of trauma studies, so why not visual theorists?

From this study I have tried to retrieve a sense of the political as a mode of thought embedded in a particular set of practices. This outcome arises from the initial problem I raised in relation to the designation of a category of trauma art and derives directly from the strategy of focusing on the dynamic operations of art. To invoke the political in this relationship to art implicitly challenges conventional notions of "political art" (particularly insofar as these construe art in an instrumental role, implementing an agenda predetermined in the realm of political theory). Moreover, it aligns with a more radical rethinking of the relationship of art to thought—a development that is at once a reflection of the maturation of the discipline of art theory and of the interdisciplinarity that now characterizes any study of culture.

One cannot write about trauma in art without incorporating trauma theory in some way—nor could one write about the postcolonial or the political without moving beyond the bounds of an art theoretical discipline. Yet, as Mieke Bal has shown, the notion that theory is *applied to*, rather than *conceived through* art implies a certain separation of the conceptual and visual domains.[1] Art history has taken readily to critical theory, deriving theoretical models from elsewhere (from philosophy, from literary studies, from psychoanalysis). We produce psychoanalytic or deconstructionist *readings of . . .* , but art is invariably cast as the *object* of theoretical inquiry. We have rarely asked what it might mean to derive theory *from* the visual.

In focusing on affectivity in art—on *what art itself does*—I have, in effect, attempted to derive a politics of empathy from a body of visual art-work. Hence, I have not offered a genealogy of empathy, except insofar as this is grounded in contemporary art practice; the study proceeds *from* this artwork *toward* a concept of empathic vision. As I have suggested, such a concept has resonances with Dominick LaCapra's notion of "em-pathic unsettlement," but it does not orient toward or emerge out of the historiographical arguments or the psychoanalytic foundations of literary trauma studies.

My focus on process in art has, nevertheless, revealed certain trends within contemporary art practice. There is, for example, an abundance of work that deals with affectively charged space and with an evocation of place in the aftermath of conflict. In addition to the works of Doris Salcedo, and of the various artists discussed in Chapter 4, recent biennials have in-cluded Zarina Bhimji's images of desolate buildings and open spaces in Uganda, Tony Chakar's haunting video work, describing the inhabitation of contemporary Beirut, and Steve McQueen's celebrated *Western Deep*, a video shot in a South African mine, developing what Okwui Enwezor has referred to as McQueen's "haptic vision."[2] Paul Seawright has also produced a series of commissioned photographs of postwar Afghanistan, document-ing a war-scarred landscape.

It might be argued that content can always be specified at some level. These works are often inspired by real events, and they sometimes manifest the trace of a person or narrative (Salcedo's fragments of clothing, bone, and so forth come to mind), but in the process of viewing them, recognition is invariably subordinated to an embodied perception or an affective register.

Collectively, these works move our conception of trauma beyond the realm of the interior subject into that of inhabited place, rendering it a po-litical phenomenon. At the same time, such works confound old-style no-tions of political art. They are not didactic images, mediating a message, but incline toward the expressive in the way they play on a certain affec-tive quality of space and objects to evoke modes of subjective experience, and specifically of loss. Thus, the question becomes, how is politics en-acted through such works, if not through the communication of an iden-tifiable proposition?

We have perhaps grown a little complacent in our theorization of the political in art under the sway of poststructuralism. No longer the predicate of the intentional act, politics has become simply that which infuses repre-sentation or art; hence, there is a tendency to regard this kind of art, pro-

duced around sites of political tension as political merely by virtue of its ostensible subject matter and conditions of production. But this in itself fails
to account for the distinctive properties of political critique or analysis conducted through art. To me, it begs the question of whether in fact there is
a qualitative difference between work that simply bears the imprint of a
particular time and place and politics, and work that is actively political by
virtue of engendering critical insight. Thus, I have tried to find the measure of art and thought: to suggest how art might constitute a substantive
critique or inquiry—a contribution to understanding.

It would, of course, be a mistake to attempt to translate the insights
of art back into a set of propositions—or to assume that the ideas emerging from art equate with those produced by philosophy. Consequently, I
have been concerned throughout this book to determine where art leaves
us, if not in the place of the other. By focusing on the aesthetic experience
—on the affective experience of art—I have endeavored to trace a process
of embodied perception through to a kind of critical awareness: a particular mode of understanding, engendered through the visual.

The painter Francesco Clemente suggests that a kind of "thinking
through the body" is fundamental to this process.[3] Ernst van Alphen has
worked such a concept into a full-blown theory of "thinking visually," arguing that art itself "thinks" or constitutes ideas, and that the specificity
(Deleuze might say "singularity") of art promotes more general philosophical questions.[4] Such a formulation echoes Deleuze's conception of thought
coming after. In a certain sense, then, we can say that the knowledge within
art is "unthought."[5] This does not of course imply that the artist does not
conceptualize. The more appropriate contrast is between this form of *unthought knowledge* in art and work that simply reproduces or illustrates the
pre-thought or *already thought.* Thus we can distinguish a process by which
art might shift perception and thereby engender new ways of thinking.

In describing instances in which affective operations open up a set of
questions, I have tried to show that the registration of affect is neither an
end in itself nor simply the measure of art's capacity to represent already
felt sensation. It is rather, a manner of doing politics: a politics that emerges
from a formal style. And it is certainly timely for art theory to review its
approach to the political at a point where the old "communicational" models that rest on the assumption that content is transmitted via text and image begin to haunt discussions around imagery relating to war, violence,
terror, and trauma; Hal Foster, indeed, suggests that the *return to the real*

heralds a return to the referential. I am proposing that the preponderance of work conducting its politics through an imagery of affectively charged space signals, in itself, what amounts to a theoretical strategy in practice: a counter to the turn to the real.

But I made the point at the outset that this study is not a genre study that merely takes as its object a distinct grouping of works. It is the tracing of a process—and in that spirit, it becomes an argument for a method. If visual arts practice is to be distinguished as generative rather than representational, so too may art theory be distinguished from the interpretative act that seeks to uncover the meaning of the object. Writing similarly may be a mode of "thinking visually," of deriving thought from an engagement with the visual. If there is a hierarchy of theory and practice within the liberal arts or humanities that traditionally privileges philosophy over visual art as the source of the idea, then visual arts disciplines have inevitably privileged the production of the object over interpretative discourse, insofar as the latter is construed as a secondary practice: a *writing about* the object. But the values of the old disciplinary structures are not those of the interdisciplinary future; neither do they provide us with the methods for a genuinely interdisciplinary practice in which all manner of inquiries can, through their distinct formal means, advance the analysis of culture. This study is an attempt to push forward onto newer ground.

REFERENCE MATTER

Notes

CHAPTER 1. *On the Subject of Trauma*

Epigraph: Michael Serres and Mary Zournazi, "The Art of Living: A Conversation with Michael Serres," in Mary Zournazi, *Hope: New Philosophies for Change* (New York: Routledge; Annandale, NSW: Pluto Press, 2002), 204.

1. "Telling Tales," curated by Jill Bennett and Jackie Dunn; see the exhibition catalogue, *Telling Tales*, ed. Jill Bennett and Jackie Dunn (Sydney: Ivan Dougherty Gallery, College of Fine Arts, University of New South Wales, 1998; Graz: Neue Galerie, 1999).

2. "Trauma," curated by Fiona Bradley, Katrina Brown, and Andrew Nairne; see the exhibition catalogue, *Trauma* (London: Hayward Gallery Publishing, 2001).

3. Leo Bersani, *The Culture of Redemption* (Cambridge, Mass.: Harvard University Press, 1990).

4. Ernst van Alphen, *Caught By History: Holocaust Effects in Contemporary Art, Literature and Theory* (Stanford: Stanford University Press, 1997).

5. Kali Tal, *Worlds of Hurt: Reading the Literatures of Trauma* (Cambridge: Cambridge University Press, 1996), 17.

6. Hal Foster, *The Return of the Real: The Avant Garde at the End of the Century* (Cambridge, Mass.: MIT Press, 1996), 168.

7. Ibid., 166.

8. Andreas Huyssen, "Trauma and Memory: A New Imaginary of Temporality," in *World Memory: Personal Trajectories in Global Time*, ed. Jill Bennett and Rosanne Kennedy (London: Palgrave Macmillan, 2003), 16–29; John Mowitt, "Trauma Envy," *Cultural Critique* 46 (Fall 2000): 272–97; Mark Selzer, "Wound Culture: Trauma in the Pathological Public Sphere," *October* 80 (Spring 1997): 3–26; Ghassan Hage, "Multi-Cultural Ethics" (paper presented at "Postcolonial + Art: Where Now?" symposium, Artspace, Sydney, October 28, 2000).

9. Hal Foster, "Trauma Culture," http://www.artnet.com/magazine/features/ foster/foster7-26-96.asp (accessed October 30, 2002), 2.

10. Cathy Caruth, *Unclaimed Experience: Trauma, Narrative and History* (Baltimore: Johns Hopkins University Press, 1996); Shoshana Felman and Dori Laub, eds., *Testimony: Crises of Witnessing in Literature, Psychoanalysis and History* (New

York: Routledge, 1992); Antjie Krog, *Country of My Skull: Guilt, Sorrow and the Limits of Forgiveness in the New South Africa* (New York: Three Rivers Press, 1999). For a critique of Caruth and Felman, see Amy Hungerford, "Memorizing Memory," *Yale Journal of Criticism* 14, no. 1 (2001): 67–92. For comments on Krog's appropriation of testimony, see Yazir Henri [Henry], "Where Healing Begins," in *Looking Back, Reaching Forward: Reflections on the Truth and Reconciliation Commission of South Africa*, ed. Charles Villa-Vicencio and Wilhelm Verwoerd (Cape Town: University of Cape Town Press, 2000).

11. For an outline of the philosophical critique of "communicational" understandings of representation, invoking Deleuze, in particular, see Brian Massumi, "Introduction: Like a Thought," in id., ed., *A Shock to Thought: Expression After Deleuze and Guattari* (New York: Routledge, 2002), xiii–xxxix.

12. Gilles Deleuze, *Proust and Signs*, trans. Richard Howard (1964; New York: George Braziller, 1972).

13. Ibid., 161.

14. Ibid.

15. Deleuze's formulation here derives from Proust (ibid., 163).

16. Dominick LaCapra, *Writing History, Writing Trauma* (Baltimore: Johns Hopkins University Press, 2001); Dominick LaCapra, *History and Memory After Auschwitz* (Ithaca, N.Y.: Cornell University Press, 1998).

17. See esp. LaCapra, *Writing History*, 41.

18. Ibid., 1–42.

19. LaCapra, *History and Memory*, 95–138.

20. LaCapra quotes Neal Ascherson's argument that Lanzmann wanted his interviewees to be "characters," including only those testimonies that offered a dramatic "re-living" of the traumatic event. LaCapra, *History and Memory*, 126.

21. Geoffrey Hartman, "Tele-Suffering and Testimony in the Dot Com Era," in *Visual Culture and the Holocaust*, ed. Barbie Zelizer (New Brunswick, N.J.: Rutgers University Press, 2000), 119.

22. LaCapra, *History and Memory*, 135–36

23. Luc Boltanski, *Distant Suffering: Morality, Media and Politics*, trans. Graham Burchell (Cambridge: Cambridge University Press, 1999).

24. Hartman, "Tele-Suffering," 122–23.

25. LaCapra, *Writing History*, 40.

26. Ibid., 40; Kaja Silverman, *The Threshold of the Visible World* (New York: Routledge, 1996). For a further application of Silverman's concept, see Jill Bennett, "*Tenebrae* After September 11: Art, Empathy and the Global Politics of Belonging," in *World Memory*, ed. id. and Kennedy.

27. Bertolt Brecht, "A Short Organum for the Theatre" (1948), trans. John Willett, in *Avant-Garde Drama, 1918–1939*, ed. Bernard F. Dukore and Daniel C. Gerould (New York: Crowell, 1976), 518.

28. Nikos Papastergiadis and Mary Zournazi, "Faith Without Certitudes: A

Conversation with Nikos Papastergiadis," in Mary Zournazi, *Hope: New Philosophies for Change* (New York: Routledge; Annandale, NSW: Pluto Press, 2002), 94–95.

29. Maurice Blanchot, *The Writing of the Disaster* (1980), trans. Ann Smock (1986; Lincoln University of Nebraska Press, 1995). Hartman also makes reference to this concept of Blanchot's; Hartman, "Tele-Suffering," 123.

30. Massumi, *Shock to Thought*.

31. Cf. Massumi's account in "Introduction: Like a Thought," in id., *Shock to Thought*, of the problems of understanding expression as communicative.

32. Ruth Leys, *Trauma: A Genealogy* (Chicago: University of Chicago Press, 2000).

33. Foster, *Return of the Real*, 156. With reference to the concept of abjection, Foster identifies three possible ways of understanding transgression in art. In doing so, he points toward a new conception of the avant-garde and its political possibilities. Ibid., 156–57.

34. *The Essential Frankfurt School Reader*, ed. Andrew Arato and Eike Gebhardt (1978; New York: Continuum, 1982), 312.

35. Clare Colebrook, *Understanding Deleuze* (Sydney: Allen & Unwin, 2002), 179.

36. Aesthetics and politics are not mutually exclusive in Deleuze's work, although it is in the books on cinema that these are most intertwined. Whereas Deleuze's discussion of postwar cinema engages with cinema as a post-Holocaust art form, his theorization of painting is much less politically engaged. See esp. Gilles Deleuze, *Cinema 2: The Time Image*, trans. Hugh Tomlinson and Robert Galeta (Minneapolis: University of Minnesota Press, 1989). For a comprehensive treatment of Deleuze's politics, see Paul Patton, *Deleuze and the Political* (New York: Routledge, 2000).

37. Friedrich Nietzsche, *The Gay Science*, trans. Walter Kaufmann (New York: Random House, 1974), 302.

38. I am referring principally to the works *Tenebrae, Noviembre 7, 1985* and *Noviembre 6, 1985*, about which I interviewed Salcedo in 2001; see "Jill Bennett Interviews Doris Salcedo," in the exhibition catalogue *Doris Salcedo* (London: Camden Arts Centre, 2001). And see Bennett, *"Tenebrae,"* for further discussion of this work.

39. See Chapter 2 for discussion of Deleuze's concept of art and sensation.

40. See, e.g., Huyssen, "Trauma and Memory."

41. Mike Davis, "The Flames of New York," *New Left Review* 12 (November–December 2001).

42. Serres with Latour, *Conversations*, 191.

43. The notion that "explication" of the larger causes of the terrorist attacks might exonerate the terrorists and thereby condone the suffering of victims pervades much of the U.S. discourse on the attacks. See, e.g., many of the U.S. contributions and letters to the *London Review of Books*, esp. 23, no. 19 (October 4, 2001) and no. 21 (November 1, 2001).

44. Carolyn Christov-Bakargiev, *William Kentridge* (Brussels: Société des expositions du Palais des beaux-arts de Bruxelles, 1998), 111.

45. One Internet poll determined that 73 percent of Americans considered themselves to have been "traumatized" by the attacks at some point in the aftermath (for the breakdown of results in this particular poll, see http:///topic/attackpoll [accessed December 2001]). Talk shows featured supposed cases of post-traumatic stress as far afield as California, where victims claimed to have been unable to leave home after September 11. See Bennett, *"Tenebrae,"* for further discussion.

CHAPTER 2. *Insides, Outsides: Trauma, Affect, and Art*

Epigraph: Édouard Claparède, "La Question de la 'mémoire' affective," *Archives de psychologie* 10 (1911): 361–77, quotation at 367–69, cited and discussed in Ruth Leys, "Traumatic Cures: Shell Shock, Janet and the Question of Memory," in *Tense Past: Cultural Essays in Trauma and Memory*, ed. Paul Antze and Michael Lambek (New York: Routledge, 1996), 113–14.

1. Claparède, "Question," 368; Leys, "Traumatic Cures," 113.

2. William James, *Principles of Psychology* (1890; Cambridge, Mass.: Harvard University Press, 1983); see Leys, "Traumatic Cures," for discussion of James in relation to Claparède.

3. See Leys, "Traumatic Cures," 95.

4. Pierre Janet quoted in Bessell A. van der Kolk and Onno van der Hart, "The Intrusive Past: The Flexibility of Memory and the Engraving of Trauma," in *Trauma: Explorations in Memory*, ed. Cathy Caruth (Baltimore: Johns Hopkins University Press, 1995), 160.

5. Kolk and Hart, "Intrusive Past," 160. For an overview, see also Leys, *Trauma*, esp. 7. Leys develops a sustained argument against the notion that trauma stands outside representation, criticizing both van der Kolk and cultural adaptations of this work such as Cathy Caruth's.

6. See esp. Felman's discussion of Paul Celan in Shoshana Felman and Dori Laub, *Testimony: Crises of Witnessing in Literature, Psychoanalysis, and History* (New York: Routledge, 1991).

7. Within art historical discourse, "expressionism" is characteristically grounded in an uncritical subjectivism. However, as Brian Massumi argues, Deleuze and Guattari offer a radically different conception of expression (Massumi, "Introduction: Like a Thought," in id., *Shock to Thought*, xiii–xxxix).

8. Charlotte Delbo, *Days and Memory*, trans. Rosette Lamont (Marlboro, Vt.: Marlboro Press,1990); id., *Auschwitz and After*, trans. Rosette Lamont, with an introduction by Lawrence Langer (New Haven, Conn.: Yale University Press, 1995); for further discussion, see Lawrence Langer, *Holocaust Testimonies: The Ruins of Memory* (New Haven, Conn.: Yale University Press, 1991), 1–38.

9. Delbo, *Days and Memory*, as quoted in Langer, *Holocaust Testimonies*, 5.

10. On the use of the phrase "seeing truth," see Langer, *Holocaust Testimonies*, xv.

11. The exhibition "Telling Tales" (see Chapter 1 n. 1, above, and Bennett and

Dunn, *Telling Tales*) explored how languages of sense memory are developed by artists against the background of common language, history, and popular discourse, as, for example, in relation to the recent history of Aboriginal people in Australia, where the lived effects of the past are frequently disavowed.

12. Michel Foucault, *The History of Sexuality*, vol. 1: *An Introduction* (1976), trans. Robert Hurley (New York: Random House, 1978).

13. Leys, *Trauma*, argues that the generalization of this understanding of trauma works to produce a victim-subject, absolved of responsibility; thus, for example, in the case of Vietnam veterans, those who have committed atrocities and who are visited by repetitive nightmares and other symptoms are seen as victims.

14. Hage, "Multi-Cultural Ethics."

15. The body of writing, painting, photographic collage, and performance work of the late David Wojnarowicz exemplifies this well; see, e.g., David Wojnarowicz, *Close to the Knives: A Memoir of Disintegration* (New York: Vintage Books, 1991).

16. This interpretation is developed further in my essay for the exhibition catalogue *Dennis Del Favero: Parting Embrace* (Sydney: Mori Gallery, 1998), and in Jill Bennett, *Dennis Del Favero: Fantasmi* (Sydney: University of New South Wales Press, 2004).

17. Felman and Laub, *Testimony*, 1991.

18. Deleuze, *Cinema Two*, 206.

19. Elinor Fuchs, "Staging the Obscene Body," *Tulane Drama Review* 33, no. 1 (1989): 33–57, at 47.

20. Karen Finley, "The Constant State of Desire," in *Shock Treatment* (1988; San Francisco: City Lights Books, 1990).

21. Janneke Lam, "Whose Pain? Childhood, Trauma, Imagination" (PhD diss., University of Amsterdam, 2002), makes extensive use of the Winnicottian notion of "potential space" in relation to the analysis of trauma and film/visual art.

22. See Massumi, "Introduction: Like a Thought," in id., *Shock to Thought*, on the theoretical problems of the communicative model.

23. The term "corporeal promiscuity" is drawn from the work of the philosopher Roslyn Diprose, further expounded in Chapter 6; Roslyn Diprose, *Corporeal Generosity: On Giving with Nietzsche, Merleau-Ponty, and Levinas* (New York: State University of New York Press, 2002).

24. Lam makes use in "Whose Pain?" of the concept of "feeling into," drawn from Winnicott, to describe the construction of an empathic response.

25. Hartman, "Tele-Suffering," 117.

26. Alphen, *Caught by History*.

27. See Mary J. Carruthers, *The Book of Memory: A Study of Memory in Medieval Culture* (Cambridge: Cambridge University Press, 1990). On the production of affect in relation to visual imagery, see Jill Bennett, "Stigmata and Sense Memory: St Francis and the Affective Image," *Art History* 24, no. 1 (February 2001): 1–16.

28. The notion of "affect contagion" is drawn from the work of the psychologist Silvan Tomkins; see *Shame and Its Sisters: A Silvan Tomkins Reader*, ed. Eve Kosofsky Sedgwick and Adam Frank (Durham, N.C.: Duke University Press, 1995). For further discussion of the mechanisms for transmission of affect, particularly in relation to what neurologists call "entrainment," see Teresa Brennan, *The Transmission of Affect* (Ithaca, N.Y.: Cornell University Press, 2004).

29. See Bennett, "Stigmata," 2001.

30. Deleuze, *Proust and Signs*.

31. Ibid., 163.

32. Ibid., 164.

33. Gilles Deleuze, *Francis Bacon: Logique de la sensation* (Paris: Éditions de la Différence, 1981).

34. Quoted in Daniel W. Smith, "Deleuze's Theory of Sensation: Overcoming the Kantian Duality," in *Deleuze: A Critical Reader*, ed. Paul Patton (Oxford: Blackwell, 1996), 45. See now Gilles Deleuze, *Francis Bacon: The Logic of Sensation*, trans. Daniel W. Smith (Minneapolis: University of Minnesota Press, 2003).

35. The inscription of the star was repeated in *Biography* in 1992, when Abramovic reenacted highlights of her life. The documentation of this work has also had a considerable afterlife.

36. Franz Kafka, *In the Penal Colony*, trans. Malcolm Pasley (London: Penguin Books, 1992), 31.

37. Darwin describes the physiological symptoms of affects in *The Expression of the Emotions in Man and Animals*, a work glossed and developed by Silvan Tomkins in his four-volume study *Affect, Imagery, Consciousness*; see *Shame and Its Sisters*, ed. Kosofsky Sedgwick and Frank.

38. See Smith, "Deleuze's Theory of Sensation: Overcoming the Kantian Duality," 42.

39. Cathy Caruth, *Unclaimed Experience: Trauma, Narrative, and History* (Baltimore: Johns Hopkins University Press, 1996), 4.

40. See Bennett and Dunn, *Telling Tales*, for illustration.

41. Maurice Blanchot, *The Gaze of Orpheus*, ed. P. Adams Sitney, trans. Lydia Davis (Barrytown, N.Y.: Station Hill Press, 1981), 84.

42. Charlotte Delbo, *La Mémoire et les jours* (Paris: Berg International, 1985), as quoted by Langer, *Holocaust Testimonies*, 6–7.

43. See Bennett and Dunn, *Telling Tales*, for further examples related to the experiences of abuse, grief, and Aboriginal family memory.

44. I am indebted to Sara Chesterman for her insights and for permission to quote from an unpublished student assignment. All subsequent citations are from that source.

45. Brian Massumi, "The Autonomy of Affect," in *Deleuze: A Critical Reader*, ed. Patton, 217–39.

46. See "Francesco Clemente," interview with Giancarlo Politi, *Flash Art*, April–May 1984, 1.

47. Deleuze, *Cinema Two*, 206.

48. Ibid., 207.

CHAPTER 3. *The Force of Trauma*

1. Veena Das, "Language and Body: Transactions in the Construction of Pain," in *Social Suffering*, ed. Arthur Kleinman, Veena Das, and Margaret Lock (Berkeley: University of California Press, 1997), 86–87.

2. Ibid., 86–87

3. Eric Santner, *Stranded Objects: Mourning, Memory, and Film in Postwar Germany* (Ithaca, N.Y.: Cornell University Press, 1990), 25.

4. Das, "Language and Body," 88.

5. Stanley Cavell, "Comments on Veena Das's Essay 'Language and Body: Transactions in the Construction of Pain,'" in *Social Suffering*, ed. Kleinman et al., 94.

6. Das, "Language and Body," 78.

7. Ibid., 70.

8. Ibid., 78.

9. Nadia Seremetakis, *The Last Word: Women, Death, and Divination in Inner Mani* (Chicago: University of Chicago Press, 1991).

10. Nancy Princenthal, Carlos Basualdo, and Andreas Huyssen, *Doris Salcedo* (London: Phaidon, 2000), 14.

11. Das, "Language and Body," 68.

12. Ibid.

13. Quotations are from unpublished letters to the author unless otherwise stated.

14. Sandra Johnston, "Numbing Repetitive Acts," *Creative Camera* 331 (December–January 1995): 20–23, at 22.

15. Roland Barthes, *Camera Lucida: Reflections on Photography*, trans. Richard Howard (New York: Hill & Wang, 1981), 27.

16. Christopher Bollas, *Being a Character: Psychoanalysis and Self-Experience* (New York: Hill & Wang, 1992), 69–70.

17. Sigmund Freud, "Remembering, Repeating and Working-through" (1914), in *The Standard Edition of the Complete Works of Sigmund Freud*, 12 (London: Hogarth Press and the Institute of Psycho-Analysis, 1958).

18. Dominick LaCapra, *Representing the Holocaust: History, Theory, Trauma* (Ithaca, N.Y.: Cornell University Press, 1994); Dominick LaCapra, "Lanzmann's *Shoah*: Here There Is No Why," *Critical Inquiry* 23, no. 2 (Winter 1997).

19. LaCapra, "Lanzmann's *Shoah*."

20. Edward Casey, *Getting Back into Place: Toward a Renewed Understanding of the Place World* (Bloomington: Indiana University Press, 1993), 48.

21. Charles Merewether, "To Bear Witness," in *Doris Salcedo*, ed. Dan Cameron (New York: New Museum of Contemporary Art, 1998), 16–24; Doris Salcedo, "Memoirs from Beyond the Grave," *Tate*, no. 21 (2000): 84.

22. Dan Cameron, "Doris Salcedo," *Grand Street* 61, "All-American," 16, no. 1 (Summer 1997): 81.

23. Elaine Scarry, *The Body in Pain: The Making and Unmaking of the World* (Oxford: Oxford University Press, 1985), 13.

24. This is also, of course, ancient sympathetic magic. "It is constantly Received, and Avouched, that the Anointing of the Weapon, that maketh the Wound, wil heale the Wound it selfe," Francis Bacon writes (*Sylva Sylvarum: or, A Natural History*, 6th ed. [1651], p. 217). The idea goes back at least to Paracelsus. I am grateful to Peter Dreyer for drawing my attention to this.

25. See Merewether, "To Bear Witness," 22.

26. Ibid.

27. Salcedo, "Memoirs," 84.

28. Ibid.

29. Geoffrey Hartman, "Public Memory and Its Discontents," *Raritan* 13, no. 4 (1994): 24–40.

30. Henri makes this argument in relation to his own experience of testifying at the South African Truth and Reconciliation Commission, discussing the way in which reporters subsequently characterized his testimony and appearance on the witness stand. He does not specifically address either art or visual imagery in this regard. Henri, "Where Healing Begins"; see also Bennett, *"Tenebrae."* Following his experience of testifying at the TRC, Henry changed the spelling of his name (from Henry).

31. Barbie Zelizer discusses the reception of documentary photographs of the Nazi camps in these terms; see Barbie Zelizer, *Remembering to Forget: Holocaust Memory Through the Camera's Eye* (Chicago: University of Chicago Press, 1998).

32. See the exhibition catalogue, Silvia Velez, Lisa Byrne, and Blair French, *Madre Patria/Motherland* (Canberra: Canberra School of Art, 2000).

33. Merewether, "To Bear Witness," 20.

34. Princenthal et al., *Doris Salcedo*, 14.

35. Interview with Jill Bennett, Camden Art Centre, September 11, 2001.

36. Princenthal et al., *Doris Salcedo*, 14.

37. Bollas, *Being a Character*, 21.

38. Salcedo, "Memoirs," 84.

39. Princenthal et al., *Doris Salcedo*, 140.

40. See esp. Bennett, *"Tenebrae."*

CHAPTER 4. *Journeys into Place*

1. Casey, *Getting Back into Place.*

2. Michael Godby, "Memory and History in William Kentridge's *History of the Main Complaint*," in *Negotiating the Past: the Making of Memory in South Africa*, ed. Sarah Nuttall and Carli Coetzee (Oxford: Oxford University Press, 1998), 102–4.

3. Godby, "Memory and History," 101

4. Christov-Bakargiev, *William Kentridge,* 110.

5. Gilles Deleuze, *Cinema One: The Movement Image* (1983), trans. Hugh Tomlinson and Barbara Habberjam (Minneapolis: University of Minnesota Press, 1986).

6. Christov-Bakargiev, *William Kentridge*, 111.

7. Ibid., 112.

8. Godby, "Memory and History," 110.

9. José Gil, *Metamorphoses of the Body*, trans. Stephen Muecke, Theory Out of Bounds 12 (Minneapolis: University of Minnesota Press, 1998), 132.

10. Ibid., 120–24.

11. Ibid., 131.

12. The preceding examples of metaphor are Gil's (ibid., 131).

13. Christov-Bakargiev, *William Kentridge*, 111.

14. Gisela Pankow cited in Gil, *Metamorphoses of the Body*, 122.

15. Casey, *Getting Back into Place*, 312.

16. *Willie Doherty: No Smoke Without Fire, Matt's Gallery, London 1996* (exhibition catalogue), Matt's Gallery, London Arts Board, Arts Council of England.

17. See esp. Maite Lorés, "The Streets Were Dark with Something More Than Night: Film Noir Elements in the Work of Willie Doherty," in *Willie Doherty: Dark Stains* (Madrid: British Council; [Donostia]: Gipuzkoako Foru Aldundia, 1999), 110–17.

18. Murray Cox, *Shakespeare Comes to Broadmoor: The Performance of a Tragedy in a Secure Psychiatric Hospital* (London: Jessica Kingsley, 1992).

19. Diprose, *Corporeal Generosity*, 68. See Chapter 6 of this book for further exemplification of Diprose's concept of generosity.

20. The billboards were accompanied by photographic installations at a gallery, and video works projected at night onto the wall of a church. Some community pinhole workshops formed part of the project.

21. Jo Ractliffe, "End of Time: A Point of Access," in *End of Time: Jo Ractliffe*, exhibition catalogue (Cape Town: Mark Coetzee Fine Art Cabinet, 1999), no page numbers. Subsequent quotations of Ractliffe are from this source.

22. Brenda Atkinson, "End of Time," in *End of Time: Jo Ractliffe*; Marc Augé, *Non-Places: Introduction to an Anthropology of Supermodernity* (1992), trans. John Howe (New York: Verso, 1995).

23. Paul Virilio, *The Lost Dimension* (New York: Semiotext(e), 1991), 83.

24. Victor Burgin, *In/different Spaces: Place and Memory in Visual Culture* (Berkeley: University of California Press, 1996), 185.

25. Other artists were subsequently invited to contribute work made from different perspectives outside Angola, but I'm most interested in this core group because their project was born of a "reengagement" with Angola at that time.

26. Angola is, of course, far from neutral territory for a South African. Throughout the 1970s, the former Portuguese colony was riven with conflict as a struggle for control of government took place between the MPLA (supported by the Soviet Union and Cuba) and other nationalist parties, including UNITA (backed by South Africa with Western support). During the 1970s, South African troops invaded and occupied parts of Angola, making repeated incursions up until 1988. In the following years, the civil war—an increasingly ethnic conflict—escalated and

there were accusations of massive civilian massacres on both sides. Although estimates vary, something like a million people died in the war in Angola; 97 percent of the population are deemed to have been "materially affected," and 200,000 have been mutilated. For further information, see reports linked to http://hrw.org/doc?t=africa&c=angola (accessed July 25, 2004).

27. At one point we hear the voice of former South African Prime Minister John Vorster, the only overt reference to South Africa's involvement in Angola.

28. David Bunn has noted that Younge does not use symbols to stand in for human suffering in any straightforward way, even as images of dilapidation and the struggles of small creatures seem to be metonyms for the larger damage. I would suggest that, like Salcedo, he is less concerned with metaphor than with metamorphosis. Careful examination of the bikes reveals that each one is covered in vellum, tightly sutured around the frame to appear like a growth upon the original structure. This is a conceit Younge has deployed in other works. In the *Memorias* exhibit, he included a work consisting of roughly sutured vellum animals along with images of birds on fragments of wood, covered with vellum and layers of varnish, which Bunn has evocatively related to the "nacreous layers of meaning that accumulate around an original wounding event." This phrase might also call to mind Salcedo's *Atrabiliarios* in its use of hewn skin and stitching to cover over signs of life, like a kind of regrowth on a wound that remains in place. In Younge's work, as in Salcedo's, damage is revealed through regeneration. See David Bunn, "Gavin Younge's Distant Catastrophes" (catalogue essay), in *Memorias intimas marcas* (Brussels: Sussuta Boé, 1998).

29. Invoking Merleau-Ponty, Casey argues that as we acknowledge the limits of our bodily "implacement" and the specificities of our inclusion in a field, so we realize a corresponding occlusion. Casey, *Getting Back into Place*, 69.

30. Okwui Enwezor, "Reframing the Black Subject: Ideology and Fantasy in Contemporary South African Representation," *Third Text* 40 (Autumn 1997): 32–34. For further theoretical elaboration of this case, see also Ernst van Alphen, "Colonialism as Historical Trauma," in *Grey Areas: Repression, Identity and Politics in Contemporary South African Art*, ed. Brenda Atkinson and Candice Breitz (Johannesburg: Chalkham Hill Press, 1999), 269–81; and Patricia Davidson, "Museums, Memorials and Public Memory," in *Negotiating the Past: The Making of Memory in South Africa*, ed. Sarah Nuttall and Carli Coetzee (Oxford: Oxford University Press, 1998), 143–60, esp. 158–60.

31. On the *Miscast* exhibition as a whole and its relationship to Khoisan memory and trauma, see Steven Robbins, "Silence in My Father's House: Memory, Nationalism, and Narratives of the Body," in *Negotiating the Past*, ed. Nuttall and Coetzee, 120–40.

32. Alphen, "Colonialism as Historical Trauma."

33. Zygmunt Bauman, *Globalization: The Human Consequences* (New York: Columbia University Press; Cambridge: Polity Press, 1998), 88. See also Ulrich Beck, *What Is Globalization?* (Cambridge: Polity Press, 2000), 56.

34. Sara Ahmed, *Strange Encounters: Embodied Others in Post-Coloniality* (New York: Routledge, 2000).

35. Enwezor, "Reframing the Black Subject."

36. Ahmed, *Strange Encounters*, 150–51. Ahmed cites and argues against Derrida here.

37. Bunn, "Gavin Younge's Distant Catastrophes."

38. This is a paraphrase of Ahmed, *Strange Encounters*.

39. Younge recorded this testimony in an interview with the man and his wife, who does not appear in the final edit.

40. Bunn, "Gavin Younge's Distant Catastrophes."

41. Slavoj Žižek suggests that Western First World nations find it relatively easy to deal with images of Third World suffering because passive suffering connotes helplessness and dependence, implying that the victims need us, our help, our medicine, and our money. The victim image thereby offers us a sense of relative control and renews our conception of First World power and magnanimity. This control is lost when "victims" are represented as assertive or as actively assisting themselves. See esp. Žižek, *The Plague of Fantasies* (London: Verso, 1997), 17–18, 61–61.

42. Younge's approach here could be compared with that of Chris Marker's 1983 film *Sans soleil*, which Silverman discusses as offering the spectator access to memories of others from Guinea Bissau to Tokyo. See Kaja Silverman, *The Threshold of the Visible* (New York: Routledge, 1996), 185–93.

43. Christov-Bakargiev, *William Kentridge*, 97. *Felix in Exile* deals with the mining and industrial wasteland surrounding Johannesburg as this is "surveyed" by an African woman. Kentridge has spoken about the work as a "geography of memory."

44. On January 30, 1972, fourteen unarmed civilians were shot dead by British paratroopers during an anti-internment march in Derry.

45. Casey, *Getting Back in Place*, 278.

46. Ibid., 289.

47. Ibid., 68.

48. James Young, *At Memory's Edge: After-Images of the Holocaust in Contemporary Art and Architecture* (New Haven, Conn.: Yale University Press, 2000); see especially ch. 5, "Memory Against Itself in Germany Today," for a discussion of the "counter-monument" that operates to promote critical reflection.

49. Gillian Warren-Brown, "Soldier Henry Comes Home," *Leadership*, December–January 1999–2000, 92–96

50. Heidi Grunebaum, "Re-placing Pasts, Forgetting Presents: Narrative, Place and Memory in the Time of the Truth and Reconciliation Commission," *Research in African Literatures* 32, no. 3 (Fall 2001).

51. See Grunebaum, "Re-placing Pasts" for a more extensive discussion of this case in relation to the WECAT tour. For an account of this and other TRC investigations, including that of the Guguletu Seven, see Zenzile Khoisan, *Jakaranda Time: An Investigator's View of South Africa's Truth and Reconciliation Commission* (Cape Town: Garib Communications, 2001).

52. Heidi Grunebaum and Yazir Henri, "Re-membering Bodies, Producing Histories: Holocaust Survivor Narrative and Truth and Reconciliation Commission Testimony," in *World Memory*, ed. Bennett and Kennedy, 111.

CHAPTER 5. *Face-to-Face Encounters*

Epigraph: Friedrich Nietzsche, *The Gay Science* (1882), trans. Walter Kaufmann (New York: Random House, 1974), 302.

1. See, e.g., Massumi, "Autonomy of Affect," in *Deleuze: A Critical Reader*, ed. Patton, 221, which treats affect as "intensity," distinguishing emotion as "subjective content" or "qualified intensity."

2. I am quoting a paraphrase of Brecht from Frederic Jameson, *Brecht and Method* (New York: Verso, 1998), 25.

3. William Kentridge, "Director's Note: The Crocodile's Mouth," in *Ubu and the Truth Commission* (Cape Town: University of Cape Town Press, 1998), viii–xv.

4. Hartman, "Tele-Suffering," 117.

5. Ibid.

6. See esp. Gayatri Chakravorty Spivak, "Translator's Preface and Afterword to Mahasweta Devi, 'Imaginary Maps,'" in *The Spivak Reader*, ed. Donna Landry and Gerald MacLean (New York: Routledge, 1996), 267–86; also Landry and MacLean, "Subaltern Talk," in ibid., 287–308. Sara Ahmed introduces the term "face-to-face" in her gloss, in *Strange Encounters*, of Spivak's notion of encounter.

7. See *Shame and Its Sisters*, ed. Kosofsky Sedgwick and Frank, esp. ch. 6, "Shame-Humiliation and Contempt-Disgust."

8. Ibid., 134.

9. Jacques Derrida, "On Forgiveness," in id., *On Cosmopolitanism and Forgiveness*, trans. Mark Dooley and Michael Hughes (New York: Routledge, 2001).

10. Ibid., 55.

11. Ibid.

12. Ibid., 49.

13. I am grateful to Nkululeko Booysen of the Direct Action Centre for Peace (Cape Town), who has worked with the Guguletu Seven mothers, for sharing his insights in this regard.

14. Brecht, "Short Organum for the Theatre," 518.

15. Hartman, "Telesuffering and Testimony," 122.

16. Yazir Henri, "Reconciling Reconciliation: A Personal and Public Journey of Testifying Before the South African Truth and Reconciliation Commission" (MS). I am grateful to Yazir Henri for providing a copy of this manuscript and for discussions on this issue. See also id., "Where Healing Begins."

17. *Ubu Roi* has been interpreted as an allegory, before the fact, of the Vietnam War and also of totalitarianism in Eastern Europe.

18. *Ubu Roi*, as Keith Beaumont has suggested arises "from a superimposition of the characteristics of the puppet theatre or *guignol* upon a subject, themes and dramatic framework belonging to traditional live theatre in its most serious, and

even most 'noble' and 'heroic' forms." Keith Beaumont, *Jarry: Ubu Roi* (London: Grant & Cutler, 1987), 30–31.

19. In Michael Meschke's acclaimed 1964 production of *Ubu Roi* (first staged in Stockholm and subsequently performed in over a dozen countries), live actors were combined with puppetlike cutouts, animated by actors concealed behind them. In *Ubu and the Truth Commission*, this mixing of the puppet and human world is continued. Ubu, for example, rides upon a menacing many-headed dog puppet, echoing not just the Meschke production but also a tradition of political caricature, including works such as the *Dream and Lie of Franco* etchings by Jarry's great admirer Picasso.

20. The *grand guignol* tradition is, as Beaumont notes, carried on today through animation or cartoons; see Beaumont, *Jarry: Ubu Roi*, 30, and, for further discussion, Keith Beaumont, *Alfred Jarry: A Critical and Biographical Study* (Leicester: Leicester University Press, 1984). Kentridge has also developed an eight-minute animation film titled *Ubu Tells the Truth*, which is shown independently of the play.

21. In the stage play, Ma Ubu is given the rotund form and pointy head. The Ubu of the projected animation makes an appearance on stage as a life-sized three-dimensional body puppet, representing Ubu's conscience.

22. Christov-Bakargiev, *William Kentridge*, 67.

23. Georges Bataille, *Eroticism*, trans. Mary Dalwood (New York: Marion Boyars, 1987), 177–96. Bataille notes that "the torturer does not use the language of the violence exerted by him," distinguishing the language of the marquis de Sade as essentially that of the victim (ibid., 187). See also Gilles Deleuze, "Coldness and Cruelty," in id., *Masochism* (New York: Zone Books, 1991), 15–23.

24. Deleuze, "Coldness and Cruelty," 15–23, contrasts the sadistic text with the masochistic text in light of such features.

25. Rosalind Krauss, "The Rock: William Kentridge's Drawings for Projection," *October* 92 (Spring 2000): 3–35, at 23.

26. Kentridge, "Director's Note," viii.

27. Bataille, *Eroticism*, 188.

28. Ibid.

29. Ibid., 189.

30. The puppeteers Basil Jones and Adrian Kohler discuss how the illusion of facial expression is produced on the roughly carved surfaces, well keyed for illumination: "under the lights, the movement of tiny shadows cast by the gouging chisel, particularly in the contrast between looking up, looking forward and looking down, assists in the illusion of changing expressions on an otherwise immobile face." Basil Jones and Adrian Kohler, "Puppeteers' Note," in *Ubu and the Truth Commission* (Cape Town: University of Cape Town Press, 1998); xvi–xvii, xvii.

31. Jones and Kohler have written that: "Puppet movement, particularly that of the witnesses, needs to find its correct speed. This is generally slower than the human equivalent to allow the audience to observe clearly what the figure is trying to do" (ibid., xvii).

32. Bertolt Brecht, *Brecht on Theatre: The Development of an Aesthetic*, trans. John Willett (New York: Hill & Wang, 1964), 37.

33. Taylor and Kentridge took heed of a short-lived experiment in which TRC translators did, in fact, try to impart some of the feeling with which the witnesses delivered their testimony.

34. Bataille, *Eroticism*, 188, 189.

35. The translator is often positioned incongruously in a shower recess. This is the same shower used by Ubu to wash away his sins, evidence of which—rendered through animation—literally vanishes down the plug hole as he is caught in reverie.

36. The published script, based upon actual TRC testimony, reads "he didn't have this of the head." Jane Taylor explains: "Many of these strategies emerged in the workshop, as we attempted to create a particular singularity in the modes of performance with each of the different testimonies. It is something of the shock of reception that the performances reach for, so that one cannot entirely anticipate the structures of one's own emotional engagement, within a relatively stable logic of 'truth telling.'" Communication to the author, January 29, 2002. I am grateful to Jane Taylor for this correspondence and for extended discussions of her work.

CHAPTER 6. *Global Interconnections*

1. See the exhibition catalogue, Greg Dimitriadis, Cameron McCarthy, and Ian McLean, *Gordon Bennett—Notes to Basquiat: 911* (Adelaide: Greenway Art Gallery, 2002).

2. Basquiat's planes feature in the works *Notes to Basquiat (City)* and *Notes to Basquiat (911)*. The fighter planes were drawn by Bennett, the passenger planes by his ten-year-old daughter Caitlin.

3. See Ian McLean, "Gordon Bennett's Existentialism," in id. and Gordon Bennett, *The Art of Gordon Bennett* (Roseville East, NSW: Craftsman House, 1996), 70.

4. See the exhibition catalogue *Gordon Bennett, 5 November–4 December 1999* (Sydney: Sherman Galleries, 1999).

5. Somewhat uncannily, an exhibition of Bennett's work at his Melbourne gallery in September 2001 included images of planes flying through buildings. I am grateful to Ian McLean for pointing this out.

6. One of the effects of the globalization of culture is that, as a result of exposure to U.S. TV, Australians have been known to call 911 (instead of the correct 000) in an emergency.

7. See Ian McLean, "Angel of History," *Third Text* 58 (June 2002): 212–15. McLean draws this connection with the work of the Gunwinggu people from Oenpelli, who live in the Kakadu region, south of Darwin and are known for their X-ray-style rock and bark paintings depicting the skeleton and organs of various animals.

8. For further discussion of this, see Bennett, *"Tenebrae."*

9. See McLean, "Angel of History."

10. Dick Hebdige, "Welcome to the Terrordome: Jean-Michel Basquiat and the 'Dark' Side of Hybridity," in *Jean-Michel Basquiat*, ed. Richard Marshall (New York: Whitney Museum of American Art, 1993), 61.

11. Ibid., 62.

12. Ibid.

13. Ibid., 66.

14. See Rukmini Bhaya Nair, *Lying on the Postcolonial Couch: The Idea of Indifference* (Minneapolis: University of Minnesota Press, 2002), esp. ch. 4.

15. See, e.g., Richard Marshall, "Repelling Ghosts," in *Jean Michel Basquiat*, ed. id. (New York: Whitney Museum of American Art, 1993), 15–27.

16. Jean-Michel Basquiat, *Discography, CPRKR, Charles the First, Cherokee, Horn Players, Ornithology*, and so on.

17. Hall is cited in Hebdige "Welcome to the Terrordome." It was through this essay that Bennett came to know Hall's work, as Bennett explains in an open letter to Basquiat published in the catalogue to his 1999 exhibition at the Sherman Galleries, Sydney.

18. Paul Gilroy, *The Black Atlantic* (Cambridge, Mass.: Harvard University Press, 1993), 71.

19. For an account of Bennett's childhood, see Gordon Bennett, "The Non-Sovereign Self (Diaspora Identities)," in *Global Visions: Towards a New Internationalism in the Visual Arts*, ed. Jean Fisher (London: Kala Press, 1994), 120–30; also McLean and Bennett, *Art of Gordon Bennett*.

20. Gordon Bennett, "Non-Sovereign Self," 120.

21. Ibid., 121.

22. Ibid., 127.

23. Ibid., 124.

24. David McNeill, "If You Took It the Wrong Way I'm Sorry, Mate: Football, Race and Transnationalism in the 1990s" (paper delivered at the Art Association of Australia and New Zealand annual conference, Sydney, December 6, 2002).

25. Gordon Bennett, "Non-Sovereign Self," 126.

26. Appadurai, "Putting Hierarchy in Its Place," 37.

27. On the history of "native title" and the response of artists, see Joan G. Winter, ed., *Native Title Business: Contemporary Indigenous Art* (Southport, Queensland: Keeaira Press, 2002).

28. Cf. Ian McLean's analysis of the relationship of globalization to indigenous art practice in id., "Global Indigeneity and Australian Desert Painting: Eric Michaels, Marshall McLuhan, Paul Ricoeur and the End of Incommensurability," *Australian and New Zealand Journal of Art* 3, no. 2, globalization issue (2002).

29. Appadurai, "Putting Hierarchy in Its Place," 46.

30. Ibid. The term "polythetic" derives from Rodney Needham, "Polythetic Classification: Convergence and Consequences," *Man* 10 (1975): 349–69.

31. Appadurai, "Putting Hierarchy in Its Place," 46.

32. McLean, "Gordon Bennett's Existentialism," in *Art of Gordon Bennett*, 70.

33. Sara Ahmed, *Strange Encounters: Embodied Others in Post-Coloniality* (New York: Routledge, 2000).

34. Gilroy, *Black Atlantic.*

35. McLean, "Angel of History."

36. The subtitle "The Coming of the Light" references an earlier work of this title by Bennett, which incorporates the motif of an arm with hands at both ends; one holding the torch of reason and signifying the ideology of enlightenment, the other a dog's collar, signifying the humiliation of Aboriginal people. This same motif appears in the 911 work, bisecting the tower labeled "morte" and constituting an apparent division between worlds.

37. Ulf Hannerz, *Transnational Connections: Culture, People, Places* (New York: Routledge, 1996), 22. Hannerz uses Dan Sperber's notion of an "epidemiology of representations" to suggest the way in which cultural languages become globalized, linking people of different cultures.

38. Lam, "Whose Pain?" 142.

39. Ibid.

40. Cf. the reference to Solzhenitsyn in ch. 4, n. 14.

41. Diana Crane, *Invisible Colleges: Diffusion of Knowledge in Scientific Communities* (Chicago: University of Chicago Press, 1972).

42. See, e.g., James Meyer, "Tunnel Visions," *Artforum* 41, no. 1 (September 2002): 168–69.

43. Diprose, *Corporeal Generosity*, 4–5.

44. See Nair, *Lying on the Postcolonial Couch*, and Spivak's comments on it.

45. Marianne Hirsch, *Family Frames: Photography, Narrative and Postmemory* (Cambridge, Mass.: Harvard University Press, 1997).

46. Arjun Appadurai, *Modernity at Large: Cultural Dimensions of Globalization* (Minneapolis: University of Minnesota Press, 1996), 65; Paul Gilroy, *There Ain't No Black in the Union Jack* (Chicago: University of Chicago Press, 1987), 153.

47. This position is both exemplified and opposed in the many contributions and letters to the *London Review of Books* cited in Chapter 1 n. 45 above.

48. Cf. Deleuze's critique of metaphor—and Clare Colebrook's discussion of this in relation to Sylvia Plath's use of the Holocaust to discuss her own experience of abuse; Clare Colebrook, *Understanding Deleuze* (Sydney: Allen & Unwin, 2002), 136–39.

49. Nair, *Lying on the Postcolonial Couch*, 226.

AFTERWORD: *Beyond Trauma Culture*

1. Mieke Bal, *Travelling Concepts in the Humanities: A Rough Guide* (Toronto: University of Toronto Press, 2000).

2. Okwui Enwezor, "Haptic Visions: The Films of Steve McQueen," in *Steve McQueen*, ICA exhibition catalogue (Manchester: Cornerhouse Publications, 1999), 37–50.

3. See "Francesco Clemente," interview with Giancarlo Politi, *Flash Art*, April–May 1984, 1.

4. Ernst van Alphen, *Art in Mind: How Contemporary Images Shape Thought* (Chicago: University of Chicago Press, forthcoming).

5. Christopher Bollas has coined the term "unthought known" to refer to that which is perceived through the senses but cannot be grasped by rational thought; Christopher Bollas, *The Shadow of the Object: Psychoanalysis of the Unthought Known* (New York: Columbia University Press, 1987). This concept is developed by Mieke Bal to describe a mode of thought in art and literature; Bal, *Travelling Concepts*, 10, 92.

Select Bibliography

Ahmed, Sara. *Strange Encounters: Embodied Others in Post-Coloniality.* New York: Routledge, 2000.

Alphen, Ernst van. *Caught by History: Holocaust Effects in Contemporary Art, Literature and Theory.* Stanford: Stanford University Press, 1997.

———. "Colonialism as Historical Trauma." In *Grey Areas: Repression, Identity and Politics in Contemporary South African Art,* ed. Brenda Atkinson and Candice Breitz. Johannesburg: Chalkham Hill Press, 1999.

———. *Art in Mind: How Contemporary Images Shape Thought.* Chicago: University of Chicago Press, forthcoming.

Appadurai, Arjun. "Putting Hierarchy in Its Place." *Cultural Anthropology* 3 (February 1, 1988): 37–50.

———. *Modernity at Large: Cultural Dimensions of Globalization.* Minneapolis: University of Minnesota Press, 1996.

Atkinson, Brenda. "End of Time." *End of Time: Jo Ractliffe.* Cape Town: Mark Coetzee Fine Art Cabinet, 1999.

Augé, Marc. *Non-Places: Introduction to an Anthropology of Supermodernity.* Translated by John Howe. New York: Verso, 1995. Originally published as *Non-lieux: Introduction à une anthropologie de la surmodernité* (Paris: Seuil, 1992).

Bal, Mieke. *Travelling Concepts in the Humanities: A Rough Guide.* Toronto: University of Toronto Press, 2000.

Barthes, Roland. *Camera Lucida: Reflections on Photography.* Translated by Richard Howard. New York: Hill & Wang, 1981.

Bataille, Georges. *Eroticism.* Translated by Mary Dalwood. New York: Marion Boyars, 1987.

Bauman, Zygmunt. *Globalization: The Human Consequences.* New York: Columbia University Press; Cambridge: Polity Press, 1998.

Beaumont, Keith. *Alfred Jarry: A Critical and Biographical Study.* Leicester: Leicester University Press, 1984.

———. *Jarry: Ubu Roi.* Critical Guides to French Texts 69. London: Grant & Cutler, 1987.

Beck, Ulrich. *What is Globalization?* Cambridge: Polity Press, 2000.

Bennett, Gordon. "The Non-Sovereign Self (Diaspora Identities)." In *Global Visions: Towards a New Internationalism in the Visual Arts*, ed. Jean Fisher. London: Kala Press, 1994.

Bennett, Jill. Essay. In *Dennis Del Favero: Parting Embrace*. Exhibition catalogue. Sydney: Mori Gallery, 1998.

———. "Jill Bennett Interviews Doris Salcedo." In *Doris Salcedo*. London: Camden Arts Centre, 2001.

———. "Stigmata and Sense Memory: St Francis and the Affective Image." *Art History* 24, no. 1 (February 2001): 1–16.

———. "*Tenebrae* After September 11: Art, Empathy and the Global Politics of Belonging." In *World Memory: Personal Trajectories in Global Time*, ed. id. and Rosanne Kennedy. London: Palgrave Macmillan, 2003.

———. *Dennis Del Favero: Fantasmi*. Sydney: University of New South Wales Press, 2004.

Bennett, Jill, and Jackie Dunn, eds. *Telling Tales*. Exhibition catalogue. Sydney: Ivan Dougherty Gallery, 1998; Graz: Neue Galerie, 1999.

Bennett, Jill, and Rosanne Kennedy, eds. *World Memory: Personal Trajectories in Global Time*. London: Palgrave Macmillan, 2003.

Bersani, Leo. *The Culture of Redemption*. Cambridge, Mass.: Harvard University Press, 1990.

Blanchot, Maurice. *The Gaze of Orpheus, and Other Literary Essays*. Edited by P. Adams Sitney. Translated by Lydia Davis. Barrytown, N.Y.: Station Hill Press, 1981.

———. *The Writing of the Disaster*. 1980. Translated by Ann Smock. Lincoln: University of Nebraska Press, 1995.

Bollas, Christopher. *Being a Character: Psychoanalysis and Self-Experience*. New York: Hill & Wang, 1992.

———. *The Shadow of the Object: Psychoanalysis of the Unthought Known*. New York: Columbia University Press, 1987.

Boltanksi, Luc. *Distant Suffering: Morality, Media and Politics*. Translated by Graham Burchell. Cambridge: Cambridge University Press, 1999.

Bradley, Fiona, Katrina Brown, and Andrew Nairne, curators. *Trauma*. Exhibition catalogue. London: Hayward Gallery, 2001.

Brecht, Bertolt. *Brecht on Theatre: The Development of an Aesthetic*. Translated by John Willett. New York: Hill & Wang, 1964.

———. "A Short Organum for the Theatre." 1948. Translated by John Willett. In *Avant-Garde Drama, 1918–1939*, ed. Bernard F. Dukore and Daniel C. Gerould, 501–32. New York: Crowell, 1976.

Brennan, Teresa. *The Transmission of Affect*. Ithaca, N.Y.: Cornell University Press, 2004.

Bunn, David. "Gavin Younge's Distant Catastrophes." In *Memorias intimas marcas*. Brussels: Sussuta Boé, 1998.

Burgin, Victor. *In/different Spaces: Place and Memory in Visual Culture*. Berkeley: University of California Press, 1996.

Cameron, Dan. "Doris Salcedo." *Grand Street* 61, "All-American," 16, no. 1 (1997).

Carruthers, Mary J. *The Book of Memory: A Study of Memory in Medieval Culture*. Cambridge: Cambridge University Press, 1990.

Caruth, Cathy. *Unclaimed Experience: Trauma, Narrative and History*. Baltimore: Johns Hopkins University Press, 1996.

Casey, Edward S. *Getting Back into Place: Toward a Renewed Understanding of the Place-World*. Bloomington: Indiana University Press, 1993.

Cavell, Stanley. "Comments on Veena Das's Essay 'Language and Body: Transactions in the Construction of Pain.'" In *Social Suffering*, ed. Arthur Kleinman, Veena Das, and Margaret Lock. Berkeley: University of California Press, 1997.

Christov-Bakargiev, Carolyn. *William Kentridge*. Brussels: Société des expositions du Palais des beaux-arts de Bruxelles, 1998.

Claparède, Édouard. "La Question de la 'mémoire' affective." *Archives de psychologie* 10: (1911): 361–77.

Colebrook, Clare. *Understanding Deleuze*. Sydney: Allen & Unwin, 2002.

Cox, Murray. *Shakespeare Comes to Broadmoor: The Performance of a Tragedy in a Secure Psychiatric Hospital*. London: Jessica Kingsley, 1992.

Crane, Diana. *Invisible Colleges: Diffusion of Knowledge in Scientific Communities*. Chicago: University of Chicago Press, 1972.

Das, Veena. "Language and Body: Transactions in the Construction of Pain." In *Social Suffering*, ed. Arthur Kleinman, Veena Das, and Margaret Lock. Berkeley: University of California Press, 1997.

Davidson, Patricia. "Museums, Memorials and Public Memory." In *Negotiating the Past: The Making of Memory in South Africa*, ed. Sarah Nuttall and Carli Coetzee. Oxford: Oxford University Press, 1998.

Davis, Mike. "The Flames of New York." *New Left Review* 12 (November–December 2001).

Delbo, Charlotte. *La Mémoire et les jours*. Paris: Berg International, 1985.

———. *Days and Memory*. Translated by Rosette Lamont. Marlboro, Vt.: Marlboro Press, 1990.

———. *Auschwitz and After*. Translated by Rosette Lamont. With an introduction by Lawrence Langer. New Haven, Conn.: Yale University Press, 1995.

Deleuze, Gilles. *Proust and Signs.* Translated by Richard Howard. New York: George
    Braziller, 1972. Reprinted as Theory Out of Bounds 17 (2000). Originally
    published as *Proust et les signes* (Paris: Presses universitaires de France, 1964).
———. *Francis Bacon: Logique de la sensation.* Paris: Éditions de la Différence,
    1981.
———. *Cinema One: The Movement Image.* Translated by Hugh Tomlinson and
    Robert Galeta. London: Athlone Press, 1989.
———. *Cinema Two: The Time Image.* 1985. Translated by Hugh Tomlinson and
    Robert Galeta. Minneapolis: University of Minnesota Press, 1991.
———. "Coldness and Cruelty." In id., *Masochism.* New York: Zone Books, 1991.
Derrida, Jacques. "On Forgiveness." In id., *On Cosmopolitanism and Forgiveness.*
    Translated by Mark Dooley and Michael Hughes. New York: Routledge,
    2001.
Dimitriadis, Greg, Cameron McCarthy, and Ian McLean. *Gordon Bennett—Notes
    to Basquiat: 911.* Exhibition catalogue. Adelaide: Greenway Art Gallery, 2002.
Diprose, Roslyn. *Corporeal Generosity: On Giving with Nietzsche, Merleau-Ponty,
    and Levinas.* Albany: State University of New York Press, 2002.
The Essential Frankfurt School Reader. Edited by Andrew Arato and Eike Geb-
    hardt. Introduction by Paul Piccone. 1978. New York: Continuum, 1982.
Enwezor, Okwui. "Reframing the Black Subject: Ideology and Fantasy in Contem-
    porary South African Representation." *Third Text* 40 (Autumn 1997): 21–40.
———. "Haptic Visions: The Films of Steve McQueen." In *Steve McQueen.* ICA
    exhibition catalogue. Manchester: Cornerhouse Publications, 1999.
Felman, Shoshana, and Dori Laub, eds. *Testimony: Crises of Witnessing in Litera-
    ture, Psychoanalysis and History.* New York: Routledge, 1992.
Finley, Karen. "The Constant State of Desire." 1988. In id., *Shock Treatment.* San
    Francisco: City Lights Books, 1990.
Foster, Hal. *The Return of the Real: The Avant Garde at the End of the Century.*
    Cambridge, Mass.: MIT Press, 1996.
———. "Trauma Culture." http://www.artnet.com/magazine/features/foster7-
    26-96.asp (accessed October 39, 2002).
Foucault, Michel. *The History of Sexuality,* vol. 1: *An Introduction.* 1976. Translated
    by Robert Hurley. New York: Pantheon Books, 1978.
Freud, Sigmund. "Remembering, Repeating and Working-through." 1914. In *The
    Standard Edition of the Complete Works of Sigmund Freud,* vol. 12. London:
    Hogarth Press and the Institute of Psycho-Analysis, 1958.
Fuchs, Elinor. "Staging the Obscene Body." *Tulane Drama Review* 33, no. 1 (1989):
    33–57.
Gil, José. *Metamorphoses of the Body.* Translated by Stephen Muecke. Theory Out
    of Bounds, 12. Minneapolis: University of Minnesota Press, 1998.

Gilroy, Paul. *There Ain't No Black in the Union Jack.* Chicago: University of Chicago Press, 1987.

——. *The Black Atlantic.* Cambridge, Mass.: Harvard University Press, 1993.

Godby, Michael. "Memory and History in William Kentridge's *History of the Main Complaint.*" In *Negotiating the Past: The Making of Memory in South Africa,* ed. Sarah Nuttall and Carli Coetzee. Oxford: Oxford University Press, 1998.

Grunebaum, Heidi. "Re-placing Pasts, Forgetting Presents: Narrative, Place and Memory in the Time of the Truth and Reconciliation Commission." *Research in African Literatures* 32, no. 3 (Fall 2001).

Grunebaum, Heidi, and Yazir Henri [Henry]. "Re-membering Bodies, Producing Histories: Holocaust Survivor Narrative and Truth and Reconciliation Commission Testimony." In *World Memory: Personal Trajectories in Global Time,* ed. Jill Bennett and Rosanne Kennedy. New York: Palgrave Macmillan, 2003.

Hage, Ghassan, "Multi-Cultural Ethics." Paper presented at "Postcolonial + Art: Where Now?" symposium, Artspace, Sydney, October 28, 2000.

Hannerz, Ulf. *Transnational Connections: Culture, People, Places.* New York: Routledge, 1996.

Hartman, Geoffrey. "Public Memory and Its Discontents." *Raritan* 13, no. 4 (1994): 24–40.

——. "Tele-Suffering and Testimony in the Dot Com Era." In *Visual Culture and the Holocaust,* ed. Barbie Zelizer. New Brunswick, N.J.: Rutgers University Press, 2000.

Hebdige, Dick. "Welcome to the Terrordome: Jean-Michel Basquiat and the 'Dark' Side of Hybridity." In *Jean-Michel Basquiat,* ed. Richard Marshall, 60–70. New York: Whitney Museum of American Art, 1993.

Henri [Henry], Yazir. "Where Healing Begins." In *Looking Back, Reaching Forward: Reflections on the Truth and Reconciliation Commission of South Africa,* ed. Charles Villa-Vicencio and Wilhelm Verwoerd, 166–73. Cape Town: University of Cape Town Press, 2000.

——. "Reconciling Reconciliation: A Personal and Public Journey of Testifying Before the South African Truth and Reconciliation Commission." MS. 2001.

Hirsch, Marianne. *Family Frames: Photography, Narrative and Postmemory.* Harvard, Mass.: Harvard University Press, 1997.

Hungerford, Amy. "Memorizing Memory." *Yale Journal of Criticism* 14, no. 1 (2001): 67–92.

Huyssen, Andreas. "Trauma and Memory: A New Imaginary of Temporality." In *World Memory: Personal Trajectories in Global Time,* ed. Jill Bennett and Rosanne Kennedy. London: Palgrave Macmillan, 2003.

James, William. *Principles of Psychology.* 1890. Cambridge, Mass.: Harvard University Press, 1983.

Jameson, Frederic. *Brecht and Method.* New York: Verso, 1998.

Johnston, Sandra. "Numbing Repetitive Acts." *Creative Camera* 331 (December–January 1995): 20–23.

Jones, Basil, and Adrian Kohler. "Puppeteers' Note." In *Ubu and the Truth Commission.* Cape Town: University of Cape Town Press, 1998.

Kafka, Franz. *In the Penal Colony.* Translated by Malcolm Pasley. London: Penguin Books, 1992.

Kentridge, William. "Director's Note: The Crocodile's Mouth." In *Ubu and the Truth Commission.* Cape Town: University of Cape Town Press, 1998.

Khoisan, Zenzile. *Jakaranda Time: An Investigator's View of South Africa's Truth and Reconciliation Commission.* Cape Town: Garib Communications, 2001.

Kolk, Bessell A. van der, and Onno van der Hart. "The Intrusive Past: The Flexibility of Memory and the Engraving of Trauma." In *Trauma: Explorations in Memory,* ed. Cathy Caruth. Baltimore: Johns Hopkins University Press, 1995.

Kosofsky Sedgwick, Eve, and Adam Frank, eds. *Shame and Its Sisters: A Silvan Tomkins Reader.* Durham, N.C.: Duke University Press, 1995.

Krauss, Rosalind. "The Rock: William Kentridge's Drawings for Projection." *October* 92 (Spring 2000): 3–35.

Krog, Antjie. *Country of My Skull: Guilt, Sorrow and the Limits of Forgiveness in the New South Africa.* New York: Three Rivers Press, 1999.

LaCapra, Dominick. *Representing the Holocaust: History, Theory, Trauma.* Ithaca, N.Y.: Cornell University Press, 1994.

———. "Lanzmann's *Shoah*: Here There Is No Why." *Critical Inquiry* 23, no. 2 (Winter 1997).

———. *History and Memory After Auschwitz.* Ithaca, N.Y.: Cornell University Press, 1998.

———. *Writing History, Writing Trauma.* Baltimore: Johns Hopkins University Press, 2001.

Lam, Janneke. "Whose Pain? Childhood, Trauma, Imagination." PhD diss., University of Amsterdam, 2002.

Landry, Donna, and Gerald MacLean, eds. *The Spivak Reader.* New York: Routledge, 1996.

Langer, Lawrence L. *Holocaust Testimonies: The Ruins of Memory.* New Haven, Conn.: Yale University Press, 1991.

Leys, Ruth. "Traumatic Cures: Shell Shock, Janet and the Question of Memory." In *Tense Past: Cultural Essays in Trauma and Memory,* ed. Paul Antze and Michael Lambek. New York: Routledge, 1996.

———. *Trauma: A Genealogy.* Chicago: University of Chicago Press, 2000.

Lorés, Maite. "The Streets Were Dark with Something More Than Night: Film Noir Elements in the Work of Willie Doherty." In *Willie Doherty: Dark*

Stains: Erakusketa, 1999ko maiatzak 13–uztailak 10 = Exposición, 13 de mayo–10 de julio 1999, Koldo Mitxelena Kulturunea, Donostia–San Sebastián. Madrid: British Council; [Donostia]: Gipuzkoako Foru Aldundia, 1999.

Marshall, Richard. "Repelling Ghosts." In *Jean-Michel Basquiat,* ed. id. New York: Whitney Museum of American Art, 1993.

Massumi, Brian. "The Autonomy of Affect." In *Deleuze: A Critical Reader,* ed. Paul Patton. Oxford: Blackwell, 1996.

———. "Introduction: Like a Thought." In id., ed. *A Shock to Thought: Expression After Deleuze and Guattari.* New York: Routledge, 2002.

McLean, Ian. "Gordon Bennett's Existentialism." In id. and Gordon Bennett, *The Art of Gordon Bennett.* Roseville East, NSW: Craftsman House, 1996.

———. *Gordon Bennett, 5 November–4 December 1999.* Exhibition catalogue. Sydney: Sherman Galleries, 1999.

———. "Angel of History." *Third Text* 58 (June 2002): 212–15.

———. "Global Indigeneity and Australian Desert Painting: Eric Michaels, Marshall McLuhan, Paul Ricoeur and the End of Incommensurability." *Australian and New Zealand Journal of Art* 3, no. 2, Globalization issue (2002).

McNeill, David. "If You Took It the Wrong Way I'm Sorry, Mate: Football, Race and Transnationalism in the 1990s." Paper delivered at the Art Association of Australia and New Zealand annual conference, Sydney, December 6, 2002.

Merewether, Charles. "To Bear Witness." In *Doris Salcedo,* ed. Dan Cameron. New York: New Museum of Contemporary Art, 1998.

Meyer, James. "Tunnel Visions." *Artforum* 41, no. 1 (September 2002): 168–69.

Mowitt, John. "Trauma Envy." *Cultural Critique* 46 (Fall 2000): 272–97.

Nair, Rukmini Bhaya. *Lying on the Postcolonial Couch: The Idea of Indifference.* Minneapolis: University of Minnesota Press, 2002.

Nietzsche, Friedrich. *The Gay Science.* 1882. Translated by Walter Kaufmann. New York: Random House, 1974.

Papastergiadis, Nikos, and Mary Zournazi. "Faith Without Certitudes: A Conversation with Nikos Papastergiadis." In Mary Zournazi, *Hope: New Philosophies for Change,* 78–95. New York: Routledge; Annandale, NSW: Pluto Press, 2002.

Patton, Paul. *Deleuze and the Political.* New York: Routledge, 2000.

Politi, Giancarlo. "Francesco Clemente." Interview with Giancarlo Politi. *Flash Art,* April–May 1984, 1.

Princenthal, Nancy, Carlos Basualdo, and Andreas Huyssen. *Doris Salcedo.* London: Phaidon, 2000.

Ractliffe, Jo. "End of Time: A Point of Access." *End of Time: Jo Ractliffe.* Cape Town: Mark Coetzee Fine Art Cabinet, 1999.

Robbins, Steven. "Silence in My Father's House: Memory, Nationalism, and Narratives of the Body." In *Negotiating the Past: The Making of Memory in South Africa*, ed. Sarah Nuttall and Carli Coetzee. Oxford: Oxford University Press, 1998.

Salcedo, Doris. "Memoirs from Beyond the Grave." *Tate* 21 (2000): 84.

Santner, Eric. *Stranded Objects: Mourning, Memory, and Film in Postwar Germany.* Ithaca, N.Y.: Cornell University Press, 1990.

Scarry, Elaine. *The Body in Pain: The Making and Unmaking of the World.* Oxford: Oxford University Press, 1985.

Selzer, Mark. "Wound Culture: Trauma in the Pathological Public Sphere." *October* 80 (Spring 1997): 3–26.

Seremetakis, Nadia. *The Last Word: Women, Death, and Divination in Inner Mani.* Chicago: University of Chicago Press, 1991.

Serres, Michel, with Bruno Latour. *Conversations on Science, Culture and Time.* Translated by Roxanne Lapidus. Ann Arbor: University of Michigan Press, 1995.

Serres, Michel, and Mary Zournazi. "The Art of Living: A Conversation with Michael Serres." In Mary Zournazi, *Hope: New Philosophies for Change*, 192–208. New York: Routledge; Annandale, NSW: Pluto Press, 2002.

Silverman, Kaja. *The Threshold of the Visible World.* New York: Routledge, 1996.

Smith, Daniel W. "Deleuze's Theory of Sensation: Overcoming the Kantian Duality." In *Deleuze: A Critical Reader*, ed. Paul Patton. Oxford: Blackwell, 1996.

Tal, Kali. *Worlds of Hurt: Reading the Literatures of Trauma.* Cambridge: Cambridge University Press, 1996.

Tomkins, Silvan. "Affect, Imagery, Consciousness." In *Shame and Its Sisters: A Silvan Tomkins Reader*, ed. Eve Kosofsky Sedgwick and Adam Frank. Durham, N.C.: Duke University Press, 1995.

Velez, Silvia, Lisa Byrne, and Blair French. *Madre Patria/Motherland.* Exhibition catalogue. Canberra: Canberra School of Art, 2000.

Virilio, Paul. *The Lost Dimension.* New York: Semiotext(e), 1991.

Warren-Brown, Gillian. "Soldier Henry Comes Home." *Leadership*, December–January 1999–2000, 92–96

Winter, Joan G., ed. *Native Title Business: Contemporary Indigenous Art.* Southport, Queensland: Keeaira Press, 2002.

Wojnarowic, David. *Close to the Knives: A Memoir of Disintegration.* New York: Vintage Books, 1991.

Young, James. *At Memory's Edge: After-Images of the Holocaust in Contemporary Art and Architecture.* New Haven, Conn.: Yale University Press, 2000.

Zelizer, Barbie. *Remembering to Forget: Holocaust Memory Through the Camera's Eye.* Chicago: University of Chicago Press, 1998.

Žižek, Slavoj. *The Plague of Fantasies.* London: Verso, 1997.

Index

Cultural Memory | *in the Present*

Stanley Cavell, *Emerson's Transcendental Etudes*

Stuart McLean, *The Event and its Terrors: Ireland, Famine, Modernity*

Beate Rössler, ed., *Privacies: Philosophical Evaluations*

Bernard Faure, *Double Exposure: Cutting Across Buddhist and Western Discourses*

Alessia Ricciardi, *The Ends Of Mourning: Psychoanalysis, Literature, Film*

Alain Badiou, *Saint Paul: The Foundation of Universalism*

Gil Anidjar, *The Jew, the Arab: A History of the Enemy*

Jonathan Culler and Kevin Lamb, eds., *Just Being Difficult? Academic Writing in the Public Arena*

Jean-Luc Nancy, *A Finite Thinking*, edited by Simon Sparks

Theodor W. Adorno, *Can One Live after Auschwitz? A Philosophical Reader*, edited by Rolf Tiedemann

Patricia Pisters, *The Matrix of Visual Culture: Working with Deleuze in Film Theory*

Andreas Huyssen, *Present Pasts: Urban Palimpsests and the Politics of Memory*

Talal Asad, *Formations of the Secular: Christianity, Islam, Modernity*

Dorothea von Mücke, *The Rise of the Fantastic Tale*

Marc Redfield, *The Politics of Aesthetics: Nationalism, Gender, Romanticism*

Emmanuel Levinas, *On Escape*

Dan Zahavi, *Husserl's Phenomenology*

Rodolphe Gasché, *The Idea of Form: Rethinking Kant's Aesthetics*

Michael Naas, *Taking on the Tradition: Jacques Derrida and the Legacies of Deconstruction*

Herlinde Pauer-Studer, ed., *Constructions of Practical Reason: Interviews on Moral and Political Philosophy*

Jean-Luc Marion, *Being Given That: Toward a Phenomenology of Givenness*

Theodor W. Adorno and Max Horkheimer, *Dialectic of Enlightenment*

Ian Balfour, *The Rhetoric of Romantic Prophecy*

Martin Stokhof, *World and Life as One: Ethics and Ontology in Wittgenstein's Early Thought*

Gianni Vattimo, *Nietzsche: An Introduction*

Jacques Derrida, *Negotiations: Interventions and Interviews, 1971–1998*, ed. Elizabeth Rottenberg

Brett Levinson, *The Ends of Literature: The Latin American 'Boom" in the Neoliberal Marketplace*

Timothy J. Reiss, *Against Autonomy: Cultural Instruments, Mutualities, and the Fictive Imagination*

Hent de Vries and Samuel Weber, eds., *Religion and Media*

Niklas Luhmann, *Theories of Distinction: Re-Describing the Descriptions of Modernity*, ed. and introd. William Rasch

Johannes Fabian, *Anthropology with an Attitude: Critical Essays*

Michel Henry, *I am the Truth: Toward a Philosophy of Christianity*

Gil Anidjar, *"Our Place in Al-Andalus": Kabbalah, Philosophy, Literature in Arab-Jewish Letters*

Hélène Cixous and Jacques Derrida, *Veils*

F. R. Ankersmit, *Historical Representation*

F. R. Ankersmit, *Political Representation*

Elissa Marder, *Dead Time: Temporal Disorders in the Wake of Modernity (Baudelaire and Flaubert)*

Reinhart Koselleck, *The Practice of Conceptual History: Timing History, Spacing Concepts*

Niklas Luhmann, *The Reality of the Mass Media*

Hubert Damisch, *A Childhood Memory by Piero della Francesca*

Hubert Damisch, *A Theory of /Cloud/: Toward a History of Painting*

Jean-Luc Nancy, *The Speculative Remark: (One of Hegel's bon mots)*

Jean-François Lyotard, *Soundproof Room: Malraux's Anti-Aesthetics*

Jan Patočka, *Plato and Europe*

Hubert Damisch, *Skyline: The Narcissistic City*

Isabel Hoving, *In Praise of New Travelers: Reading Caribbean Migrant Women Writers*

Richard Rand, ed., *Futures: Of Jacques Derrida*

William Rasch, *Niklas Luhmann's Modernity: The Paradoxes of Differentiation*

Jacques Derrida and Anne Dufourmantelle, *Of Hospitality*

Jean-François Lyotard, *The Confession of Augustine*

Kaja Silverman, *World Spectators*

Samuel Weber, *Institution and Interpretation: Expanded Edition*

Jeffrey S. Librett, *The Rhetoric of Cultural Dialogue: Jews and Germans in the Epoch of Emancipation*

Ulrich Baer, *Remnants of Song: Trauma and the Experience of Modernity in Charles Baudelaire and Paul Celan*

Samuel C. Wheeler III, *Deconstruction as Analytic Philosophy*

David S. Ferris, *Silent Urns: Romanticism, Hellenism, Modernity*

Rodolphe Gasché, *Of Minimal Things: Studies on the Notion of Relation*

Sarah Winter, *Freud and the Institution of Psychoanalytic Knowledge*

Samuel Weber, *The Legend of Freud: Expanded Edition*

Aris Fioretos, ed., *The Solid Letter: Readings of Friedrich Hölderlin*

J. Hillis Miller/Manuel Asensi, *Black Holes/J. Hillis Miller; or, Boustrophedonic Reading*

Miryam Sas, *Fault Lines: Cultural Memory and Japanese Surrealism*

Peter Schwenger, *Fantasm and Fiction: On Textual Envisioning*

Didier Maleuvre, *Museum Memories: History, Technology, Art*

Jacques Derrida, *Monolingualism of the Other; or, The Prosthesis of Origin*

Andrew Baruch Wachtel, *Making a Nation, Breaking a Nation: Literature and Cultural Politics in Yugoslavia*

Niklas Luhmann, *Love as Passion: The Codification of Intimacy*

Mieke Bal, ed., *The Practice of Cultural Analysis: Exposing Interdisciplinary Interpretation*

Jacques Derrida and Gianni Vattimo, eds., *Religion*

The authorized representative in the EU for product safety and compliance is:
Mare Nostrum Group
B.V Doelen 72
4831 GR Breda
The Netherlands

www.ingramcontent.com/pod-product-compliance
Lightning Source LLC
Chambersburg PA
CBHW020904180526
45163CB00007B/2615